GAY SWEATSHOP
Four Plays and a Company

'I was lucky enough to work for Gay Sweatshop in one of its very first seasons, and it was a revelation both as an actor and as a gay man. I don't think I've ever had before or since quite such a direct sense of contact with an audience, passionately hungry for some kind of account of its own life.

The work that Gay Sweatshop has done since then has constantly enlarged the understanding by both gay and straight people of what it really means to be gay in our time – the limitations to be overcome and the possibilities to be aspired to. Gay Sweatshop is one of the few points at which the theatre engages directly with people's lives. Its continued existence is vital to both the theatre and the community.'

Simon Callow

In this personal account of the work of Gay Sweatshop, actor, playwright and director Philip Osment gives an insider's view of the Company. Gay Sweatshop includes interviews with past and present members, a detailed chronology, and four highly-acclaimed plays demonstrating the breadth of the company's concerns.

In **The Dear Love of Comrades** Noël Greig goes back to the nineteenth century in a play about Edward Carpenter, socialist pioneer and campaigner for gay and women's rights.

Compromised Immunity, Andy Kirby's painfully funny play, takes a brave look at AIDS, friendship and compassion. **This Island's Mine** by Philip Osment is about a group of people coming to terms with different, often conflicting, needs and principles. Jackie Kay's **Twice Over** is about a schoolgirl's discovery that her grandmother was a lesbian.

A Methuen Theatrefile

*This anthology first published in Great Britain in 1989 by
Methuen Drama, Michelin House, 81 Fulham Road, London SW3 6RB.
Distributed in the USA by HEB Inc. 70 Court Street, Portsmouth, New Hampshire 03801.*

Copyright in the introduction and chronology © *Philip Osment 1989*
The Dear Love of Comrades © *Noël Greig 1989*
Compromised Immunity © *Andy Kirby 1989*
This Island's Mine © *Philip Osment 1989*
Twice Over © *Jackie Kay 1989*

A CIP catalogue record for this book is available from The British Library.

Caution
This paperback is fully protected by copyright. All rights are reserved and all enquiries concerning the rights for professional and amateur stage productions should be made before rehearsals begin to:
The Dear Love of Comrades: *Michael Imison Playwrights Ltd,
28 Almeida Street, London N1 1TD*
Compromised Immunity: *Methuen Drama, Michelin House,
81 Fulham Road, London SW3 6RB*
This Island's Mine: *Michael Imison Playwrights Ltd, 28 Almeida Street,
London N1 1TD*
Twice Over: *Methuen Drama, Michelin House, 81 Fulham Road, London SW3 6RB*

This paperback is sold subject to the condition that it shall not, by way of trade or otherwise, be lent, resold, hired out, or otherwise circulated without the publisher's prior consent in any form of binding or cover other than that in which it is published and without a similar condition, including this condition, being imposed on the subsequent purchaser.

The front cover photograph shows (above) Margaret Robertson as Miss Rosenblum *in* **This Island's Mine** *(photo © Sunil Gupta) (below) Alan Pope as* Lenny *in* **As Time Goes By** *(photo © Rolf Fischer).*

Gay Sweatshop
Four Plays and a Company

edited by Philip Osment

The Dear Love of Comrades
Noël Greig

Compromised Immunity
Andy Kirby

This Island's Mine
Philip Osment

Twice Over
Jackie Kay

Contents

	page
Finding Room on the Agenda for Love A History of Gay Sweatshop	vii
The Dear Love of Comrades by Noël Greig	1
Compromised Immunity by Andy Kirby	51
This Island's Mine by Philip Osment	81
Twice Over by Jackie Kay	121
A Chronology of the work of Gay Sweatshop	147

Acknowledgements

I agreed to write a history of Gay Sweatshop knowing I was able to rely only partly on my own memories and perceptions. When I joined the company it had already done a great deal of important work and had established its reputation. I am indebted to past members for their help and advice. Alan Pope spent considerable time talking to me about the early days and gave permission for me to quote from his own essay about how the company started and I would also like to thank Roger Baker, Jill Posener, Kate Crutchley, Nancy Diuguid, Noël Greig, Angela Stewart-Park and Kate Owen for letting me interview them. Noël also read the first draft, pointed out where it was unclear, and helped me edit.

Many people influenced the company and its work; if I have failed to mention anyone then I would ask them to forgive me. There are also countless people who have given their support and without whom the company would never have survived. Not all their names appear but this does not diminish their contributions.

Finally I would like to thank Pamela Edwardes and Linda Brandon at Methuen and my friend Nina Ward for their help and encouragement.

Three of the four plays in this collection are from the eighties – the fourth, *The Dear Love of Comrades*, was originally published in a Gay Men's Press volume which is now out of print. It is included because it seems as relevant in 1989 as it was in 1979 when it was first performed. Other Gay Sweatshop plays that have been published include: *One Person, Fred and Harold* and *The Haunted Host* by Robert Patrick, *Thinking Straight* by Laurence Collinson, *Ships* by Alan Wakeman in *Homosexual Acts* (Ambiance/ Almost Free playscripts 1); *Any Woman Can* by Jill Posener (*Lesbian Plays I*, Methuen); *Care and Control* by Michelene Wandor (*Strike While the Iron is Hot*, Journeyman Press); *As Time Goes By* by Noël Greig and Drew Griffiths with *The Dear Love of Comrades* by Noël Greig in *Two Gay Sweatshop Plays*, (Gay Men's Press); *Poppies* by Noël Greig (Gay Men's Press). Gay Sweatshop Times Ten productions: *More* by Maro Green and Caroline Griffin (*Plays by Women VI*, Methuen); *Julie* by Cathy Kilcoyne (*Lesbian Plays II*, Methuen).

Finding Room on the Agenda for Love

A history of Gay Sweatshop

Philip Osment

Dedicated to the memory of Drew Griffiths (1947–1984)

Prologue

In March 1974 a letter appeared in Gay News:

Season of Gay Plays

The Almost Free is planning a Gay Season (along the lines of last year's highly successful Women's Season) for autumn '74 and is interested in hearing from anyone with a play (*not* professionally produced previously if possible) suggestions etc. Write to Sue Carroll, Inter-Action, 14 Talacre Rd., London NW5.

Members of the gay community were quick to take up the invitation and a core-group soon came together. This provided the impetus for setting up Gay Sweatshop – a company those work over the last fourteen years has affected the lives of countless individuals and has played a significant role in changing attitudes towards homosexuality within the world of theatre and within society as a whole.

The company became part of a communications network voicing the concerns of the Gay Movement. On many occasions it found itself in direct conflict with the State and having to fight prejudice and bigotry. Devon Education Officers, Dublin councillors, churchmen in Golders Green and Aberdeen, Dr Rhodes Boyson, Ian Paisley, homophobic journalists, all have fulminated against the company and its work, usually without having seen it.

The plays themselves have been much less sensational but have brought hope and strength to audiences, and have pointed the way to change. They have put the experiences of lesbians and gay men centre-stage. They have also spoken to wider political concerns and any history of the company is also a history of radical movements in Britain over the past two decades.

The company's influence is not limited to this country; there have been tours to Ireland and Europe and there have been productions of its plays in Canada, Europe, the United States, and Australia. Company members have gone on to work in other areas of theatre from the West End and mainstream national companies through to young people's theatre and Theatre-in-Education.

If there was ever any doubt about the usefulness of theatre then a company such as Gay Sweatshop dispels it most forcefully proving conclusively that 'theatre can change your life'.

It's not all Gaiety

Images on the stage and on the screen can have an enormous effect on our lives, not always a positive one. It is not the purpose of this introduction to give a comprehensive history of the portrayal of homosexuality in British theatre but in the sixties and early seventies, plays and films in general reflected the fear and prejudice of the whole society.

As a teenager in North Devon in the sixties I have some painful memories of the confusion and sense of isolation that my growing awareness of my sexuality caused me. This was exacerbated by the images of homosexuality presented to me in films and on the stage. I remember sitting with my family watching Otto Preminger's 1962 film *Advise and Consent*, the story of an American senator blackmailed by political opponents because of a homosexual affair during his army days. In desperation he goes to New York to look for his friend and finds himself in a seedy house with an effeminate fat man who seems to know where his friend, Ray, might be found. The man sits the senator down and gives him tea. My memory of this scene is particularly vivid – a clean-cut all-American in the clutches of someone whose degeneracy and effeminate nature were being linked and embodied in the way he poured out the tea – a woman's task if ever there was one! For years afterwards, whenever I was asked to pour out tea I would quite seriously ask myself why I had been asked to do this: was it because they sensed what I was? Would they be able to tell by the way I held the teapot?

The senator finds his friend in a club for homosexual men. He is revolted by the idea that Ray is no longer a real man. Their relationship had been above love and friendship but Ray has spoilt all this by continuing to be a homosexual . As the senator rushes away in horror Ray clings to the door of the cab but is thrown to the ground and left lying in a puddle in the road. The senator returns to his office in Washington where he cuts his throat with a razor. I found the film profoundly upsetting and was terrified that this would be noticed by my family. On the one hand, the film was holding out to me a concept that was exciting and hopeful – that it was possible for two men to love each other – but this only made its effect more painful because, on the other hand, it was arguing that such a relationship was doomed.

Another film that I saw about this time, mercifully this one I watched on my own, was *The Loudest Whisper* which was also made in 1962 and was based on Lillian Hellman's stage play *The Children's Hour*. Although it is a much better film than *Advise and Consent* it, too, had a deeply disturbing effect by presenting lesbianism in a similarly doomed fashion. A precocious and spiteful pupil starts to spread rumours about two of her teachers played by Audrey Hepburn and Shirley MacLaine. These two have a close relationship and, although it has never been sexual, it becomes clear during the film that the Shirley MacLaine character has feelings for her colleague that go beyond platonic friendship. It is her guilt at this realization rather than the accusations themselves which she finds unbearable. This film, too, ends with a suicide.

The Loudest Whisper also raised the issue of homosexuality in relation to schools and young people. This continues to obsess the so-called guardians of morality. During my schooldays I can remember one play with a homosexual character being brought to my school by the Northcott Theatre. It was Shaffer's *Black Comedy* in which the gay character was portrayed as a camp, predatory figure to be ridiculed. In 1968 Devon Education officers saw nothing wrong with presenting images like this to schoolchildren but in 1983 they did see fit to ban Gay Sweatshop for fear of the effect the company might have on their pupils. People who talk about the need to protect children give little thought to the well-being of young lesbians and gays, and to combatting the ignorance and prejudice that goes unchallenged in schools all over the country.

There is a danger of becoming censorious and ungenerous in examining images of homosexuality in films and plays of the past. It is important, however, to see that they often had an oppressive and damaging effect on the self-esteem of people who were struggling to accept themselves and their sexuality. In theatre the clichés were used again and again: the camp gay man, the butch lesbian. Plays like *Boys in the Band* and *The Killing of Sister George* did little to dispel myths or to flesh out the stereotypes. Gay people learnt to accept these images of themselves, even applaud them. A founding member of Gay Sweatshop, Alan Pope, remembers the relentless bitchiness of *Boys in the Band* and the famous line which seemed to sum up the play: 'Show me a happy homosexual and I'll show you a gay corpse.' As Alan points out, 'You can't get more negative than that!' Yet there was a feeling among gay people that the play accurately portrayed a certain section of the New York gay scene and that the line was rather wonderful and witty. Oddly, the play is less offensive in 1989 than in 1969 when a play with an all-gay cast of characters was a rarity, and seemed to be making universal statements about gay men. Now it can be seen as a period piece and has been set in context by recent more positive gay plays. It is little wonder that when Gay Sweatshop was founded *Boys in the Band* was often quoted as the type of play which was particularly damaging to the gay community and the struggle for self-respect and pride.

When the first season at the Almost Free was launched there was a press conference. Roger Baker, one of the founding members of Gay Sweatshop, was reported in an editorial in *The Times* as saying: 'The conventional theatre is, in myth, supposed to house a number of homosexuals. But it presents distorted stereotypes of what homosexual's are like.' Gay Sweatshop was set up in response not only to the way homosexuality was portrayed onstage but also to the way in which gay people working in theatre were often put in the position of colluding with those portrayals. Since its inception the company has worked to dispel the myth that theatre provides a haven for gay people.

In the early seventies women and Black people working in theatre were coming to realize that they had to take control of the way they were being portrayed. In both fringe and mainstream theatre men always outnumbered women onstage and there were few Black characters. And so the Women's Theatre Group and Monstrous Regiment, Temba and Black Theatre co-operative were set up.

Gay people, or at least gay men, on the other hand, were thought to occupy a privileged position as they hadn't been excluded to the same degree. So, why a gay theatre company? Ever since it was set up Gay Sweatshop has had to justify its existence and every Arts Council application, every programme or publicity blurb has had to ask and answer this question. The truth lies, of course, in the fact that because they were able to pass for straight, gay actors, writers, directors, designers, technicians were able to become invisible within the profession and to be involved in the presentation of shows which either denied their existence altogether or else portrayed lesbians and gay men as figures of fun or as objects of disgust and pity. Gay Sweatshop was to provide a context for gay people to work together and to allow their sexuality to inform their work in a positive way.

There are countless examples of discrimination against gay performers which went unnoticed because the oppression had been internalized, because no one wanted to rock the boat or just because it was accepted that that was the way things were. Gay male actors were told that they were 'too camp' to play certain roles – because the actor was known to be gay it was assumed that he wasn't able to play a part. The irony is that most gay people spend their adolescence trying to pass for straight which makes them expert at aping heterosexuals. The prejudice often worked in reverse where a director casting a gay role would deliberately cast a heterosexual in that role and claim that it was because she/he would bring more objectivity to the part – a mad logic which is still sometimes used by casting directors today. Of course, that heterosexual actor, when interviewed in the press, would be sure to mention the existence of a girlfriend or a wife and children just in case anyone should get the wrong idea.

All members of Gay Sweatshop have memories which belie the popular belief that it is easy to be gay in the theatre. Nancy Diuguid who joined the company in 1976 remembers how her openness about her sexuality was received at drama school by both staff and students. Fellow-students admitted to her later that they used to change in the opposite corner of the dressing-room for fear of being attacked. At another time someone said, 'I've been dying to ask you, who sleeps on top?' Luckily, she had a sense of humour: 'Well', she replied. 'We have a blue nightgown and a pink nightgown and whoever is wearing the blue nightgown that night sleeps on top.' But it wasn't just the students who were homophobic. The teachers also felt threatened – the gay male teachers because they were closeted about their own sexuality and the heterosexual men because they didn't know how to respond to a woman they couldn't chat up. The students, at least, responded openly; some of the teachers responded in a more hidden, snide way such as casting her in the role of Lesbia in one of Shaw's plays. One would like to think she was given this part out of a concern that she should be allowed to play a strong woman-identified character, but, sadly, it had more to do with having a joke at her expense and giving expression to the hostility which her sexuality aroused.

Kate Crutchley who worked in rep for many years and in the West End before joining Gay Sweatshop recalls that the social life of the reps and the casting of plays was organized in such a way as to make coming out as a lesbian impossible or, at least, inadvisable. For an actress to make herself so clearly 'unavailable' to men would both threaten and anger them. Given that there were even fewer female directors then than there are now, this would have been tantamount to professional suicide. Indeed, more recently, actors have been told that working for Gay Sweatshop might be detrimental to their careers. If they do act for the company it indicates that they see their sexuality as a vital and positive aspect of themselves which they can bring to their work. There is no doubt that many directors still find this disturbing, while agents, casting directors and publicity departments pressurize performers to hide their sexuality to 'protect' their public image. In 1989 many actors and actresses are still scared of resisting this but more and more are doing so. Twenty years ago hardly anyone would have dared to resist.

The internalization of society's attitude to homosexuality had an insidious effect upon gay artists leading to self-hatred and self-censorship. This made them sublimate and hide their true selves in their work. But if they did try to deal openly with their sexuality they had a difficult and lonely task. Because of the taboos surrounding the expression of homosexual desire they had to go into unmapped territory with no role-models. There were few artists of the past whose work and example could help to sustain them. If they did manage to create something which was true to their own experience then they were at the mercy of a society which would accuse them of perversion and degeneracy. It is incredible that the publication of a book as seemingly respectable and innocuous as *The Well of Loneliness* should have provoked the outcry it did. But the people with power – the critics, judges, the Lord Chamberlain, self-appointed moral arbiters – carry prejudices with them destroying the work and the happiness of many gay artists.

Even if they escaped censorship, homosexual artists were often treated by critics and biographers in a way that betrayed latent homophobia. Their homosexuality would either be seen as a fatal flaw, which prevented them from creating truly great art, or else it would be considered unworthy of mention and irrelevant – as if Michelangelo's appreciation of the male nude had nothing to do with his sexual orientation. It is little wonder then that most artists chose either silence or disguise and often concealed homosexual relationships in heterosexual characters.

It is the greatest irony of all that E M Forster who was an apostle of integrity, should have been scared of publishing his homosexual novel *Maurice*. Forster advocated being true to oneself by dispensing with the hypocrisy and respectability of bourgeois society. His credo was summed up in the two words 'only connect'. Much has been said elsewhere about the morality of his decision not to publish, and about the artistic merit of the novel itself, but the fact is that as a homosexual writer he was gagged by his own self-denial, by the attitudes of the society around him and by the laws of this country. In his terminal note to the novel he writes:

> A happy ending was imperative. I shouldn't have bothered to write it otherwise. I was determined that in fiction anyway two men should fall in love and remain in it for the ever and ever that fiction allows, and in this sense Maurice and Alec still roam the greenwood. I dedicated it 'To a Happier Year' and not altogether vainly. Happiness is its keynote – which by the way has had an unexpected result: it has made the book more difficult to publish. Unless the Wolfenden report becomes law, it will probably have to remain in manuscript. If it ended unhappily, with a lad dangling from a noose or with a suicide pact, all would be well, for there is no pornography or seduction of minors. But the lovers get away unpunished and consequently recommend crime.

The producers of *Advice and Consent* took great care not to recommend crime. I can only imagine what it would have felt like if, as that teenager, I had been watching a film which which promised personal fulfilment and happiness instead of degradation and death.

Changing Times

Chapter One painted a dismal one-sided picture of the position of gay people in theatre and the arts during the sixties and early seventies. There were movements afoot to bring change. The emergence of Gay culture and pride didn't just happen overnight: the way was being prepared by the social and cultural revolution that was taking place in this country and in the United States.

In Britain, the Welfare State and the Education Act meant that art and ideas were no longer the preserve of an élite. For the first time, working-class people were able to go on to further education in significant numbers, creating a demand for new ideas and new ways of expressing them, for new political aims and new political groupings to achieve them. It was a movement which had started in the fifties with the Aldermaston marches and the beatniks. It heralded the break-up of the traditional Left and the formation of the New Left – which took on issues that were not necessarily on the agenda of the Labour Party. There was a growing awareness that Britain had a multi-cultural pluralistic society which challenged the socialism of the old guard with its strictly class basis.

In the United States where class divisions were less clear and socialist traditions less strong the emphasis, from the start, was on pluralism and civil rights. Most notably, Black people were making demands for equality and dignity which galvanized whole sections of the population into action and set an example of how a popular movement could 'overcome'. The State could be resisted and forced to change. It was an example that other groups such as women and, later, gay people were to follow. The anti-Vietnam War movement, too, was part of this revolution, both in Britain and in the US. It motivated young people to reject the values of a capitalist society which could send them off to fight a war they didn't believe in to protect a system which was corrupt. Many decided to drop out rather than embrace the life that their parents wanted for them with its respectable trappings of a job, a mortgage and a family. Instead they opted for peace, personal fulfilment, development of spirituality and free love.

From here it was a short step to homosexual emancipation but the path was not without obstacles. Without wanting to jump on the fashionable bandwagon of ridiculing hippy culture, it has to be said there is some truth in the stereotype of the long-haired hippy who referred to a woman as 'my chick' or 'my old lady' and expected her to fulfil a nurturing 'earth-mother' role while he was free to reap all the benefits of the new permissive age. The modern Women's Liberation movement was still in its infancy. Women were caught in the double-bind of having to accommodate male demands for greater sexual freedom whilst being unable to make any demands of their own. If they expressed their needs they were likely to be accused of trying to trap men or of being scared of sex. Neither should one be deceived by the less macho image that these men projected. The hair, the bracelets, the beads and the flowing garments did not mean that they were necessarily ready to embrace their gay brothers. Hippy ideals created a climate where liberation was possible but in the end gay people had to take the final step for themselves – no one was going to take it for them.

The 1967 Sexual Offences Act made legal homosexual acts in private between males over twenty-one in England and Wales. (Owing to Queen Victoria's refusal to believe that lesbianism existed there was no law prohibiting sex between women and so no reform was necessary.) As a piece of legislation it was still highly discriminatory. It indicated that legal reform alone was not going to change prevalent attitudes to homosexuality. Instead of going cap-in-hand to those in power, homosexuals needed a movement that would assert their sense of identity and pride just as the Black Consciousness movement had done for Black people in the States. Prejudice and injustice were fuelling the growing sense of anger that gay people were feeling. The spark that fired the gay men's movement came from the US, from a bar in Greenwich Village called the Stonewall.

It is fitting that the section of the gay community responsible for starting the Stonewall Riots of the summer of 1969 was far from respectable. The drag queens were the first to stand up and resist. The police had been raiding gay bars for years, closing them down, making arrests, and gay people had accepted it, not wanting to make a fuss for fear of publicity, of their family finding out, of losing their jobs. But a point was reached when the attacks were so regular and their effect so demoralizing that they felt they had nothing to lose. It was the day of Judy Garland's funeral. Judy Garland became almost an icon for many gay men who through their adolescence had been unable to fit into the masculine mould of the jock on the baseball field and had been called 'cissy' and 'pansy'. The image of a woman such as Judy who survived no matter how hard the knocks, was a source of comfort and inspiration. She showed that strength was not solely the preserve of macho men. And so many gay men attended her funeral. In the gay bars in Greenwich Village that night the drag queens were out in strength to mourn the passing of their idol. Then the police raided.

For the first time there was united resistance. The drag queens, helped by the rest of the gay community, trapped the police inside the Stonewall bar. The riots which followed gave gay people a visibility and strength. They showed homosexuals throughout the world that we do not have to hide and be isolated, that it is possible to join together in solidarity. The cry went up – 'Out of the closets and into the streets!' In London, regular Gay Liberation Front (GLF) meetings were organized at the LSE in 1970 and there were demonstrations and marches – most notably the Gay Days in Hyde Park.

The theatricality of many of those early demonstrations was striking. Outrageous costume was used to challenge images of masculinity and femininity. Members of the gay commune Bethnal Rouge and the Notting Hill Street Theatre Group walked the streets wearing dresses, with glitter in their beards. This mixing of masculine and feminine was known as gender-bending. The emphasis was on big open-air spectacles and making theatre in the streets. There was the demonstration against the Festival of Light, which was campaigning against what people like Lord Longford and Mary Whitehouse saw as the evils of the permissive society, when members of GLF turned up dressed as nuns. At other times, GLF would link up with women's street theatre groups as happened at the demonstrations against the Miss World contest in 1971. It was a theatre of the streets practised by activists who saw themselves as part of the counter-culture and therefore avowedly amateur. It was a long way from professional theatre and even from the theatre of the fringe and the alternative movement.

Founding members of Gay Sweatshop, Alan Pope and Drew Griffiths, were trying to make their way in professional theatre at this time. Alan remembers that there were few, if any, images of gay people in the work of the alternative companies, many of which were still dominated by men. Left-wing touring groups were often committed to an ideology which saw sexual politics as a diversion, and homosexuality as a manifestation of bourgeois decadence. In trying to appeal to working-class audiences these companies would use stereotypes taken from light entertainment which were often sexist and anti-gay. The notion of strong parts for women – let alone positive gay characters – was still very much a novelty. Noël Greig, who was to join Gay Sweatshop in 1977, was working in alternative theatre during the late sixties and early seventies where he saw no context for any debate around sexuality. With friends he had set up the Brighton Combination. He remembers working on a play about the Cuban revolution and then catching the train up to London to go to one of the GLF meetings at the LSE and not being able to link up the two experiences. The performances by Notting Hill Street Theatre in Hyde Park seemed to have little to do with his own life and work.

And so we return to the sense of being invisible and to the feeling of schizophrenia which was experienced by gay people working in theatre. For Bette Bourne who had been involved with the Notting Hill group the answer was to build on the tradition of gender-bending street theatre. He formed *Bloolips* whose work owes much to those early days of radical drag. Others decided to work within professional alternative theatre and to bring the politics of Gay Liberation into that realm. Some of these were the people who became founding members of Gay Sweatshop.

Almost Free

Inter-Action was a community arts resource centre based in Kentish Town, now known as Inter-Change. It was a radical organization, run co-operatively, that had sprung from the ideology of the late sixties. It described itself as a 'charitable trust founded in 1968 by Ed Berman to stimulate community involvement in the arts, especially through the use of drama and creative play, and to experiment in theatre/media and their social applications.'

The Almost Free Theatre which was in Rupert Street just off Shaftesbury Avenue, was the home for Inter-Action's new plays production unit. The theatre's name arose from its policy of not having a fixed ticket price and asking audiences to contribute instead what they could afford, which itself is a reflection of those more optimistic times, but the name also had a second, artistic, significance. The aim was to produce plays that would lead people to the brink of liberation – to a state of being 'almost free' – at which point they could choose to take action.

At the Almost Free, Inter-Action had a lunchtime theatre club called Ambiance. They had already produced a women's season and a Black season and, at the height of the Gay Liberation Movement, they saw the need for a season produced by gay people. Roger Baker, a freelance writer and theatre reviewer for *Gay News*, met up with Suresa Galbraith and Ed Berman and had a meal with the Inter-Action collective. Suresa Galbraith, the co-ordinator of the Almost Free, was responsible more than anyone for nurturing and supporting the idea of Gay Sweatshop. Her aim was to get a group of gay people together who would put on a season of gay plays and might then go on to form a company. It was assumed that the group would be made up of people with little theatrical experience and so Inter-Action was offering to provide the theatre, the technical staff and the know-how so that they could learn about all aspects of production from ticket-tearing through to directing the plays. Ed Berman would retain artistic control and would have final approval on the choice of plays for the season.

Roger rang up friends he thought might be interested and it was decided to hold open meetings at his flat in Great James Street every Thursday. The meetings were advertized in Gay News. The group fluctuated and decisions and policies had to be constantly re-assessed and explained to newcomers. Who ever said that forging radical alternatives was an easy process? On the other hand, it did mean that the work could legitimately claim to be the voice of the (male) gay community and there were many people who became involved who would have been excluded from a more structured professional grouping. People like Lloyd Vanata who was a particularly dedicated and reliable volunteer. He ended up building scenery, tearing tickets, fixing lights, sweeping floors or running the bookstall and all because of his commitment to the idea of gay people coming together to make statements about their lives. Indeed it was obvious that the project was going to entail a lot of work and consequently the name chosen for the group was The Gay Sweatshop.

The first task was to elicit scripts and to choose plays for the season. The scripts that were sent in, however, did not necessarily reflect the politics and the ideals of the group. How could they? Many of them were written by people who had grown up in more repressive times and who had not had the chance to be part of the Gay Liberation movement. The plays had not yet been written which would represent these wider horizons. In the end the scripts selected for the first half of the season had to be generated from within the group.

The meetings were held throughout the summer and autumn of 1974 and eventually a core group of about ten people came together, which included Alan Wakeman, Laurence Collinson and John Roman Baker, who wrote the plays for the season. Other regular attenders were Suresa Galbraith and Norman Coates who worked as a designer at the Almost Free. From the start there was a mixture of gay activists and professional theatre workers so the group was not as amateur in make-up as had been envisaged initially and, as time went on, the professionals played an increasingly important role. Among these were a Cambridge graduate, Gerald Chapman, who was just embarking on a career as a director, and Drew Griffiths who already had considerable experience and had worked in rep both as an actor and as a director.

Drew was brought up in Manchester and his family background was working class. In 1968, having worked as an ASM at Dundee Rep, he went to the Birmingham School of Speech Training and Dramatic Art where he met Alan Pope who was also from a Northern working-class family and a Scottish student, Gordon MacDonald. The three of them became friends and kept in touch after drama school. Drew went back to Dundee Rep for a while and then to Manchester Polytechnic where he did a postgraduate drama course at the Stables Theatre. At the same time, Alan and Gordon were working together in Theatre-in-Education in Chester. Alan remembers how they would all three meet up at weekends and visit the gay clubs in Liverpool and Manchester. Drew's course finished and the contract in Chester came to an end and so they decided to move to London. In the summer of 1974 when the *Gay News* advertisement for meetings at Robert Baker's appeared they were sharing a flat in Balham with Philip Howells, a young actor from Merseyside with whom Alan had worked on a tour of *The Rupert Bear Show*. Drew went to the meetings and even submitted a script – an adaptation of *Maurice* which was turned down. This rejection coincided with the offer of work in Basingstoke and Drew dropped out of the group. Alan was working at Windsor Rep at the time and recalls how they both felt out-of-place down South in a very middle-class environment. For both of them their first perception of being oppressed was in terms of class. They read *The Uses of Literacy* by Richard Hoggart:

> It had a profound effect on us and sowed the first seeds of understanding self-oppression, but then it was in terms of class not sexual orientation. Those who claim class divisions don't exist or that they don't matter are generally from the middle-class. What is certainly true is that working-class expectations are lower, and that being transplanted into an alien environment like the theatre can make you feel cut off from your roots and yet not really part of the society you find yourself in. This was certainly how Drew felt at Basingstoke, and I was going through something similar at Windsor where I was appearing in pantomime. We were primed for change, and sexual politics were about to radicalise us. (Alan Pope, unpublished essay about Gay Sweatshop, *No Retreat no Surrender*)

Gay Sweatshop had planned a lunchtime season to take place during the autumn of 1974. As chance would have it the season was postponed. Drew was back from Basingstoke and available to direct *Thinking Straight* by Laurence Collinson. Alan and then Gordon and Philip also became involved. In 1978, *Gay Left* magazine published a series of statements from Sweatshop members entitled *Why I'm in Gay Sweatshop*. Drew said:

> From 1967 to 1974 I was busy pursuing a career in the straight theatre. I'd heard somewhere about painted freaks in the south wearing silly clothes and saying ridiculous things and assumed it was part of the queenery I found so unappealing. When I arrived in London in 1973 I saw them for myself and decided what they

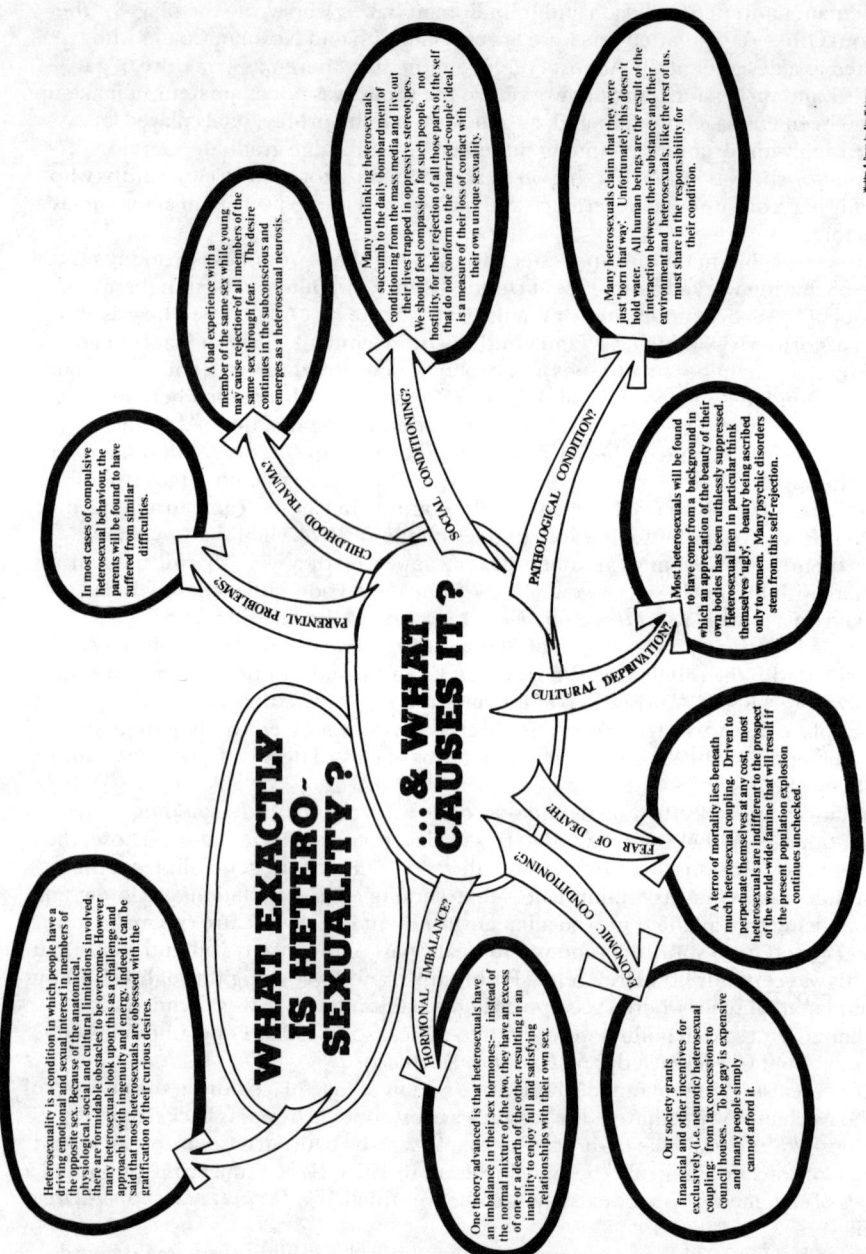

represented was definitely not for me. But there was a nagging doubt: perhaps these people were having a better time than I was; perhaps my weekend gay status was incompatible with the hardworking a-sexual, professional actor image I presented during the rest of the week. The doubt remained until I joined Gay Sweatshop in 1975. I joined with great fear and trepidation – after all, I could be ruining my career – (I remember vividly the first press call when I deliberately disassociated myself from the group, sat with my back to the cameras, afraid of being publicly identified as homosexual) but somehow found the courage to direct two of the plays in the first season. At the end of the first six months I knew that the previous seven years had been a preparation for this.

Homosexual Acts, as the lunchtime season was called, was a huge success. People queued around the block which was unheard of for lunchtime plays. The distinctive posters, designed to look like the front page of a tabloid newspaper, featuring three footballers holding hands and hugging, were seen all over London and made a statement all on their own. The three plays scheduled, *Limitations, Thinking Straight* and *Ships* were to take the season to the end of April. Roger Baker remembers particularly Drew's witty production of *Thinking Straight* by Laurence Collinson with its clever design by Norman Coates. The play dealt with a scriptwriter's attempts to come to terms with his homosexuality whilst having to write heterosexual plays and ended with a hymn to Gay Liberation which was a spoof of *That's Entertainment.* Everyone involved remarks on the excitement the season created, the audience's response to the truthful depiction of their lives, the friendly atmosphere. The foyer had been given over to an exhibition and a bookstall which sold all the radical gay literature that had been published – there were no gay bookshops at that time and anyone looking for gay publications had to hunt around for them. Alan Wakeman's Causes of Heterosexuality poster was painted on one of the walls in the foyer and most importantly there were discussions after the plays which were led by Alan Pope and which often continued late into the afternoon. These discussions were free-ranging and afforded people the opportunity to talk about things which they had perhaps never been able to express before. Sometimes the discussions became therapeutic with people ending up in tears or there were bitter arguments about sexual politics and about what was right-on. Always new ground was being broken and new ideas were being shared.

In any radical organization which is exploring hitherto uncharted areas, where the rules have to be made up as you go along, there is bound to be conflict and Gay Sweatshop was (and is) no exception. One of the earliest disputes was about the company's policy on employing heterosexuals. For the Almost Free season the rule was that the writers and directors should be gay but that the actors need not necessarily be. Then, one of the actors wrote a biography for the programme which said that he had a wife, two children and three cats and lived in married bliss in Clapham. It is understandable that many people found it offensive that he should have asserted his heterosexuality in this way. As Drew later pointed out, it proved that 'straight actors were terrified of being thought of as gay almost as much as gay actors.'

It wasn't only actors who were uneasy about what their participation in the season might mean. The audiences were wary of giving their names and addresses for the Ambiance's club list. When the Almost Free mailed them about future productions a large proportion of the letters were returned because so many people had given fictitious names and addresses.

The success of the plays was such that the run of *Ships*, directed by Gerald

Chapman, was extended. *Thinking Straight* transferred to another lunchtime venue, The Act Inn, and both plays were booked to go the Mickery theatre in Amsterdam. The Gay Sweatshop were also asked to come up with more plays to continue the season to the end of June.

It will not have gone unnoticed that all the plays were by men and contributions by lesbians were conspicuous by their absence. When the season was extended a young stage manager who was working on a production of Robert Patrick's *Kennedy's Children*, at the Arts Theatre, came along to the group with a rough outline for a play and a few pages of script. She had been encouraged by Robert Patrick to develop her ideas for a semi-autobiographical play about a lesbian. The story was to follow the woman's developing awareness of her sexuality. The writer, Jill Posener, felt diffident about her ability to write a play in the conventional sense, but the success of *Kennedy's Children* showed her that it was possible to write interesting and dramatic theatre in monologue form. She read what she had written to the Gay Sweatshop. The group agreed unanimously to stage the play. In the end, however, Ed Berman vetoed it. Jill remembers him taking her out for a meal and explaining that the play lacked conflict and that to be dramatic it needed dialogue. With hindsight, it is clear that this was a mistake – it prolonged the period when the company was solely producing work by men, such that when women did join there was an imbalance in the company's profile which had to be redressed.

Of the plays that were chosen for the extended season three were by Robert Patrick (one of which was a monologue!) and their content caused another dispute which led in the end to resignations. Some members felt that the Almost Free was being opportunistic in wanting to produce plays with good box-office potential following the success of *Kennedy's Children*. They felt that although they were witty and well-written the plays perpetuated lies about gay people. It was also thought that because the plays were written by an American they were less relevant to English audiences. It is ironic, then, that the final play in the season, which was the most accomplished and the most successful, was also by an American writer.

Martin Sherman's *Passing By* tells the story of two gay men who pick each other up and then go on to develop hepatitis. They convalesce together and come to know and love each other. The play's strength lies in the fact that it shows gay male love as something natural – even ordinary – and it struck a chord with audiences who had been starved of portrayals of gay romance. The production, which was directed by Drew and acted by Simon Callow and Michael Dickinson, seems to have been particularly fine. For Martin Sherman it marked a watershed:

> Until then, my plays had been produced in haphazard and deeply unsatisfying ways and I was in despair. There seemed little reason to carry on as a writer. The Sweatshop's production of *Passing By* changed all that. For the first time a play of mine came alive, truly alive, as I had imagined it originally, and the cause of that life was a group committed to an ideal, an ideal of professional gay theatre, that I passionately subscribed to. The Sweatshop was led then by Drew Griffiths who was a visionary and that vision gave my artistic dreams purpose and reality. (Martin Sherman, 1988)

It would seem that with this production the company was coming of age but there was, as yet, no guarantee that after the season had finished Gay Sweatshop would continue to exist. An Arts Council application for funding had been turned down and the ad hoc group of people, amateurs and professionals, were still very dependant on the support of Inter-Action. When the Almost Free closed for its summer break they were left with nothing but the desire to carry on doing what they had so greatly enjoyed.

Getting the Show on the Road

By 1975 the Campaign for Homosexual Equality (CHE) was riding on the crest of a wave. The 1974 conference in Malvern – known as the happy hippy conference – had been particularly successful and the membership increased dramatically, with local groups setting up in most large towns and cities. The 1975 conference, to be held in Sheffield in August, promised to be the biggest ever. CHE approached Inter-Action to invite Gay Sweatshop to perform in Sheffield. This posed problems: many of the actors involved were in other shows and there were no resources to build and transport a touring set, but Suresa Galbraith was keen that Gay Sweatshop should participate. It was clear that the four men who shared the flat in Balham, Drew, Alan, Gordon and Philip, together with Gerald Chapman formed the nucleus of a potential company. Inter-Action managed to find a small amount of money for production costs (about £80 as Alan recalls) and offered technical and administrative support. Work began on what was to become *Mister X*. As Alan now says, they were caught up in the 'Let's put on a show!' syndrome which continued to operate in Gay Sweatshop throughout those early years.

One of the publications sold on the bookstall at the Almost Free was a booklet by Andrew Hodges and David Hutter entitled *With Downcast Gays* (Pomegranate Press). In it, the writers set down clearly and uncompromisingly the way homosexual self-oppression operates, and show how society's attitudes are internalized and become self-hatred. It ends with a challenge to gay people to bring about change by being open about their sexuality:

External oppression we can only fight against; self-oppression we can tear out and destroy.

If *The Uses of Literacy* caused Alan and Drew to reassess their working-class background, then *With Downcast Gays* was as crucial in terms of their sexuality. Alan recalls the profound change that reading the booklet brought about, how it made them all analyse their behaviour and the attitudes of others towards them. A neighbour used to invite them to parties; on the one occasion they were unable to go, her response was: 'But you've got to come, you're the cabaret'. On reading *With Downcast Gays* they realized how true this had been. They used to attend the parties and put on a bitchy, queeny act in order to disarm people. The logic being that if I put myself down first then it doesn't hurt so much if you put me down afterwards.

And so they decided to do a play about self-oppression which would use *With Downcast Gays* as a starting-point. Roger Baker and Drew both went away and wrote material which was then worked on in rehearsals. Gerald was made production manager. One of the first pieces Drew wrote was a speech for himself at the climax of the play; this established a tradition for Drew of always writing himself a good part! In the speech a gay Entertainer tells oppressive anti-gay, racist and misogynist jokes and abuses the audience in a way which when Drew performed it was dangerous and shocking. Much of the rehearsal time was spent in discussion, reminiscence and improvisation. Alan, Drew and Philip all had in common their northern working-class background, all four of them had known the gay bars in Northern provincial towns and cities and the play became in many ways a collective autobiography. Because of this it had a distinctly provincial working class setting. The main character, *Mister X*, played by Alan, went on a journey similar to the ones that Alan and Drew had travelled from being scared and closeted to being self confident and proud to be gay.

Gay Sweatshop is often accused of preaching to the converted. In fact the company regularly performs to audiences whose prejudices need challenging but the self-critical or celebratory elements in the plays also mean that everyone can learn and take strength from them. *Mister X* was a positive gay play that attacked the sort of apolitical gay man who would go to gay bars but ridicule the idea of Gay Liberation and pretend that he didn't need it. The play was primarily a price of agit-prop for the Gay Movement and was reaching out to people who were themselves Mister Xs.

As the end of August approached the four performers became more and more nervous about the piece they had created; because it was so personal they were not sure whether it would reach anyone else. They used some of their production budget to buy some yellow loons (flared) and the cheapest t-shirts they could find (which were to fall apart after their first wash). They had Gay Sweatshop printed on the t-shirts and packed the rest of their set – Brechtian signboards announcing each scene and a feather boa for Drew to wear as the Entertainer – and caught the train to Sheffield.

If the Malvern conference had been one of unity then Sheffield was one of discord. It was a very angry, radical conference and although it marked the high-point of CHE's influence it also marked the beginning of the organization's demise. CHE was and always had been reformist in its policies. The influx of lesbians and gay men whose politics were informed by anarchism, socialism and radical feminism inevitably caused ructions. Women were represented for the first time in significant numbers which only emphasized how much the organization was dominated by men. The rows started when, at the opening civic reception, it became known that the waitresses were being paid less than the waiters. When challenged by women attending the conference the mayor told them they should keep quiet and go through their chairman! This was nothing compared to the near-riot which occurred during the entertainment laid on at The Crucible. Some bright spark had booked the Yetties to perform. The sexism in their act caused the audience to become increasingly hostile. When the band tried to make amends things only got worse because they didn't understand why they were causing offence – quite a common phenomenon when sexist entertainers are challenged. In the end they were unplugged by women in the audience. One can imagine then that the four actors, booked to perform *Mister X* the next day in the hotel ballroom, looked forward to the event with a certain sense of trepidation:

> The opening in Sheffield was the most frightening moment of our lives. Nerves, yes, every actor knows them, but in rehearsal this play had developed into a very revealing statement of the four of us involved. We were telling the truth and exposing our lives to public scrutiny. (Drew Griffiths, in *Touching our lives, Gay News*, 1977)

Indeed, the way the play ended emphasized that it wasn't like other plays where actors could discard their roles after the performance. Having been jeered at by the Entertainer for refusing to call himself queer, and for claiming that being gay need not be seen as a problem, Mister X walked to centre stage, faced the audience and said, 'My name is Mister . . . My name is Alan Pope and I live at 10 Marius Mansions, Marius Road., London SW17 and I'm gay.' This simple and straightforward way of identifying the actor with the character was a vital element in the play and later work was to retain the sentiment of this statement. It is one thing to go and watch a play with gay characters, but another altogether to watch a play put on by a gay company where connections are being made between the audience, the actors and the material. The audience in that ballroom in Sheffield knew they were being addressed directly. They stood, many of them in tears, and cheered.

The play said the right thing at the right time and the company were inundated by requests from CHE members to come and perform *Mister X* in their town for their local group.

Gay Sweatshop was not the only theatre group performing at the conference; there was also a street theatre group from Nottingham called Green Noses and the Bradford based General Will who performed a play entitled *Present Your Briefs* which looked at the way the law treated gay people.

During Gay Sweatshop's season at the Almost Free a banner headline had appeared on the front of *Gay News: Gay Actor in Showbiz Row*. This was not a story about a fight in the chorus-line but rather about a gay performer in the Bradford based General Will theatre company who went on strike in the middle of a performance. The gay actor in question was Noël Greig who, for some years had been living and working in Bradford. His 'strike' occurred at a time when the General Will was composed mainly of heterosexual men. Its work reflected strictly applied Marxist attitudes and appraised the world in an objective 'male' fashion which left little room for the feminist and radical gay politics which were opening up new debates in the town. These debates were not only around sexuality. GLF was making its presence felt in local politics generally, particularly in anti-fascist work. Most significantly, of all the radical groups in Bradford the lesbian and gay movement had large working-class support because its membership was made up of local working-class people. Noël had been working with these people on a community play called *All Het Up* and was becoming frustrated by the contrast between the vitality of this work and the arid stalemate which had occurred in the General Will. Noël's strike was, in effect, a seventies-style 'zap' and resulted in the lesbian and gay community taking over the company. Drew had seen *All Het Up* in the early summer of 1975 when the group had performed for South London GLF in Brixton. When the *Gay News* article appeared, a member of Gay Sweatshop had written a letter of support to Noël. The Sheffield conference was not the first contact between the two groups. Neither was it to be the last.

Given the response at Sheffield it was clear that *Mister X* must go on tour. CHE agreed to send out booking forms in their next mailout and the company tried once more for Arts Council funding. Ed Berman gave valuable support to the successful application. They heard later that the grant was nearly refused again, on the grounds that the company would be catering to a minority. It was then that a woman on the panel pointed out a contradiction: another grant that they had just approved was for a production touring only to Church of England venues. In the end the panel approved a small grant to tour *Mister X* until Christmas.

That first Gay Sweatshop tour in the autumn of 1975 set the tone for all later tours. The response was almost overwhelming – in all senses. From the first performance the battles started. The company had been booked to perform at the Golders Green Unitarian Church as part of the 50th anniversary celebrations. The following week's Hampstead and Highgate Express had the headline: *Vicar in Gay Play Rumpus* – 'Heckling Minister Ejected During Show at Church'. *Mister X* opens with a scene where the actors play a group of adolescent boys and simulate masturbation. As soon as it started some people in the front row led by the Revd Edward Walton from the neighbouring Christ Church in Hendon stood up and called down the wrath of God on the actors and the Unitarian Minister who had booked the show. They produced from under their chairs placards which they had conveniently brought with them and which said things like, 'Man Shall Not Lie With Man'.

The company tried to start the show three times and it became almost like a pantomine with the actors asking the audience if they wanted the show to begin and the bulk of the audience saying 'Yes, we do,' but the protesters bellowing back, 'Oh no, we don't.' Eventually Revd Walton was asked to leave but his wife and friends stayed to barrack for another twenty minutes before they too left. The Ham and High printed a photo on its front page that week of the vicar with his daughter in a bunny girl costume with the caption:

There's no question that the Revd Edward Walton is as broad-minded as they come. His daughter, Christine, was once a Bunny Girl and is now a night-club singer, and he's proud to boast about her.

But a gay play at Golders Green Unitarian Church was more than even the liberal-minded minister could stand.

As Roger Baker and Drew pointed out in their letter to the editor:

To produce a bunny from his beretta is scarcely a guarantee of open-mindedness since the bunny girls represent one of the most blatant examples of commercial exploitation and objectification of women.

It was obviously a frightening experience for the actors and the show suffered that night. The effect of the demonstration though was that the Unitarian Church congregation, who might have been quite shocked by some aspects of the play, were totally won over by it because they had been given such a blatant example of the persecution of homosexuality by bigots.

After Golders Green the company set off around the country in a Budget Rent-a-Van with half the living-room furniture from the Balham flat to sit on in the back, together with copies of *Gay News* and pamphlets and books for the bookstall, the Brechtian signboards, an easel to put them on and, of course, Drew's feather boa. The first touring date was in Exeter where there was also a considerable furore in the press about their visit – Devon, too, seems to have more than its fair share of bigots – from there they went to the Traverse in Edinburgh; homosexuality was still illegal in Scotland and the Procurator Fiscal was consulted to see if the performance constituted a homosexual act! Throughout Gay Sweatshop's history the stories of such battles abound. What has given the company the strength to fight these battles, and win them, is the effect the plays had on audiences.

News of *Mister X* spread like wildfire among the gay community and many people who might have thought twice about going on a gay demonstration plucked up the courage to go and see the play. Given that it was often being performed in their home town this was in itself a brave thing to do. Reactions to the play varied. Many people were deeply moved. The company would receive letters from audience members saying the performance had caused them to completely re-evaluate their lives. Others found the play shocking or even terrifying in the way that it challenged them to accept their sexuality and to be open about it. In the discussions after the show people would express their fear of coming out and then realize that they'd just told a hundred people in the audience that they were gay. During these discussions the company would hear people talking about their sense of isolation or of how they'd been thrown out of the home by their families because they were gay – perhaps sharing their hurt and anger for the first time. They also heard tales of incredible bravery – of young people coming out at school for instance. There were negative responses to the play as well, from gay people who were threatened by it. They would claim that things were better before the 1967 Sexual Offences Act when being a homosexual was like being part of an exclusive male club, an attitude very similar to that of the character of Mister X in the play.

However the audiences were not solely gay; many heterosexuals also came to see the performances. (The insecure heterosexual man could often be spotted by the way he kept his arm around his girlfriend all the way through the show.) The company discovered that the play had wider reverberations, that by presenting a truthful view of the world from a gay perspective they were able to speak to and enlighten everyone. Comments such as 'I didn't think I'd have anything in common with you', were frequently heard. GLF had always asserted that Gay Liberation encompassed everyone because it challenged everyone to re-assess attitudes towards gender and sexuality – this has been powerfully demonstrated by Gay Sweatshop audiences over the years. There was one memorable occasion at The Heriot Watt Students' Union in Edinburgh when four aggressively heterosexual male students bought four 'Lesbians Ignite!' badges and one 'Gay Love' badge. A few minutes later they were to be seen camping about and demonstrating exactly what they felt about 'queers'. After the show one of them approached Drew with the badges and said, 'We bought these before the show for a laugh. Now we don't want to laugh anymore.' He handed them back. And they didn't want their money back.

In many ways the five members of the company were like ambassadors for the Gay movement and it was crucial that they were themselves gay. Through travelling around the country with the play, holding the discussion and providing *Gay News* and gay publications on the bookstall, the company became part of a network of information. They were spreading ideas which were censored by the press and the media and were forging links with people all over the country. Sometimes the performances provided the first impetus for the setting up of a local gay group because it brought people together, or it helped local groups to gain new members and to consolidate their activities. Often campaigns against the company would backfire, as happened in Golders Green, and people who might otherwise have sat on the fence would be politicized by seeing intolerance and prejudice masquerading as morality and decency.

It was a very demanding job. Alan Pope says:

We weren't able to be just actors in a play and to walk away from it. We had a responsibility to our audience which actors don't normally have. You had to be ready to deal with any situation, ready for any questions. You could never get bored. We used to get asked the same questions every night but you had to deal with it as if it was the first time you had ever heard it. You got better at answering, that was all.

It was also a 24-hour job. The Arts Council grant did not cover accommodation and the company had to rely on the hospitality and generosity of CHE members and people in the towns where they were performing. This meant that after the show they would be going to someone's home where more discussion about the play would take place. But there were many compensations:

The contacts and friendships forged then were often the major rewards in a punishing schedule involving cross-country treks which looked impossible on the map. Daily journeys of between 200 and 400 miles became commonplace as did the acquisition of speeding fines and parking tickets. (Drew Griffiths, *Touching Our Lives, Gay News.* 1977)

This was obviously a sore point for Drew who must have been worried about the strain placed on the budget by these unforeseen expenses. In the newsletter that Christmas he wrote of Gerald, the driver:

> It's difficult to know what to say – if you ever see a headline saying 'Gay Hell-Driver Prosecuted for 24 Speeding Offences and 15 Parking Tickets', it'll be him. But one thing in his favour is – he always got us there. 'There' might not have been where we were supposed to be, but we always made it somehow.

In spite of the hard work, and the gruelling journeys, the tour was exciting and exhilarating. Writing this in 1989 one can't help feeling slightly envious of the optimism:

> At the end of the tour five people looked back on a unique experience which had proved the power of theatre as a force of change and enlightenment. (Drew Griffiths, *Touching our Lives*)

The angry debates at the Sheffield conference, the activities of the lesbian and gay community in Bradford, the battles and the euphoria of the *Mister X* tour were all part of an amazing world of change and hope summed up by a song written by Noël Greig for the Bradford GLF group, which became almost a gay anthem:

> There are people in the cities
> And the towns throughout the land,
> Who are saying to themselves,
> 'This is the time to make a stand.'
> Workers, women, gays and black and white,
> Now opening our eyes,
> To the need to take control
> Of both our bodies and our lives.
>
> All you gay women,
> All you gay men,
> Come together, stand together,
> And each other's rights defend.

In 1989 there is a sense of gay people retreating and being on the defensive. In 1975, as Alan Pope recalls, the barricades were up and we were storming over them and attacking the very foundations of a world that had oppressed us and denied our existence for far too long.

A Mixed Company

1976 was a particularly busy and productive year for Gay Sweatshop. A second season of six lunchtime plays was put on at the Institute of Contemporary Arts (ICA) which ran from February through to June, *Mister X* continued to tour and the same company produced a sequel, *Indiscreet*. There were visits to Holland and to Dublin, and, at Christmas, a lunchtime show and a late-night pantomime at the ICA. All in all, Gay Sweatshop produced nine shows that year and completed two major tours. But the most important development was that women joined the company and work for and by lesbians was produced for the first time.

There are subtle differences between the response of straight society towards lesbianism and towards male homosexuality. As Jill Posener points out, 'The Lesbian is a monstrous and mythological creature.' (A view with which Queen Victoria would

have probably agreed.) Gay men were accorded a modicum of acceptance as long as they conformed to stereotype and did not rock the boat. The response to lesbianism is in many ways more complex because it is threatening in a different way:
> The Lesbian is the stuff of so much male imagination: she's an ideal for men within pornography; she represents a threat for men in relationship to their girlfriends.
> (Jill Posener interviewed by the author.)

In more recent years the acceptance of gay men by certain sections of the society has meant that there have been sympathetic portrayals in West End plays and gay male characters on TV soap operas. It is true that often these characters have been presented in a way that makes them not at all threatening or subversive but they have been there. Images of lesbianism are still very rare – the idea that women can have an active sexuality, independent of men, continues to shock.

The first women to join Gay Sweatshop were the women who worked on Jill Posener's *Any Woman Can* – the play that was turned down for the Almost Free season. Jill's introduction to radical politics began whilst she was at school in Berlin when she became involved in protests against the war in Vietnam. She was already aware of her sexuality but the anti-war movement was not a context in which this could be expressed and explored. Once again we see someone faced with the difficulty in making links between a radical struggle which has political validity and their own personal struggle. But by the time she was a student at LAMDA on the stage management course she was used to confrontation and came out as a lesbian in class. She also began to take part in the Women's movement.

For many women feminism now provides a context where they can begin to explore sexual feelings towards other women that may have been hidden or suppressed for years. And, for Jill, feminism was attractive because it meant 'women together'. But 'women together' within the context of the Women's Liberation movement of the early seventies did not necessarily have a sexual dimension. Feminists often criticized *Any Woman Can* because it didn't deal with issues such as class and race, there was no mention of how the central character earned her living, of her relationship with her parents. Jill says that this is because the play was informed not by socialist-feminist politics but by her own need to write something which reflected her own experiences, her personal struggle as a lesbian. There was hardly any work around that provided lesbians with insights into their own lives. She didn't see herself as a pioneer or a playwright. She did have a strong desire to express her feelings creatively and, if she hadn't written *Any Woman Can*, then she would probably have written a book or joined a band instead.

When *Any Woman Can* was vetoed by Ed Berman, Jill showed her script to Kate Crutchley whom she had met whilst working at The Orange Tree in Richmond. Kate had attended drama school in Birmingham and gone on to work in rep, first as an ASM and then as an actress in pantomimes, musicals, old time music-hall shows, as well as the stock rep plays. She also worked with television in the Birmingham-based serial, *United*. In her early twenties Kate remembers that she was only interested in her career, in 'singing and showing off and living out of a suitcase!'; consequently, she didn't have time for a personal life and it wasn't until her mid-twenties that she became aware of her sexuality when she met the designer Mary Moore. In her late twenties Kate started directing – her first production was *The Boyfriend* at St. Andrews. She also came into contact with alternative theatre and played a part in Steve Gooch's *Female Transport* at the Half Moon. However, when Kate met Jill at the Orange Tree, she saw her career as still being very much in mainstream theatre and, as Jill remembers, she was quite discreet about her personal life and her relationship with

Mary. All the same, Jill took the step of asking Kate and Mary to read *Any Woman Can*. The next day they phoned her and were very enthusiastic about it. This response was very encouraging and meant that Jill had allies who knew what she was trying to say and were keen to see the play produced.

In the autumn of 1975 Jill went up to the Leicester Haymarket to work in the studio theatre as stage manager for a women's theatre season. Jill approached the management to stage her script as part of the season. The management were very nervous about putting on a lesbian play and Jill remembers endless meetings about it. Monday evenings were open nights when more experimental pieces were given an airing and eventually it was agreed that the play could be given a one-off performance at one of these open nights. Jill asked Miriam Margolyes to play the central role and Kate and Mary Moore worked with the cast in London and brought the play to the Haymarket for the one night. The response was very favourable and a glowing review appeared in the *Morning Star*.

Meanwhile Gay Sweatshop was touring *Mister X* and was planning a second lunchtime season of plays to be held at the ICA. The Arts Council had agreed a grant for the first half of the year and, for the first time, union rates could be paid. In order to attract scripts a slightly different tack had been taken; Gerald Chapman reasoned that Gay Sweatshop was an important theatre company for which the most prestigious playwrights in the country should be writing and so he had approached a number of them. One of the few who responded to this approach was Edward Bond who sent in his play *Stone*.

Drew and Gerald had both wanted *Any Woman Can* performed at the Almost Free and so they asked Jill, Kate and Mary to bring it to the ICA as a Gay Sweatshop production. At the same time they invited them to join the company. The women's contribution to the season was considerable; as well as *Any Woman Can*, Kate directed Andrew Davies' play *Randy Robinson's Unsuitable Relationship* and Mary Moore worked wonders designing the whole season from one basic set.

This second lunchtime season was, if anything, more successful than the first and, like the Almost Free season, it was extended running from February through to July. The atmosphere at the ICA was particularly friendly and the building became home for the company and a drop-in centre for London lesbians and gays. Again there were discussions, an exhibition and a bookstall. This last was run by Ernest Hole who used the experience to start 'Gay's The Word' bookshop a couple of years later. *Mister X* broke records for the size of audience attending a lunchtime play and *Any Woman Can* was equally popular and was booked to play the Kings Head after its ICA performances.

The responses to other plays in the season were mixed. *The Fork* by Ian Brown raised issues about fascist regimes and torture and went some way to equating homosexual oppression with Fascism. At the time Amnesty International was resisting including gay people as prisoners of conscience and the play fed into that debate. *Randy Robinson's Unsuitable Relationship* was criticized by some because the central character was heterosexual and Edward Bond's *Stone* caused considerable controversy in the company because it was heavily symbolic to the point of being obscure and therefore its relevance to Sweatshop's audiences was in doubt. Once again it had proved difficult to find scripts which reflected the philosophy and the ideals of the company. Gerald's attempt to elicit work from established playwrights, irrespective of whether they were gay, had not proved wholly satisfactory and Gay Sweatshop came out of the ICA season with a renewed commitment to its identity as a company where writers, directors, designers as well as actors would all be lesbians and gay men.

The company's homegrown sequel to *Mister X*, *Indiscreet* or *The Revenge of Mister X*, was itself not totally successful. Looking back on it, Alan Pope feels that in trying to bring Mister X's story up to date and to look at the current state of the Gay movement some objectivity was lost. It was difficult to explore the events as they were happening – it was as yet not clear what the next statement from the men in the company should be.

Mister X was still in demand and continued to tour throughout the long hot summer of 1976. The company took the show to Bradford. They had been booked to play Bradford the previous autumn but the show had been cancelled because the GLF group in the city saw Gay Sweatshop's professional status as a contradiction – it was felt that Sweatshop members were setting themselves up as experts in gay theatre which was resented by some members of the new General Will. They believed that gay theatre should be created by people within the context of their own communities. Through the General Will, working-class lesbians and gay men in Bradford had taken the opportunity to make plays about their own lives and were fiercely proud of their achievement. The New York company Hot Peaches were given a hostile reception when they visited the city. They used drag in their shows but walked the streets looking very 'straight' which made their work seem like a charade to people who lived their gayness both onstage and off in Bradford. So it was with some anxiety that Gay Sweatshop went to perform to the heaviest dykes and gays in the country! The company did come in for a lot of criticism but, all the same, a dialogue was set up between the two groups and particularly between Drew and Noël Greig who was still a key figure in the General Will.

When the ICA season finished, Gay Sweatshop decided that touring was the most important aspect of their work; the priority was to find a lesbian cast for *Any Woman Can* and to send it out on tour. Kate Crutchley undertook to administrate the bookings and successfully applied for Arts Council funding. She and Jill auditioned actresses – among them Nancy Duiguid, Helen Barnaby, Julie Gretton (Parker) who had been in the year below Nancy at the Central School and Sara Hardy who had seen the play at the ICA and written in offering to help in whatever way she could. This cast became full-time members of Gay Sweatshop and for the first time there were equal numbers of men and women in the company.

What *Mister X* had achieved on tour for gay men, *Any Woman Can* achieved for lesbians. Nancy recalls sitting up late into the night hearing women talk about their lives as lesbians, their fear of losing their jobs, their fear of losing their children. Once again there was a sense of a voice being given to people who had until then been denied one. There was a memorable occasion when she and Jill Posener answered questions on a phone-in programme on the radio in Plymouth when they listened to people with a whole spectrum of opinions and attitudes ranging from cruel, angry and unthinking through to compassionate and supportive. What made it worthwhile was that the performance that evening was attended by people who had obviously come because they had heard the phone-in. The audience was composed largely of older couples, many of them women.

Later on in the year the men's company took *Mister X* to Holland where they discovered that Dutch gays didn't have things as easy as the liberated Amsterdam scene might suggest:

> We expected to be regarded as an English oddity, a nostalgia-trip for Dutch gays who'd left self-oppression behind them when the laws were changed. Sadly not

so. The English stories we'd heard of people too afraid to come to the theatre in case they were recognised were repeated.
But Holland was light years away from the next port of call.

The men and the women met up in November 1976 to take the ferry to Ireland where performances of *Mister X* and *Any Woman Can* were being hosted by the Project Arts Centre in Dublin. The Project had recently been awarded a grant for improvements of £6,000 from the City Corporation. There had already been some opposition to the grant from people who saw the Project as a subversive left-wing organization. Gay Sweatshop's visit caused a furore in the city which continued for months and which was comparable only to the occasion in 1957 when the gardai moved in and closed down Tennessee Williams' play *The Rose Tattoo*.

 The scandal really got off the ground when one theatre reviewer - Desmond Rushe of the *Irish Independent* – accused the company of being 'propagandist in the most crudely offensive manner' and 'as grotesquely obscene as one could imagine'. He began his review by saying that when Gay Sweatshop announces itself as an openly gay theatre group he expected an attempt at brainwashing – 'Just as if a company performing a play about necrophilia announced that they were all practising necrophiliacs'. Of *Mister X* he said that it 'wallows on the level of "the cottage", to use one of the perverse distortions of language popular in the deviant scene'. He finished his review by questioning the Project's policy referring to a visit some weeks earlier by 7:84 'a left-wing group from England on a boring propaganda trip'. He then asked, 'Is the substantial subsidy given by Dublin City Council and the Arts Council intended to support such a policy?'

 This review was seized upon by the Project's opponents and a campaign was mounted by organizations such as The League of Decency, Parent Concern and The Society to Outlaw Pornography to stop the City Corporation grant. There were bomb threats, wooden rosaries and illustrations of flagellation scenes were posted through the letterbox and people who had not even seen the plays were condemning them as filth.

Members of the Amenities Committee who had agreed the grant were lobbied to withdraw it. One letter to a newspaper read:

It is ironic that some City Councillors regard sodomy and lesbianism as art forms, and culturally uplifting. Ranting against society for not accommodating itself to such sexual perversions is an admission of ignorance of the vulnerability of society, and the young in particular, to the corrosive effect of unnatural vice.

But there was also support for the plays, not least from Mr Rushe's fellow critics on other publications. Some of these obviously found it hard to accept the uncompromising stance of the work, but had to recognize the skilful and imaginative way in which it was presented, and their liberal consciences forced them to see the validity of what the plays were saying. For David Norris of the Irish Gay Rights Movement (IGRM) 'the performances brought into the open some of the uncomfortable realities with which as homosexuals we have to live and from which too many uncaring and unconcerned fellow citizens are content to avert their gaze.'

 In spite of this support and enthusiastic audiences the City Corporation suspended the Project's grant. A counter campaign was mounted. The company flew back to Dublin the following January to much media attention for one-off performances of the two plays. Even though the grant was not re-instated the Project gained many friends and the Dublin Gay Movement was strengthened and given direction by it.

Gay Sweatshop's achievements in 1976 were crowned by a celebratory late-night Christmas Show at the ICA – *Jingleball 2*. (*Jingleball 1* was a lunchtime show devised and performed by Gerald Chapman and Kate Crutchley and featured music by Tom Robinson, most notably his very beautiful song, 'Truce'. Tom was making a name for himself as a singer with Cafe Society and with his own band and his period of collaboration with Gay Sweatshop was brief but fruitful.) Meanwhile, in Dublin, the *Mister X* and *Any Woman Can* companies were coming up with ideas for *Jingleball 2*. Kate remembers receiving phone-calls from Ireland telling her the subject matter for songs that were needed and then phoning Michael Richmond who was writing the lyrics and relaying the requirements to him. Tom Robinson wrote the music for one of the songs but the rest was composed by Alex Harding who had first met the company after coming to the Almost Free. Later, back home in Portsmouth, he wrote a letter asking how he could be involved in the company's work:

> I'm 25. I can type, play the piano (commercially à la Mrs Mills!) have done lots of clerical work, was box-office clerk at the Palladium, a tape operator for a recording studio and speak French . . . I know that somewhere amongst political gay men and women, there is a place for me.

The company gained a member whose contribution both as an arranger, composer and musical director was to be invaluable.

Jingleball 2 was a pantomime loosely based on *Cinderella* but with a backstage storyline. Cinders works for two nationalistic drag queens (played by Drew and Gordon) who mime to such songs as 'Land of Hope and Glory'. She is described in the programme as 'an oppressed woman' and her co-worker is a gay man called Buttons. There is 'an influence for good' in the shape of the lavender fairy who wears a boiler suit covered in lesbian badges. Cinders' talent is spotted by an impressario by the name of Miss Charming played in true principal-boy style by Nancy. The show was irreverant and celebratory and marked a high-point in the collaboration between the men and the women.

Dublin had been the first opportunity for the two companies to work together for any length of time. The trip to Ireland had an inauspicious start when the women were late for the boat. The men were waiting anxiously on the quayside. The atmosphere between some members of the two groups was decidedly frosty on the crossing. When they got to Dublin Alan remembers them all sitting down to breakfast together. He tried to break the ice by grabbing a teapot and asking, 'Shall I be Mother?' He immediately realized the unconscious sexism of the question and was mortified. He discovered afterwards that Julie, at least, had found the whole situation hilarious. But there were differences between the ways that the men and women related to each other and to the work and this had serious repercussions. In the Gay movement the gulf between lesbians and gay men was widening. Lesbian feminists felt that they weren't getting enough support from gay men, and gay men felt attacked and defensive, accusing lesbians of being anti-men. Nancy remembers that although lesbians supported men over issues such as the age of consent, this support wasn't reciprocated when it came to fighting lesbian custody cases. Within Gay Sweatshop there were long discussions: because it had originally been a men's company the women felt that it was difficult to establish a separate and autonomous identity. The women were making radical demands and looking for ways of creating work with a strong political focus. After much soul searching it was decided to split the company into two autonomous groups that would be run by a mixed collective.

Our separation into two mutually-supportive groups was necessary for the work to

proceed. A vague plan of merging and presenting plays with equal lesbian and gay male content has been seen for the pipedream it is. The current more realistic approach to our work simply amounts to doing what you know best. Who better than gay men to relate their own experience and lesbians to do likewise?
(Drew Griffiths, *Touching Our Lives*)

A note of sadness and resignation is detectable in Drew's evaluation of this decision – it was one which everyone involved had reached painfully, particularly given the success of *Jingleball*.

After Christmas the company was committed to producing a mixed show about the age of consent for school audiences at the Royal Court as part of the Young People's Theatre run by Gerald Chapman. After that the women and the men were to go their separate ways in relating their own individual experiences: the women to devise a play about lesbian custody cases and the men to explore gay male history. These were to be the first full-length plays that the company produced and both of them proved to be milestones of lesbian and gay theatre.

Living with State Control

By 1977 it was clear that Gay Sweatshop needed to put itself onto a more secure footing financially and to employ a full-time administrator. David Thompson had been completing an arts administration course at the Central London Poly during the ICA season and had undertaken a survey of the audiences. He was the obvious candidate for the administrator's job. It was David who put the company's books in order and who negotiated an annual programme award of £15,000 from the Arts Council for the year beginning April 1977. This grant, unlike revenue subsidy, was not guaranteed and had to be re-applied for each year, but it did allow the company to plan a whole year's work.

1977 had begun with yet another scandal when the company found itself plastered over the front of the *Evening News*. Alan remembers leaving a cinema with other members of Sweatshop and seeing a billboard: 'Children in Sex Play.' They remarked jokingly that it probably referred to the upcoming production of *Age of Consent* at the Royal Court, never dreaming that it would turn out to be the truth. The play was to be performed as part of a season for school parties entitled *Everyone Different*. The self-appointed protectors of youth were voicing their terrible phobia about young people being presented with a balanced and sane view of sex and homosexuality. They seemed to believe homosexuality could be caught as easily as the common cold (there is always the sinister link with disease) and that young people need to be protected from seeing positive images of lesbians and gays.

A survey by the Gay Teenage Group found that the suicide rate among gay teenagers is higher than in any other group. This situation can only change if young lesbians and gays are presented with positive role models and if young heterosexuals have their homophobia challenged. It was with this mind that Gerald Chapman presented *Age of Consent* at the Royal Court.

The media responded in its usual sensationalistic and mindless fashion. Dr Rhodes Boyson himself intervened and tried to get the performances stopped and some schools, in consequence, withdrew from the scheme in alarm. Many did not withdraw, however, and the season went ahead – a major victory.

It is clear from this type of incident that the State viewed homosexuality as something highly subversive, threatening the fabric of the society. Both Gay Sweatshop's next shows by the men and the women explored different facets of the way discrimination has been and continues to be sanctioned by the State.

Care and Control

Care and Control tackled the subject of child custody – an issue of prime importance to many lesbians. In 1977 it was unheard of for a mother to retain custody of children after divorce or separation if it became known that she was a lesbian – a situation which continues today. Only in cases that do not come to court and where there is a sympathetic local authority does a lesbian mother stand any chance of retaining custody. This legal prejudice is often exploited ruthlessly by fathers who want to maintain influence over their children and perhaps get their revenge on a wife who has wounded their sexual pride. In fact, as *Care and Control* illustrated, it was sometimes enough just to hint that a mother was lesbian, or even a feminist, for the case to go against her. One judge accepted the possession of a copy of *Spare Rib* as evidence that the woman was an unsuitable parent. For anyone who thought the *The Loudest Whisper* was melodramatic in the way it portrayed the establishment's paranoia about lesbians and children the transcripts of some of these cases make salutary reading.

When the Gay Sweatshop women were on tour with *Any Woman Can* they asked audiences what issues they would most like to see the company take on. Two subjects came up again and again: discrimination at work and child custody. Nancy Diuguid was particularly keen to develop the latter idea.

Nancy had come to this country from the States to study at the Central School of Speech and Drama in the early seventies. It is interesting that the show she helped to develop for Gay Sweatshop was a courtroom drama of sorts because her earliest ambitions had been to become a lawyer; as a child she used to read all the cases of Clarence Darrow – one of America's leading liberal lawyers. Nancy's background was Southern, upper middle-class and conservative (even if Democrat) and she remembers her growing awareness as a child of the social injustice that surrounded her: seeing Black people still working on the plantations, and the signs outside public lavatories which said 'Blacks Not Allowed'. She remembered a trip to Cuba as a child, three days before the revolution, where she saw vast wealth contrasting with the abject poverty of the hundreds of people begging on the streets. Although too young to be involved in the civil rights movement she took part in anti-war demonstrations and became involved in the Women's Liberation Movement from 1968 onwards. As a student in 1970 she attended one of the first women's conferences in Indiana and she remembers, too, the feeling of elation of being in a room with ten other lesbians at a workshop during the conference.

She started out on the production side with a particular interest in lighting design and only began to act relatively late in her time at Indiana University. Later she went to London to attend a summer school at Central and when they offered her a place on the three-year course she accepted eagerly the opportunity to stay in England. This was motivated partly by her disillusionment with the US over Vietnam, her need to escape certain aspects of her family background and her desire to take in as much of the culture and intellect of Europe as possible. Coming as she did from the Mid-

West she feels she had an inferiority complex about the intellectual and cultural superiority of people from the East Coast and moving to England was a way of going one better than them. She walked into Central as an out lesbian, covered in badges of all sorts – lesbian, feminist and left-wing. After graduating she worked with a company performing in prisons and mental hospitals before auditioning for Gay Sweatshop.

Care and Control was the first women's show generated from within the company and those involved put in the same commitment and personal investment as the men had when devising *Mister X*. Kate and Nancy started interviewing women who had lost children – working-class women as well as middle-class women, heterosexual feminists as well as lesbians. They heard many disturbing stories of heartache, frustration and loss. One of the difficulties in devising the show was to get transcripts of cases; they were less readily available then than they would be now. Nancy managed to beg and, 'borrow' them from solicitors' offices and barristers' chambers. There was a vast amount of research material and the job of sorting it out and making a play of it seemed a huge one. The company began to work on a structure, improvising and devising scenes. Two of the actresses, Kate Phelps and Tasha Fairbanks, had writing skills and made particularly relevant contributions to this process. Decisions were made about how to combine certain cases so that some characters became amalgams of two or more real-life people. In the end it was decided that they needed a writer to help them shape and refine the material. Michelene Wandor was asked to come in and fulfil this scripting role. The end result was both shocking and moving.

The women who had been interviewed were invited to a preview in order to discuss the play before it was publicly shown. Nancy can still remember vividly the atmosphere at the preview. The women were overwhelmed by seeing their experiences portrayed and transformed into a piece of theatre in such a way that their hurt could be shared and the injustice they had suffered communicated.

Care and Control is an example of a piece of documentary theatre which was collectively devised, which arose directly from people's lives. Countless women contributed to it. It revealed things that had never been properly exposed before and was uncompromising in the way that it showed how the State uses the notion of the family to control people's lives. *Time Out* described it as 'one of the most enraging, instructive and bitterly funny plays the Women's movement has yet produced.' When the production went out on tour the response was equally emotional and such was the play's success that a second production was toured later in the year.

Meanwhile a new men's show was being planned.

As Time Goes by

Early in 1977 Drew met with Noël Greig for a drink. Noël had left the General Will because of disputes within the group which eventually led to its demise. In an article for *Platform* (No.5), since reproduced in Michelene Wandor's *Carry on Understudies*, Noël wrote about his experiences in Bradford:

> The project died in the end. There were internal problems about how to run such an operation in an open way and maintain some kind of skilled

administration which did not accrue all the power and decision-making. Beyond this, and more importantly, despite support from individual members on the ACGB panels, that bureaucracy could not contain the idea of such an experiment... There is no doubt in my mind that the project could have survived an Arts Council cut. However, this occurred at just the moment where the initial energies for the first one-and-a-half years had given way to the need for a period of reflection. A long and exhausting battle over funding added to tensions, and the focus moved from the work to the political battle to retain public support.

Noël had left Bradford under duress and was not totally reconciled to being in London. In 1972 he had left the Combination after it moved from Brighton to Deptford because of the contradictions that arose from not being able to link up all the different aspects of his life – his class politics, his sexuality, his creative needs. For a brief period he had existed in a limbo, unsure of what to do next: at one point he directed at the Almost Free for Inter-Action, and, at another, became involved in commercial theatre as assistant director on the first production of *Jesus Christ Superstar*. When the opportunity arose to move to Bradford to join the General Will in 1973 he seized it because it would allow him to be creative within the context of a Northern working-class community. Subsequently his work with the lesbian and gay community gave that context an even greater pertinence to his own life. It was very important to him that the work was community-based, that it came from a collaborative process and that it was a reflection of the lives of the people onstage. When Drew had seen *All Het Up* in 1975 he had been intrigued by the large-scale epic quality of the company's work, which placed gay people within a broad political context. Gay Sweatshop's men's company were unsure of what to do next and Drew suggested to Noël that they write a play together that would be Gay Sweatshop's version of that large-scale epic theatre. Noël accepted Drew's offer although his heart was still in Bradford and the idea of returning to London and working as an individual artist, albeit in Gay Sweatshop, was not altogether appealing.

The collaboration between Drew and Noël was very productive. Noël brought historical perspective and the ability to work on a large canvas. Drew brought his considerable theatrical know-how and a discipline that was based on his experience of working in rep on 'well-made' plays. They both had similar sensibilities in terms of what they felt made a piece of theatre effective and moving and both were skilled in the art of combining pathos and humour. ('I remember one occasion, when I had just joined Gay Sweatshop as a callow 24-year-old, going to the theatre with Drew and Noël and turning to see them both sitting with tears streaming down their faces at the end of the performance. I'd never seen anything like it!')

The men's company had found it difficult with *Indiscreet* to produce a play which looked at contemporary gay issues. Drew and Noël decided to examine the past in order to gain greater understanding of the present. They explored three periods over the last 100 years during which State repression of homosexuality was linked to wider events: Victorian England, thirties Berlin and late-sixties New York.

As Time Goes By, the play that emerged, was divided into three sections. The first emphasized the class divisions in Victorian England, a society that set great store by people knowing their place, their class and their gender, motivated by the desire to maintain industrial output by having a docile workforce and to maintain the

Empire by having a population which produced men who were willing to die defending it. England was becoming increasingly militarized in preparation for the Boer War and ultimately the First World War. The class system and the Family became the bedrock of the Victorian values much lauded by present day politicians and used by the State as a means of control. Oscar Wilde and men like him flaunted these conventions by taking working-class, male lovers. This provoked the full force of State retribution. The lucky ones and those who could afford it escaped on the boat train to Paris; others, like Oscar Wilde and the working-class men who were caught, ended up in prison.

Section two, in Berlin, also showed a society where the State was becoming increasingly militarized. For a few years during the Weimar Republic there was a greater tolerance and understanding of homosexuality in Germany. A Jewish homosexual sexologist, Magnus Hirschfeld, had begun to make studies of sexual behaviour at his Institute for Sexual Sciences in Berlin and his ideas were receiving worldwide attention. But with the rise of the fascist regime it became increasingly dangerous to hold liberal opinions. One recurrent theme in this section was the attitudes of parties of both the Right and the Left towards homosexuality. Even in 1977 there was a widely-held belief that homosexuality had been somehow responsible for the Third Reich. The perverted brutality of that regime was often embodied in plays and films by the queer Brownshirt or SS guard. I remember friends who couldn't understand why Gay Sweatshop was doing a play about Nazi Germany asking, 'Weren't most of the Nazis gay anyway?' The fact that homosexuals were sent to the concentration camps was still not widely known and we were often missed out when victims of the Holocaust were listed. At the time of Hitler's rise to power the Communists used homosexuality 'as a stick to beat the Nazis' to quote *As Time Goes By*. Conversely, the Nazis caricatured the Left as being composed of Jewish intellectual queers, a description which fitted Magnus Hirschfeld on all counts: the Instititute was raided in 1933, his books and a bust of Hirschfeld were thrown onto a bonfire on the Opera Square.

This scapegoating of homosexuals by both sides of the political spectrum left them exposed and vulnerable. Ultimately, however, socialist ideals embrace human diversity whereas fascism imposes uniformity. This section of *As Time Goes By* shows gay men caught up in these political contradictions and unable to find a secure, unified base from which to resist. One scene shows a drag queen, Kurt, (played by Drew) trying to seduce a young gay communist, Hans. Hans is new to the city and quite naive about his sexuality. He is obviously attracted to, and fascinated by Kurt but tries to hide this by talking about politics. Kurt, who is working-class, is in many ways apolitical and dangerously ignorant of the threat of Nazism – which appalls Hans. He is more interested in admiring the colour of Hans' hair than talking about Communism, and regrets the passing of the time 'when all we ever did was sit around and natter about gowns'. Such a character could very easily be portrayed as being vacuous and foolish but the writing and Drew's performance gave him dignity and natural intelligence; his sense of right and wrong and his confidence in his sexuality meant that they could both learn from each other and it is Kurt who breaks the deadlock between them, taking Hans off to bed. It was a brilliant and funny illustration of the relationship between straight left politics and the politics of Gay Liberation. When it was performed some heterosexual male socialists found it very difficult to take.

The National Socialist's response to the accusations of homosexuality was the Night of the Long Knives when it purged all known homosexuals from its ranks.

The most eminent of these was Ernst Röhm the leader of the Brownshirts. Subsequently, under Himmler's direction, the regime tried ruthlessly to rid the Fatherland of all such 'perverts' and men like Kurt as well as Hans the communist were despatched to the camps in cattle-trains.

The third section dealt with the area covered by Part Two of this history. (Changing Times). It charted the journey through the civil rights movement, the Women's movement, the anti-war movement and the hippy movement to Stonewall. It was written in the monologue form of *Kennedy's Children* and was set in a gay bar in Greenwich Village on the night of Judy Garland's funeral. The characters represent aspects of all these different movements. The barman is a draft-dodger, one customer is a white business-man who has had a relationship with a Black man and was rejected by him when he joined the Black Panthers (who saw homosexuality as a white man's disease). Another customer is a student who has been introduced to feminist ideas through his sister's involvement with the Women's movement, another is a drag queen trying to understand his own place in the counter-culture and wittily explaining his identification with female Hollywood filmstars. There is a taciturn leather guy who merely grunts and chews gum throughout and a silent cruiser who turns out to be an undercover cop. When he tries to arrest him for soliciting, the drag queen resists and eventually enlists the support of the other gay men in the bar. As the actor playing the cop I can still remember the intensity of Drew's performance as the drag queen when he turned on me and refused to be arrested with one almighty 'no!' – the moment embodied the turning-point in our history when gay people found their collective voice.

For Drew the mixing of Hollywood film, images that he had seen as a child, and political struggle was not incongruous and had a particular poignancy:

> As a child I wept at the movies when a woman suffered at the hands of a man or when the pit fell in and the miners were killed because of the owners' greed: it was natural for me to weep at human suffering. Self-sacrifice was also an occasion for tears; the unmarried mother whose daughter never called her 'Mamma'; the giant ape who held the heroine aloft in his palm as the island sank and the waters closed over his head. I wept at bravery in the face of hardship ('As God is my witness, I'll never go hungry again') and single-minded determination achieving the impossible (The children marching into the village singing 'Nick, nack, paddy wack, Give the dog a bone, This old man came rolling home.') But what moved me most of all was hope, when individuals representing collective consciousness express the hope that the future will be better than the present or the past because it is within our power to make it so.

At the time the play was performed many commentators ridiculed the idea of a political message being mediated through characters such as Kurt or the New York drag queen and dismissed the play as being ghetto theatre. In his contribution to 'Why I Joined Gay Sweatshop' in *Gay Left*, Noël later wrote that hostility towards Gay Sweatshop came not just from 'the prejudiced and officious around the country' but also from members of the theatre profession:

> The real reason for their disdain, horror, or *cool* support is I suspect, that the Cissies have come out on the shop floor. We've put all those big butch numbers (whether on the stage of the National or in a touring Left group) in a nasty situation, and their response is to be even Bigger and Butcher. They don't like gays in the theatre going public; they're scared stiff of being associated with one of the cissies who'd much rather put on a cossy and some slap, than clock in at Ford's every day.

In the early seventies some members of the straight left parties saw sexual politics as a diversion from the one true struggle – the class struggle – and political theatre was expected to follow this orthodoxy. Noël's criticism of certain sections of the straight left at that time was obviously fuelled by his own experiences in Brighton and Bradford and by the way that even when feminist ideas and Black politics became more widely accepted the work of Gay Sweatshop was still undervalued:

> ... what's really interesting is that although the notion of autonomous Women's or Black groups has taken root, the same recognition has not been extended to Gay men and Lesbians. The cry of 'Ghetto' goes up from those very people who coo over the idea of autonomous Black theatre. (Why I Joined Gay Sweatshop, *Gay Left* 1978)

Drew found this especially painful and infuriating. In a letter to someone who produced *As Time Goes By* in America in 1983 Drew wrote:

> I'd invested everything – mind, heart and soul – into the show and the inevitable adverse reactions knocked me sideways. Indeed, everything printed about the play (and there were some marvellous things but not enough to satisfy me) seemed to reveal ignorance, hatred and homophobia; being so closely involved I took them as personal attacks on me.

Talking about it now, Noël feels that, for Drew, *As Time Goes By* represented the high standard of theatre he aspired to, and also reflected his relatively newly-formed gay politics and he knew that it was being attacked for unfair reasons. With this play, however, Gay Sweatshop was setting itself up to be judged on the same level as other companies and,so, taking the criticism was par for the course. As Drew acknowledged, there was also considerable acclaim for the play; in *Time Out* Richard Krupp compared the play to the recently-screened *Roots* and went on to say:

> Blacks – like women – have long known that a sense of history can produce the sense of collective oppression from which springs positive action. Noël Greig and Drew Griffith's play depicts gay men continually caught up in history but alienated from it; six versatile actors and a tireless pianist bring it triumphantly to life.

As a member of that cast I have very strong memories of the effect the play had on audiences and on me, changing the direction of my life. In the ten years between sitting in front of the telly in Devon and joining Gay Sweatshop I had myself spent six months in Berlin before going to University to read modern languages. My time at University coincided with the emergence of Gay Liberation (1971-74) but I managed to stay firmly in the closet. This was perhaps partly because I had chosen to go to Oxford where the traditional image of homosexuality was an outmoded, flamboyant, upper-class one which I found hard to reconcile with my Devonian diffidence and background. On the rare occasions when I did see a 'Glad to be Gay' badge I ran a mile and never ventured across Magdalen bridge to the pub on the Cowley Road where the GLF discos were held. The summer I left Oxford I visited a friend from school in Berlin and there, walking along the Kurfürstendamm, she asked me if I was gay – she'd picked up on a few heavy hints I'd been making – and I breathed a sigh of relief that I could now talk to someone close to me about myself. I returned to England and moved to London with a vague idea of becoming an actor. I got a job with a community theatre group in Battersea and then a touring children's company; slowly and tentatively, I began to meet other gay men.

At the same time my politics were changing. My background was non-conformist and the choice at elections was between the Tories and the Liberals – Jeremy Thorpe was still North Devon's MP. My introduction to socialist and feminist ideas was a gradual one and developed hand-in-hand with my acceptance of my sexuality. By 1976 my politics were of the left and I went on abortion campaign demos, although I had never been on a Gay Pride March. I still found it difficult to pluck up the courage to enter a gay disco, let alone talk to anyone once inside, and most of my friends were heterosexuals. I was aware of Gay Sweatshop's existence and had seen *Mister X* at the University of London Union where I met someone I knew, who was with a man called Noël down from Bradford to see the show. (I learnt later that I'd not made a particularly good impression.) I even contacted Gerald Chapman at one point and went along to a Sweatshop collective meeting where I found myself in the middle of a squabble about the poster for the ICA season. I was obviously attracted to the company but wary. In the autumn of 1976, I went to drama school on a postgraduate acting course from which I emerged in 1977 determined to pursue a career that would lead me into rep and from there into one of the big national companies (I hoped) and ever onwards and upwards to fame and fortune! Then I saw Gay Sweatshop's advert for actors in *The Stage*.

Every actor who is offered a part with Gay Sweatshop probably has the moment when they wonder what they'll tell their Mum. For a while the company became just plain Sweatshop in my telephone calls to Devon. Eventually, of course, my family had to discover not only that I was gay but that I was intending to stand up and be a homosexual on stage in front of people. In joining the company I was burning bridges – perhaps more than I realized at the time. It changed my life not only personally, socially and politically; it revolutionized my concept of theatre. It wasn't just that I learned that theatre can make you cry, I also began to make connections (of the E M Forster kind) between my own life and the work which were both exhilarating and, looking back on it, terrifying. It was, in all senses, a sentimental education and no acting job would ever be quite the same again.

The tour of *As Time Goes By* had many high spots but perhaps the most poignant and the most significant was when we played Berlin in December 1977. For me, the city had all sorts of memories from both my previous stays. We travelled in a clapped-out van called Quentin which we had to push to start and which had no heating (I still have a mental picture of Drew sitting in the back cocooned in a sleeping-bag and woolly hat). We pushed the van off the ferry in Hamburg and over the border between East and West Germany where one drunk company member had to be restrained from addressing the border guards as the 'Red Menace' and reached Berlin. We played in a cinema on a stage that was barely big enough to accommodate set and actors at the same time. The set was an ingenious white box and Paul Dart's design gave the impression of a black-and-white film which cleverly mirrored the play's cinematic references and was particularly apt in this Berlin venue. The first performance was packed out – 'Will they understand it?' we asked ourselves; after all, an average English audience wouldn't have much patience with a play in German. The warmth and enthusiasm of those Berlin audiences was unforgettable. They not only got the message but they got the jokes as well. We were the toast of Berlin (that week) and at the end of our final performance were showered with roses. We hadn't realized that to gay Berliners the play would have such significance, particularly the middle section. They, too, had seen precious little about the Nazis which didn't cast homosexuals as the villains. One member of the audience said afterwards, 'That's the first time that I've seen something about the Third Reich where I didn't feel to blame.'

Just before *As Time Goes By* opened Drew started a barbed correspondence with Peter Hall about two recent productions at the National Theatre, *Tales from the Vienna Woods* and *The Madras House*. In the former, the MC who is the only gay character turns out to be a fascist and gives a Nazi salute: in the latter, the camp Mr Windlesham was portrayed as a grotesque caricature who, according to Drew, succeeded 'in getting cheap laughs from closed minds'. He went on to point out that 'when two plays are given superb productions and set out to attack sexism and the rigidity of gender roles and yet still contribute to the prejudice against homosexuals then the blame must rest firmly with the play's producers.' A letter came back:

> The difficulty about your letter is that it presupposes a prejudice on *your* part – that homosexuals are never foolish, excessive or vicious. You cannot in all honesty lay all these faults squarely in the laps of heterosexuals only.

The fact that in 1977 there were still very few balanced portrayals of homosexuals on our major stages must have fed Drew's anger and Peter Hall's defence, that they had recently produced Harold Pinter's *No Man's Land* in which he said, 'homosexual passions were treated absolutely seriously and tenderly', did little to reassure him. It could have seemed that Drew was fighting a losing battle but *As Time Goes By* sent out ripples which were political, social and artistic and which reached the furthest shores. Alan feels most strongly that Gay Sweatshop's work had a wide-reaching effect on British and American theatre and the way homosexuality was portrayed in plays.

Martin Sherman pays tribute to the inspiration he drew from *As Time Goes By* when he was writing *Bent*. *Bent* was a success both in the West End and in New York and paved the way for later successes such as *Torch Song Trilogy* and *Cage Aux Folles* by Harvey Fierstein. Martin had been asked by Drew to come into rehearsals and help the actors with the American accents. What struck him most during those rehearsals was the second section of the play:

> That Berlin, the Berlin that had existed just before Hitler and was ultimately destroyed by Hitler, the Berlin, I suppose of Isherwood, had always had a compulsive fascination for me, and the Berlin section in *As Time Goes By* struck a nerve. At some point the ultimate fate of Germany's gays in the concentration camps was mentioned, and a cartoonist drawing that rehearsal scene would have put a lightning flash above my head, because it was like that, truly like that. I knew immediately that I wanted to write a play on the subject. I had been thinking for many months about the 'illusion' of freedom that homosexual men and women had, most particularly in America, and also about a certain hardness that had entered the world, an inability to commit, an inability to admit to the purity of loving, but I didn't know how to write about it. In the lightning flash I realized the answer was to re-examine history, just as *As Time Goes By* was doing and to draw the parallels, and there in the beloved Berlin of my imagination was the history I was looking for.

> I travelled with the Sweatshop to Edinburgh for the run of *As Time Goes By* and that play pumped adrenalin into my eager veins. Drew was particularly encouraging and promised me that Sweatshop would produce my play. So I quite literally wrote *Bent, for* the Gay Sweatshop. Months later, when I had finished the play (back in America) I sent it to Drew. He told me that the Sweatshop could only guarantee the play a limited audience, and that it deserved to be seen on a far wider basis, and urged me to take it out into the world. It was

an act of extraordinary generosity, typical of Drew, and typical, too, of the foundations of the Sweatshop, for it was an organization built not just of sweat, but wisdom, kindness and the desire to inspire. It did. (*Martin Sherman*, 1988) In trying to assess *As Time Goes By* Noël Greig argues that the play's achievement was to show that gay men had not been onlookers in history. They had either colluded with the State or taken action against it. They had been able to make their own decisions about how to operate in terms of the State. Their responses had been various in terms of their class and their perspectives and were not necessarily unified or passive. For Noël, the most important point is that the passivity of the characters decreases throughout the play, ending as it does on a note of defiance and unity.

Gay Times/Bad Times

Gay Sweatshop began an association in 1978 with the Drill Hall in Chenies Street which still continues today. The venue was run then by the resident company, Action Space, who had, in 1977, hosted a Women's Festival organized primarily by Julie Parker, Kate Crutchley and Nancy Diuguid (although it was not a Gay Sweatshop festival) and which featured a performance of Susan Griffin's *Voices*. Following on from the success of this, Action Space invited the men of the company to run a gay male event and the result was the *Gay Times* Festival. It was got together by the *As Time Goes By* company which included Drew, Alan, Gordon and Alex together with newcomers, Philip Timmins, myself, Bruce Bayley and the stage manager, Peter Charles, as well as Noël, Paul Dart and David Thompson. The company had only recently returned from Germany and the whole thing was put together in the space of a fortnight. Each of the three weeks was given a theme arising out of the three sections of *As Time Goes By* which were performed separately, one a week. There were daytime workshops organized tirelessly by Philip Timmins, discussions, films, performances by outside groups such as the play from the South London GLF community theatre group and Bloolips' show *Cheek*. There were discussions with representatives from the mass media co-ordinated by Alan and at the same time the company rehearsed three new cabarets which were performed each week. Even Paul Dart and David Thompson devised their own shows for the event.

This first *Gay Times* festival had far-reaching reverberations and the media evenings in particular were very influential. There was a discussion with a panel representing the Press to which both the *Evening Standard* and the very homophobic *Evening News* sent their deputy editors. In 1978 the *Evening News* had launched a vicious attack on lesbians through its exposé of artificial insemination with the headline 'AID for Lesbians'. Members of Gay Sweatshop had been involved in a demonstration at the newspaper's headquarters. The session was particularly heated and gave lesbians and gay men an opportunity to share their views on such stories with members of Fleet Street. It was, however, the discussion evening about the treatment of gays in news stories and in entertainment programmes on TV and radio which had the most dramatic results. There was a panel, brought together by

Robin Houston, which included Jeremy Isaacs (then director of programmes at Thames), John Birt (Controller of Features and Current Affairs for London Weekend) and Brian Hayes from LBC. In 1978 there were still no gay TV programmes. Thames had produced a discussion programme, in 1976, as part of a sex education series called *Sex in our Time* which Nancy and Drew took part in and which was shown at the *Gay Times* Festival. One of the people interviewed on the programme was a psychiatrist who was an advocate of aversion therapy for homosexuals. He had been included in order to get an argument going. He was so affected by the persuasiveness of Nancy and Drew's arguments – and freaked perhaps as well – that he did a U turn which infuriated the programme's producer. The programme was never broadcast owing to pressure from the IBA; I can remember the immense feeling of distrust that was felt at that time by gay people towards broadcasters and both John Birt and Jeremy Isaacs came in for a lot of criticism. As a result of the evening both of them undertook to do something about the shortcomings of their own particular networks. John Birt even returned on the following Saturday with his wife to watch the American section of *As Time Goes By* and the cabaret which followed it. In consequence the first gay series *Gay Life* was screened on London Weekend and of course, later, Jeremy Isaacs became head of Channel Four where he was instrumental in programming work such as the *In The Pink* series. It is on these grounds that Alan Pope can now claim with some justification that gay television came out of the *Gay Times* Festival.

The three weeks ended with a cabaret (devised in a week) called *Manmad*. At this time Anita Bryant's *Kill a Queer for Christ* campaign was at its height in the States. In England, Mary Whitehouse was, as usual, making pronouncements ('It is not the individual homosexual I am against, it is his sin'). *Manmad* saw a group of schoolboys led by a Biggles figure, alias Noël Greig, setting up camp in Mary's back garden. Mary – a delightful parody played by Alan in drag – sets out to save them from the evils of homosexuality; (one of the boys finds 'The Love that Dares to Speak its Name' by James Kirkup, the poem which was the subject of the *Gay News* blasphemy trial which was happening at the time). Mary is aided by the sudden arrival from the States of Anita – Drew in another colourful frock – and together they sing the Anita and Maria song from *West Side Story*. This brought the house down – not least because Drew's singing was appalling.

There is no doubt that the *Gay Times* Festival was a major cultural event in spite of the fact that the performances were in a small basement below the venue's current performing space which now serves as the dressing-room. Audiences crammed themselves into the tiny space which was supposed to seat sixty and on some nights seated 120 – the GLC fire officers would have spontaneously combusted in alarm. In *Gay News* Peter Robins said that the company had succeeded in organizing 'a three-week happening that should be remembered as a landmark in the progress of gay awareness in England.' For the company it was an intensely rewarding experience. It showed how well we could work together and how much could be achieved in such a short space of time through trust, commitment and love. My only regret is that we were working at such a pace and demanding so much of ourselves that, inevitably, we were putting a strain on ourselves which was impossible to sustain.

There is no doubt that being in Gay Sweatshop could (and still can) take a heavy toll. Being constantly in conflict with the State creates pressures which, at the same time as making you feel as if you're really living, can wreak havoc. In my interview with Noël he asked:

> How is someone that is essentially a highly-sensitive person, very passionate about their work, about the cause, who is thrust into this hugely public role – seeming to shoulder the burden of a whole movement, being the voice of a movement, carrying anger with them – how is that person, who may have his or her own personal problems to do with class and childhood, to contain all those pressures?

For Drew it became increasingly difficult to contain them. We have already seen how painful he found it when *As Time Goes By* was unfairly attacked. Artistic work already has a low status in our society but if that work is not even given recognition by the community of artists then there is really no support. As Drew admitted in his letter to the American producer of *As Time Goes By* his personal investment in the play and his inability to deal with the adverse reactions 'undoubtedly contributed, along with a gruelling nine month tour, to my falling ill, at first physically and then mentally.'

The pressure was always present in the touring companies; it sprang partly from the problems of trying to work collaboratively, problems which, for Noël, arise from conditioning which is antipathetic to co-operation, 'you've grown up feeling isolated and outcast and then all of a sudden you're in a situation where you're meant to be collaborating with each other'. And 'how is it possible for people to collaborate who feel that no one would want to co-operate with them if they knew who they really were?' Nancy also talked about this when recalling the difficulties of being on tour with Care and Control. (One company member at times described it as 'Hell on Wheels'!) It is of course understandable that there will be tensions and differences of opinions when producing this kind of work because feelings run high, not least because everyone cares so passionately about what they are saying. But Nancy also blames what she calls 'horizontal hostility' which arises because women are socialized to take their anger out on each other rather than see that it is caused by their own powerlessness in a patriarchal society.

In all theatre companies, heterosexual ones as well as gay ones, tensions can arise out of complex emotional relationships. With Gay Sweatshop it was inevitable, indeed necessary, that in creating art, personal feelings should intervene, but at times the blurring of the line between the personal and the professional was confusing. As in any other theatre company, relationships would occur between people which could prove creative or could cause jealousy and discord. Because there was so much commitment and love in the company, discord was all the more disturbing when it did occur.

At the end of the nine-month tour of *As Time Goes By*, the men's company was in a state of crisis. Looking back on it Alan puts much of this down to exhaustion and not understanding the demands made by the rarified atmosphere of Gay Sweatshop . Drew, Alan and Gordon had been working solidly since *Mister X* in 1975, and the whole company had been on tour with *As Time Goes By* from August 1977 to May 1978, never out of the spotlight, never able to relax, except perhaps in the van (at that time the grant still didn't allow us to stay in Bed and Breakfasts and the company continued to rely on the hospitality and generosity of local people for accommodation). The exhaustion, Alan believes, caused paranoia which meant that members of the company were unnecessarily suspicious of each other. Drew, who had cemented the touring company together, fell ill, with hepatitis. The company embarked on a tour of Holland and Belgium where, without him, tensions and arguments finally split the company apart. It seems sad that a group of people who had achieved so much together (Alan still believes that the *Gay Times* Festival could not have been produced without that unique combination of talents) should end in this way but it heralded changes which were productive and creative in their own way. Longstanding members eventually left the company and new ones took over, sometimes doing work that went over old ground or making old mistakes, sometimes finding new areas of concern and new ways of taking the company forward.

Iceberg

Over the summer of 1978 the company revived *Jingleball* and took it to Edinburgh. Out of this revival came a new nucleus of people which included Angela Stewart-Park, Stephanie Pugsley, Sharon Nassauer, Sandra Lester, Noël Greig and Philip Timmins as well as Jill Posener and the new administrator, John Hoyland. Together they devised a show, *Iceberg*, which was very much a product of its time. It was thematically linked to *As Time Goes By* in that it presented the lives of lesbians and gay men within the context of a repressive society – but that society was contemporary Britain. Looking back on it now Angela remarks wryly 'We thought we were going through difficult times.'

The National Front was very strong in the mid-seventies and there was a concerted effort by everyone on the Left to try and put a stop to their insidious influence. 1978 was the era of the Anti-Nazi League which united the resistance to right-wing ideologies and racism. The role of the police in protecting the 'right' of fascists to march through Black and Asian communities shouting racist slogans gave rise to a feeling that the police force was itself racist. There were violent clashes leading to injuries and death. 1978 was also the time of 'Reclaim the Night' marches, when women walked through Soho, past porn cinemas and sex shops, in an attempt to show the links between pornography and violence against women. Here again there were confrontations with the police and on one occasion the police lost control and attacked the women on the march. One of the women in the company was injured in this incident.

Iceberg tried to demonstrate how an awareness of the oppression of women and gay people had to be central to any anti-fascist struggle and that, for gay people, repression was a day-to-day occurrence. It used personal anecdote and songs and was very upfront in style. The show caused controversy wherever it played – in trades' clubs, for Communist Party audiences, and in Belfast at the Festival at Queen's University where Ian Paisley's Democratic Unionist Part organized a rally against it. The DUP had earlier organized a campaign called 'Save Ulster from Sodomy' (sic) and for Gay Sweatshop's arrival had plastered the city with bright yellow posters announcing, 'God Demands Righteousness not Gay Rights'. There was, however, a huge counter-demonstration and the DUP protesters were completely outnumbered. All the same it was a frightening experience.

Iceberg continued the process that *As Time Goes By* had begun, challenging the assumption that homosexual inclinations are a fundamental part of the fascist mentality. As late as 1978 the National Youth Theatre was presenting a play about the National Front where a major character representing the fascist organization was shown slobbering over the bodies of young male recruits. Left-wing playwrights were still not averse to using the vilest slander of homosexuality against fascists. They ignored the fact that the fascist philosophy seeks to repress any expression of sexuality other than heterosexual marriage. It was indicative of the Left's continuing marginalization of lesbian and gay rights. There was still a tendency to believe that they had little connection with class politics, based on the myth that homosexuals were mainly middle- and upper-class intellectuals.

The company's next major production, *The Dear Love of Comrades*, was to show how this marginalization arose from the Left's abandonment of the early roots of its ideology which embraced the concept of 'the whole human being'. In looking into the history of the socialist movement a figure had been found who was not only one of the founding fathers of the labour movement and central to radical struggles at the end of the last century; he was also gay and had working-class homosexual socialist lovers.

A Gay Comrade

Drew and Noël first came across Edward Carpenter when researching *As Time Goes By* and, indeed, he makes a fleeting appearance in the Victorian section. There is an idyllic scene portraying him and his lover at their home near Sheffield which contrasts sharply with the scenes of upper-class men hiring the services of working-class boys in the brothels of Cleveland Street. Noël Greig has written a substantial appreciation of Edward Carpenter's life and his work in the first volume of *Edward Carpenter: Selected Writings* (Gay Men's Press, Gay Modern Classics) and in it he describes this first encounter:

> There was a reference to a man who turned his back upon a well-heeled, Brighton-born and Cambridge-educated background, to settle in the North of England amongst the workers. Eventually, so the story went, he played a major role in the national drive towards a party of Labour (having been a key figure in the socialist revival of the 1880s). Eventually, too, he declared his homosexuality, discussed the issue in his writings, and celebrated it by setting up home with his lover, a working-class chap from Sheffield called George Merrill.

This came as a revelation because this story – not recorded in history books – hinted that within the working-class and its organizations at that time, there had been openly homosexual persons whose relationships were based on equality rather than prostitution.

> ... that first brief description of Carpenter and Merrill fired my imagination. Here was proof that a movement in which I held faith – the impulse towards a radical shift in the structures of society – held within its early stages an open advocation of something even closer to me – my own sexuality. Some sense of isolation dissolved – the feeling of having no personal part in the movements of history. In the early 1970s the starting point for many of us in the Gay Liberation Movement was the phrase 'the personal is political'. For myself Edward Carpenter gave this a historical dimension.

This discovery of a whole tradition of Utopian socialism also put the ideas of the sixties into a historical context, for Edward Carpenter was not only a socialist pioneer but also a poet fascinated by Eastern religion, a penal reformer, a vegetarian, an advocate of a 'simpler life', and an ardent supporter of feminist aspirations. His brand of socialism was one which attempted to seek connections between various forms of oppression; a way of looking at the world ridiculed by the apostles of greed in our current age when they talk about the 'loony left'. Indeed, at the turn of the century a cartoon appeared in *Punch* which portrayed Carpenter wrapped up in a blanket and wearing his sandals. It lampooned him and all that he stood for in much the same way that the right-wing press tries to discredit dissenting voices in present-day Britain.

Edward Carpenter was profoundly affected by his awareness of his own sexuality which he wrote about in *My Days and Dreams* (Volume 1 *Selected Writings*, Gay Men's Press). In this essay which he began work on in 1890 he even predicts the coming of a movement for Uranians, as he calls gay men:

> as these sufferings of women, of one kind and another, have been the great inspiring cause and impetus of the Women's movement ... so I do not practically doubt that the similar sufferings of the Uranian class of men are destined in their turn to lead to another wide-reaching social organization and forward movement.

Carpenter's philosophy allowed a place for desire and saw the will for change coming from within and not just from material conditions:

> The facts of his own life – of his own half-realized desires acting upon him and seeking for the light – taught him to reject mechanical Darwinism (and later encouraged him to regard a strictly Marxist approach as a useful yet limited tool). (Noël Greig, Introduction to the *Selected Writings*)

As Carpenter himself expressed it in *Towards Democracy*:

> Of that which exists in the Soul, political freedom and institutions of equality, and so forth, are but shadows (necessarily thrown); and Democracy in States or Constitutions but the shadow of that which first expresses itself in the glance of the eye or the appearance of the skin. (*Selected Writings* Vol.2)

Towards Democracy was itself a major influence for many early socialists and at a memorial for Carpenter in 1984 both Fenner Brockway and Dora Russell paid tribute to the profound effect it had on their lives and thinking. His anthem 'England Arise', which closes the first act of *The Dear Love of Comrades* became the song of the English Labour Movement. It was sung as frequently as the 'Red Flag' and in 1892 Carpenter was one of the central figures in the setting up of the Independent Labour Party.

But the man who allowed such a wide range of issues onto the socialist agenda, who published pamphlets on homosexuality ('Loves Coming of Age' *Selected Writings* Vol.1), who lived openly with his working-class male lover, became an embarassment to the Labour Party in its undignified scramble for votes and parliamentary success. *The Dear Love of Comrades* charts the way Carpenter and his ideas were shunted to one side, and the way that he himself became increasingly drawn to art, spiritualism and personal relationships.

For Noël, Carpenter's story afforded the opportunity to examine the conflict between organized politics, focused on parliamentary parties, and the possibilities of late nineteenth- century socialism that embraced the philosophy of anarchism. While working on the play it became clear that this was not at the centre of Drew's interest. Drew himself was still physically and mentally exhausted by the experiences of the past three years and the cumulative effect of all this was that the valuable period of collaboration between himself and Noël (which had also produced the excellent BBC2 play *Only Connect* about the continuing effects of Carpenter's teachings on our lives) came to an end. It was agreed that the final presented version of the play should be accredited to Noël.

Nancy Diuguid, who had resigned from the management committee in 1977, was asked to return to the company to direct. She thought it was a beautiful play and admired the writing but was also excited because it was dealing with a new and interesting area of politics. In the States political movements are parochial in their concerns, they tend to centre on one particular group. There are not the same all-embracing traditions as in this country. Nancy's politics had come to her intuitively and she had not been exposed to a strong socialist movement, so she found this historical aspect of the play fascinating. She was also drawn to the idea of a woman directing an all-male show. (I remember visiting the company with Nancy while they were performing at Birmingham Rep. After the show she gave notes in the Indian restaurant across from the theatre. I can still recall the look of amazement on the faces of other customers as she sat holding forth at the head of the table surrounded by men.)

One of the criticisms levelled at the play in performance was that the wives of some of Carpenter's lovers and other women in his life, such as Olive Shreiner, did not figure. Both Noël and Nancy are adamant that they made the right decision in concentrating on the relationships between the men. The play was written at a time when many male playwrights were locating the voice of reason and right in strong women characters which meant that male characters were defined by the way they treated women rather than by the way they related to each other as men. Noël feels that female characters would have provided him with an easy get-out – all the criticisms of maleness and all the criticisms of Carpenter himself could have been voiced by these women. In the play any feminist critique arises from what is happening between the men and how they treat each other. The fact that a woman directed the piece meant that this critique was clearly delineated – as Noël points out Nancy represented the wives in the way that she directed it. She also brought a sense of domestic lives being lived and a detailed attention to texture and rhythm.

Other valuable contributions were made by Alex Harding who, as the composer and musical director, played a crucial role in the rehearsal process and by Paul Dart as designer. Respectively they had a sympathetic ear and eye for the mood of the piece. Noël found himself in the unenviable position of starting rehearsals playing the lead role in a play that he had only half-written and pays tribute to the support he got from everyone involved.

For Nancy the epic sweep of *The Dear Love of Comrades* together with the sense of poetry in the writing, and the quest to reveal inner secrets in the relationships, made it pure joy to work on. She finds it surprising that ten years later none of the major theatres which support and encourage new writing have ever commissioned a play from Noël. She attributes this to a strong female principle in his work which is threatening to these institutions, many of which are still male-dominated and display a streak of heterosexism in the way they operate.

The response both in London and on the production's extensive tour showed that once again the company had produced a topical piece of work which addressed issues which were of concern to both men and women. The company toured arts centres, rep studios, university campuses and venues hired by local lesbians and gay groups. There was a visit to Northern Ireland and a tour of Germany where the production won an award at the Munich Theatre Festival. Countless people who saw the play continue to value the effect it had on their lives and their thinking. One member of the audience at Leeds Trades' Club describes the occasion as his 'Road to Damascus'! At a time when people like Jeffrey Weeks and Sheila Rowbotham were unearthing different aspects of women's history and gay history the play had a very strong appeal. It deals with a period of English history when the Labour Party was in its infancy, and was being performed at a time when it was clear that the party had got many of its priorities wrong: the year that the current Conservative government came to power. But the play's appeal was not just historical; much of the inspiration for the characters and the situations in which they find themselves came from Noël's experiences in Bradford and the play proved that working-class characters do not have to be portrayed as people in cloth-caps with simple needs. It showed that they could be as eccentric, contradictory, bloodyminded, complex and full of potential as anyone else. They are ordinary people whose lives are extraordinary and the predicaments in which they find themselves and the problems they face were recognizable. We see them trying to cope with jealousy and non-monogamy, trying to reconcile themselves to the gap between theory and practice in both their political and their personal lives – much of the humour revolves around this. It sometimes seems, looking back on the seventies, that we set ourselves Herculean tests in order to prove that we weren't possessive or jealous or monogamous. The characters in *The Dear Love of Comrades* go through the same ordeals and audiences identified with them, laughing with them rather than at them.

At the time that Section 28 was going through parliament Polly Toynbee wrote in the *Guardian* that gay people had brought the legislation down upon themselves by allowing themselves to become too closely identified with the Left. What she failed to understand is that anything that questions the notion of the family and the way it is defined by the corporate state is bound to be identified as being part of the left. There is no other arena for us given that a serious contemplation of the politics of anarchism is discredited. In the late seventies many gay people might have said that there was not a lot to choose between the two major parties but that at least the Labour Party offered them an inch in which to survive. Many responded by joining the Labour Party and fighting for lesbian and gay rights within that arena. It was a long struggle and the advances were often resisted and continue to be resisted by whole sections of the party. When, in the autumn of 1987 the Labour Party leadership allowed Clause 27 (later to become Section 28) of the Local Government Bill to go through its committee stages without opposition or amendment it was once again trying to shunt to one side an issue which it would prefer not to have on the agenda for fear that it may lose votes. For young people with left politics *The Dear Love of Comrades* offered both hope and inspiration because it showed that the radical movement for change out of which the Labour Party grew was 'a movement which demands a world where all have equal access not simply to the material comforts, but to the desires of our bodies and the joys of our souls.' (Noël Greig, Introduction to the *Selected Writings*). If the Labour Party once again chooses to ignore these roots then it should understand that it might not be able to sustain itself and is in danger of withering away. What is clear however is that the ideas of Carpenter and people like him will never die:

> The outcrop of exotic behaviour, mysticism, communes, etc. of our own times was a resurfacing of a tradition of thought and action to which Carpenter belongs. It comes back to us on the great ebb and flow of history from time to time, in various guises – sometimes in group adventures, such as the Cathars of the twelfth century, the Seekers, the Ranters and Diggers of our English Revolution, or as individual commentators such as Rousseau, George Sand, Whitman, Shelley, Blake. It will continue to come back, until the world is no

longer dragged along by the scruff of its neck by those who place our lives at the mercy of their power. Until then, these anarchistic, communitarian, free spirits will rise time and again despite repression or (in the more sophisticated world) ridicule. (Noël Greig, Introduction to the *Selected Writings*)

Enter the Eighties

The Dear Love of Comrades was hailed by some as being the most important piece of gay theatre yet produced because it showed the inter-relationship of personal lives and wider politics and because every artistic element – the writing, the music, the design, the direction, the acting – complemented the content. It represented Gay Sweatshop's work at its very best. It seems incredible then that just eighteen months later the company was told by the Arts Council that it could not expect annual funding in the future. It had to give up its recently-acquired office and rehearsal space and its full-time administrator.

In 1979 and 1980 two more major shows had been produced, *I Like Me Like This* and *Blood Green*, as well as another project commissioned by Gerald Chapman under the auspices of the Royal Court Young People's Theatre. *I Like Me Like This* was a radical lesbian musical written by Angela Stewart-Park and Sharon Nassauer and it too concerned itself with the discussion of relationship – how we, as gay people, explore alternative ways of living and relating to each other.
One of the difficulties of presenting lesbian and gay relationships onstage is the temptation to justify them, to make them seem as valid as heterosexual ones. We live in a society where it is heterosexuality that is 'promoted' and couple relationships based on the model of heterosexual marriage are seen as being the ideal to which we all aspire – whether we admit it or not. It is almost impossible to escape this dominant ideology and some lesbians and gay men, particularly in the States, even go as far as consecrating their relationships with marriage ceremonies which seems, to me at least, fraught with contradictions. All the same the need for validation of our lives and loves is a real one which should not be denied. *The Dear Love of Comrades* ends on an elegiac note as we see Edward and George choosing to live in domestic bliss at Millthorpe. At the same time, we are made aware that this choice is not a simple one, it goes hand-in-hand with a retreat from a world which no longer values Carpenter's ideas, but the play celebrates their relationship without making those of us not living in cosy coupledom feel like failures!

In the seventies, radical lesbians and gay men were trying to evolve ways of living and relating which avoided the mistakes of past generations and rejected the idea of monogamy, of being faithful to one person or expecting them to fulfil all your needs. Instead there was a philosophy of being generous with life and sharing all aspects of it – lovers included. This often led to partners making unreasonable demands on each other; the need for honesty was held up as being of paramount importance which meant, at times, talking with lovers about other relationships in ways that verged on cruelty. Often, too, it meant that it was difficult to admit to feeling jealous and hurt. With hindsight it is easy to be cynical about these experiments in alternative living and to ridicule them but it is important to realize that, in trying to define our lives on our own terms, we were making the rules up as we went along. The experiments were built on the desire for a world where a lover was not a possession and where love was not a bond.

I Like Me Like This reflected these concerns. The play was set in a collective house where all the problems of shared space and shared living occurred. At one point a character who feels that she isn't high enough on her lover's list of priorities suggests sarcastically that a rota should be set up (in the same way George Adams recommends to Carpenter that he puts his lovers in rotation). Ironically these were the same problems that theatre companies (both gay and straight) often encountered on tour and the *I Like Me Like This* company was no exception. To this day Angela Stewart-Park feels that being in a work situation with one's lover is highly problematic; if, at the same time, it is a situation where other emotional and sexual relationships are likely to occur then it is to be avoided at all costs.

Feminists were turning the spotlight on men and male attitudes to sex and sexuality in an attempt to understand women's oppression and self-oppression. Andrea Dworkin's *Pornography* and Phyllis Chesler's *About Men* both expounded the theory that these attitudes were a reflection of men's contempt for women and women's bodies. The writers show how men use sex to express their power over women and to debase women. Little boys are taught to despise and reject their mothers which leads them to repress their own femininity, to fear any expression of it within themselves. This internalized self-hatred turns into aggression against women later in life. Neither do homosexual men escape their criticisms and they attack the misogyny of many gay men and what they see as the preoccupation with power in their sexual relationships.

I Like Me Like This strongly identified men as being responsible for what was going wrong with the world and included scenes about male violence and rape. For the designer, Kate Owen, who had worked in theatre for years, it was the first time she had worked with a female director and she insists that the production has to be seen in its context. The play was a period piece which was very raw and not at all apologetic for its politics. She believes that much early political theatre presented the world as we would want it to be rather than as it was, owing to a conviction that theatre really could change the world. Now, in general, the work has become scaled-down and more personal and there is a tendency towards being more contemplative and self-critical as people try to find a balance between their outer and inner lives. But this is also a product of less optimistic times where the faith in the capacity of theatre to bring about change has been lost.

I Like Me Like This was presented at the height of a period of massive change. The play had many positive aspects; it showed lesbians living alternative lifestyles but unable to be open about their sexuality at work – at one point a nurse sings a song about her two modes of being called *Quick Change*; it also showed women playing electric guitars and using a p.a. which in those days was rarely seen – this meant that the show attracted an audience that would not normally go to theatre but would go to hear bands. The production was criticized for its lack of political and artistic sophistication and certainly it did not find favour with the Arts Council but all the same many women still remember it with affection and affirm that it changed their politics.

Meanwhile Philip Timmins was developing a piece of young people's theatre which was quite unique in Gay Sweatshop's history. Philip had trained at RADA and his professional work had included a period at The Traverse before moving to the more liberal, less homophobic climate of Amsterdam in the early seventies. In

Amsterdam he taught at a theatre school and his interest in teaching and the well-being of young people has always informed his work – his own experiences as a gay teenager growing up in the Midlands gave him a commitment to the concerns of young gays. He returned to England to be involved in the production of *As Time Goes By* in which his portrayal of the communist, Hans, was particularly memorable. When Gerald Chapman approached the company and asked if they were interested in producing a play for a season entitled *Youth and Sexuality* Philip agreed to develop a script with Bruce Bayley and Sara Hardy. The play revolved around a group of young people, some still at school, others recently left, both hetero- and homosexual and raised issues such as coming-out at school, at home and at work, as well as jealousy, male attitudes to women, love between members of the same sex and violence.

What was unique about this production was that Philip approached groups like the London Gay Teenage Group and the play was scripted and developed with a group of young inexperienced lesbian and gay performers. It was the only time that Gay Sweatshop managed to produce a piece of young people's theatre and it only came about through Philip's persistence and determination. (Once again there were letters to the *Evening Standard* and banner headlines decrying both the play and Gerald Chapman for perverting the young.)

It was very heartening to see the young audiences at the Royal Court – and at other venues on tour – respond to the play and have their prejudices challenged. They were always particularly surprised when they realized that the whole cast was gay. Earlier in the year Philip had been with *The Dear Love of Comrades* company when they had been set upon by a gang of queerbashers on their way to a gay club in Birmingham. Presenting *Who Knows* to those school audiences was a way of turning the anger and distress into something positive. Homophobia arises through ignorance and it is an ignorance which many in positions of power are still anxious to promote in our schools.

In 1980 the company produced a mixed production by Angela Stewart-Park and Noël Greig entitled *Blood Green* which was set in the future and dealt with themes such as genetic engineering, transexualism, sado-masochism and violence against women. Angela and Noël both recognize that the play was unwieldy and that it did not gel in the writing and rehearsal process. But it was also ahead of its time in terms of what it was trying to say and once again illustrates that it is much easier to write successfully about the past than about the present or the future. Many of the issues which it tried to tackle are still topical and are only just beginning to be explored in literature.

The fact that both *Blood Green* and *I Like Me Like This* had limited success meant that morale in the company was low. One of the drawbacks of being an established company and the only professional lesbian and gay theatre company in the country is that every show has quite a high profile and there is no margin for failure. Certainly it would seem that a project-funded company exists on the reputation of its last show in the eyes of the Arts Council. There is no recognition that a company's creativity ebbs and flows.

In 1980 the Arts Council announced cuts for the following financial year including forty-one revenue clients. Later it was announced that all annual programme grants were also to be suspended. There was no right of appeal and no indication of the criteria used in making the cuts. Most companies, including Gay Sweatshop, were told that they could apply for project grants for specific productions. It was a severe blow. In spite of support from individuals in the Arts

1 Gay Sweatshop

Council the bureaucracy obviously still saw Gay Sweatshop as a company catering to an insignificant minority. Work which spoke for lesbians and gay men was not given priority. The energy required to keep the company afloat is enormous and Gean Wilton, the administrator at this time, and Noël and Philip Timmins, who were still directors, felt too worn down and tired to take the risk of embarking on another project in the hope that a grant might be forthcoming. The company was wound down.

Of course this did not mean that the people who had been involved in the company stopped creating. Ex-Sweatshop members Alan Pope and Alex Harding had been working together independently since 1978 and had produced a number of two-handers including Alan's very funny show based on his impersonation of Mary Whitehouse. They went on to produce *Layers* at the ICA which was a musical about gay relationships directed by Drew. Noël, Philip Timmins, Kate Owen, Stephanie Pugsley and Gordon MacDonald teamed up with Stephen Gee and formed New Heart Theatre Company. (Stephen had worked with the Brixton Faeries, a community group which had evolved out of the South London GLF group. He had played Jeremy Thorpe in their radical gay interpretation of the Norman Scott affair, *Minehead Revisited*). New Heart's first show *The Gorgeous and the Damned*, represented an attempt to find a more visual way of working and new modes of discourse. In the early eighties there was a sense of uncertainty about where the Gay movement was going, what the best response to the most right-wing Tory government since the war should be, how gay theatre could best contribute to the debates of the new decade.

Gay Sweatshop's demise left a gap as Gean Wilton and Noël pointed out in a press release in March 1981:

> The inclusion of gay themes by other companies into their work must be encouraged and supported, but these developments should not deflect from the need for a full-time Gay Theatre Company . . . This society divides us off from each other, lines of communication are often few and fragile. A phone-line, a publication, these form part of our telegraph system. Gay Sweatshop is part of this . . . we can see the state making a concerted effort to attempt to stop us meeting and shut us up. Buildings are burnt down. Street attacks because of sex, sexuality or race are still being ignored. They want us to retreat into anonymity – again.

But there were other clouds gathering on the horizon which were to present new challenges and there were changes taking place in County Hall which were to revolutionize funding policies and put the Arts Council's lack of commitment to minority and ethnic arts to shame.

Take the Toys from the Boys

In the early eighties the main focus for dissent in this country was the Peace movement. Its revival was prompted by the aggressive stance taken by British and American administrations who saw themselves as protectors of the West from the Russian 'evil empire'. Since the 'Ban the Bomb' marches of the fifties and early sixties, CND had become less active. It re-emerged in the eighties as a key political force. Throughout Europe there were demonstrations and civil disobedience against NATO's nuclear defence policy and specifically against the deployment of the long-range cruise missiles. The campaign against nuclear weapons was part of a wider concern about environmental issues including the threat posed by nuclear power stations, the erosion of the ozone layer, the destruction of the rainforests, acid rain etc. which became known as the Green movement. Green politics stress the need for humankind to treat the planet with respect and to live in harmony with the other life forms – the plants and animals. It warns that if we don't then we are precipitating our own extinction. The movement is part of those same traditions to which Edward Carpenter belonged and which seek to make connections between the way we live our lives from day to day and the way the world is organized.

There is much common ground between these politics and the aims of the Women's movement and the Gay Liberation movement with their assertion that the personal is political. For feminists the roots of our lack of respect for the planet and of militarism lie in traditional male values which encourage competitiveness and aggression. We tend to be cut off from our emotions and unable to function as whole human beings living at peace with the world. Essentially this is caused by a lack of connection with sex and sexuality. In *Towards Democracy* Edward Carpenter emphasized the importance of sex:

Sex still goes first, and hands eyes mouth brain follow; from the midst of belly and thighs radiate the knowledge of self, religion, and immortality.

In our society sex has become split off and fetishistic; we are alienated from our sexuality. Sex is no longer a loving experience where power is shared becoming instead – as Andrea Dworkin believes – a way of exerting power over someone or of expressing contempt. The phallus and penetration become important symbols of male power which has led to connections being made between sexual obsessions and men's obsessions with guns and missiles. Feminists have gone so far as arguing that male preoccupation with weapons of destruction comes literally from 'womb envy', from a jealousy of women's reproductive capacities.

Feminism had a huge impact on the Peace movement in its eighties incarnation. The Women's movement found a new unity in organizing a fight against nuclear weapons and attention became focused particularly on the American Base at Greenham Common. On one occasion women held hands around the whole perimeter fence and pinned photos and mementoes of their children to the wire – an action which was called embracing the base. This brought to Greenham Common women from all over the country who did not necessarily identify with 'Women's Lib' but who came because they wanted a world where their children could live without the fear of ultimate destruction. Once there they began to make links with feminist principles.

The play, which saw the re-emergence of Gay Sweatshop in 1983, was inspired by the activities at Greenham Common and put forward a response to the nuclear threat and militarism from a radical gay male perspective. It was a response that was badly needed given the climate in Britain after the Falklands War of 1982 when another Tory election victory was in the offing. Early in 1983 there was a reading of *Poppies* at a Gay CND conference where the reaction to the play gave Noël the confidence to think about trying to do a fully-fledged production. He had written the play with the help of an Arts Council bursary and it had been intimated to him that the Arts Council would look favourably on an application for a project grant to stage it.

lii Gay Sweatshop

The 'telegraph system' of which Gay Sweatshop was a part was in a parlous state; there was no longer a national gay newspaper and no other company had stepped into the gap left by Gay Sweatshop. Bloolips were still captivating audiences in this country, on the continent and in the States with their joyous mixture of camp and politics; a community group, Consenting Adults In Public, had been formed by Eric Presland which did workshops for gay people interested in theatre and produced two memorable productions on midsummer's night on Hampstead Heath. There were one-off productions at the Oval House and companies such as No Boundaries and the Brighton-based Siren kept lesbian theatre alive. There were productions with gay or lesbian content from non-gay companies such as the Women's Theatre Group's *Double Vision*. The West End too had been opened up slightly by *Bent* and so male homosexuality was not quite so taboo there as it had been. But there was no other funded, professional lesbian and gay theatre company in existence which was taking shows out on tour. Barry Jackson who had supported Gay Sweatshop's work from the outset and who now worked at the Arts Council expressed his surprise about this to Noël. He told him that he would have imagined that by 1983 there should have been six state-funded companies producing gay theatre. And so, out of what he calls 'sheer bloodymindedness', Noël made the application for *Poppies* in the name of Gay Sweatshop. There was, as yet, no intention of starting the company up again on a full-time basis. He enlisted the support of his housemate, Martin Humphries, as financial administrator, and working from a room in their house as an office they made the application and started booking a tour.

Poppies is set on Parliament Hill on the eve of Remembrance Day. It is a time of national emergency and nuclear war is threatened. Two older men, Sammy and Snow, come up the hill to spend what may be their last night alive out in the open air. For Sammy the location has special significance – here, in 1939, as a student, he met a young airman, Flag, who was later to die over Dresden. His memory conjures up these two figures from the past and the story of their relationship is re-enacted before our eyes. The young Sammy and Flag have different outlooks – Sammy is a pacifist and ready to go to prison as a conscientious objector; Flag is willing to die defending his country and all that it stands for from Hitler's armies.

Sammy and Snow's picnic is interrupted by Snow's skinhead son, Hippo, who has followed them up having been out with his mates looting and burning (an echo of the inner-city riots of 1981). His antipathy towards Snow, and his homophobia, are fuelled by his sense of rejection and loneliness which is made more acute by the fact that his much-loved brother is currently in Wandsworth Jail. He and Snow have unfinished business. The structure is made more complex by the presence of two dead people, described as Mouldy Heads, who bicker about the value of living – one can only remember the pleasure, the other the pain. They threaten each other after each exchange with ever bigger bits of scrap like little boys playing with make-believe guns as they jealously watch and comment on the antics of the living.

The structure reflects a complex interplaying of themes and ideas many of which had preoccupied Noël in earlier plays; the way that possessiveness and jealousy cuts us off from each other; the way that romance and death interrelate and stop us living our lives to the full. Sammy lives in the past with dreams of his dead love and the stand he made as a pacifist. This prevents him from appreciating Snow's love and from taking any action in the present. Even though most of the play is set in the near future there is a strong sense of history going through it. Young Sammy is an undergraduate studying history (the subject that Noël read whilst at King's College, London) and lectures Flag on the Roman conquest of Britain while Flag prepares himself to fight against a threatened German invasion in 1939. This is set against the threat of nuclear war in the 1980s. The Mouldy Heads quarrel about the past as they dredge up memories of previous lives that go back through the centuries. In spite of this complexity, at its heart the play has a very simple thesis: men kill each other because they do not know how to love each other. It is a thesis that some critics found very difficult to accept and very easy to ridicule:

> Ultimately I can't help feeling that the author's conviction that world peace can be assured if enough men embrace on Hampstead Heath is a specialized viewpoint; and may even have been disproved already. (*Financial Times*)

There were reviews, in the gay press, too, that revealed a defensiveness and an inability to come to terms with what the play was saying. One of the critics in *Gay Times* said of the second production: 'By no yardstick could *Poppies* be considered a successful play. Less still a successful play for 1985' and accuses most of the actors of falling prey 'to the slimy sentiment that entraps their characters'.

In terms of success, audiences and other reviewers disagreed. *The Times* paid tribute to Noël Greig's sure dramatic skill and the effectiveness of both the production and the writing and, in *City Limits,* Jim Hiley made the point that 'this is very much the product of gay consciousness but contradicts a common criticism of gay theatre by looking out from the ghetto and addressing itself with wit and sometimes brilliance to the biggest questions of the day.' It was a point that audiences were quick to appreciate and *Poppies* was hailed as being one of the most important plays to come out of the nuclear debate. When the company went on tour, for the first time in four years, it found that the work was as popular as ever, and audiences, both men and women, flocked to see the production.

Once again the company hit controversy on the tour. There was a performance in a school in Avon which had Tory councillors condemning the play both because it was about homosexuality and because it was making a contribution to the nuclear debate. There were accusations of indoctrination and the company was called 'sinister and subversive' by the leader of the Tory Group on Bristol Council. A Gay CND leaflet which was in the programme advertizing workshops was interpreted in the most sensationalistic fashion imaginable. Some time later, Angela Browning of Women and Families for Defence wrote to the *Sunday Times* about Peace Studies in schools (which she called 'Propaganda for Defencelessness') and her concern about the 'biased indoctrination of children'. In the letter she used the performance of *Poppies* in Avon as an example of this. In his reply Noël asked her if she and her organization wanted to rid schools of all ideas of which they did not approve:

> What would she have in their place? Only ideas she and they approve of? Would that not then be biased indoctrination? Ms Browning describes Peace Studies as a 'national issue which should be of concern to all involved in the education of children.' It certainly is but not in the spirit which she intends, which is the spirit of censorship.
>
> If she is in favour of such things, might I suggest she goes and lives in Russia?

The programme gave a list of possible touring dates including Devon. This alerted the county's Chief Education Officer, Ted Pinney, who banned the play. The sixth formers at the Avon school were both enlightened and moved by the play. They talked to the company afterwards with an intelligence and perceptiveness which contrasted sharply with the prejudice and ignorance of some of their elders.

Given the interest that the play had aroused the touring department of the Arts Council, which was run by Ruth Marks, agreed to finance an extension of the tour. However the offer came too late to set up bookings immediately. It was clear that any further touring would have to happen later and would mean recasting. The amount offered by the Arts Council was not sufficient to cover another rehearsal period.

By 1984 the Labour-controlled GLC had begun to make its mark on the services provided for Londoners. These policies were greeted initially with hostility but gradually people saw the commonsense of what Ken Livingstone was advocating and they became immensely popular. Much of the hostility was generated by the press and one could hardly open a newspaper in those days without seeing a headline about 'Red Ken'. As part of the council's equal opportunities policy the GLC began to make grants to gay self-help groups and counselling services in an attempt to redress the imbalance caused by discrimination. The amounts of money involved were remarkably insignificant but the press tried to play on people's fears and prejudices by talking about 'homosexuality on the rates'. As far as the arts were concerned the new policies which emphasized the need to fund ethnic and minority arts had a radical effect. It was as if, for the first time, the capital had woken up to the fact that we were living in a multi-cultural society and that this should be reflected in concert-halls and theatres, in art galleries and libraries. Doubtless there were mistakes made; sometimes groups were given grants who did not have the structure or the experience to function as full-time funded organizations; the bureaucracy at County Hall was so clumsy and ponderous that much time and energy was spent trying to circumvent petty regulations. But the general principle was a good one and there was a flowering of Black and ethnic work which enriched the cultural life of the city beyond measure.

Gay Sweatshop had been slow off the mark in applying for funding from the GLC – primarily because it had not existed in the early years of the new administration. In 1984 Martin Humphries and Noël made an application for a grant to supplement the Arts Council's touring subsidy and eventually, a year later, a grant came through which allowed the company to stage a second production of *Poppies*. The Arts Council did not fund revivals so the opportunity to have a second look at new plays was rare. The second production built on the reputation of the first. As the director of the revival, I was able to use the insight which I had gained from acting in the original and to re-interpret certain parts – particularly the Mouldy Heads. In the first production Noël (the director) and Kate, who designed, had abstracted them and stressed their surreal nature by dressing them in grass-covered costumes; in the revival they became more human. The whole production accentuated the way the different characters represent different aspects of masculinity. This time Kate's design had the Mouldy Heads in a dress-suit and a kilt (Gordon MacDonald returned to the company to play the role with a comic acerbity which almost stole the show). The production opened in February 1985 and any concern that there was no longer an audience for the play in London proved unfounded; it played to packed houses both at the Drill Hall and on tour.

Apart from the contribution that *Poppies* made to the ideas of the Peace movement it re-established Gay Sweatshop as a company producing work of the highest standard which puts the experiences of gay people centre-stage but speaks to everyone. By 1985 it was clear that the company was back on the road again and it was about to celebrate its tenth anniversary by returning to the idea of a festival of new plays which is how it had all started in 1975 at the Almost Free.

Forging New Links

By 1984 the Gay movement seemed to have become somewhat apathetic; there was a feeling in some quarters that we had our pubs and our clubs and that was enough; the ideals which had inspired the movement were now seen as being old-fashioned and redundant and Mrs Thatcher talked about the need for society to turn its back on 'the claptrap of the sixties'. Many activists felt disillusioned and pessimistic about the future especially in the face of growing paranoia and hysteria about AIDS. This was beginning to create a backlash whilst the majority of gay people buried their heads in the sand.

The question arises as to how far the material goodies and the attentions of Style and Fashion, the relative ease with which we can conduct our lives (and it is only relative) have made the issues of Class, Race and all the matters of wider politics seem out-of-date, fuddy-duddy and irrelevant? Flick through most of the Gay glossies and it would certainly seem so. Well, if we have created a Gay Culture (complete with clubs, comics, lifestyles and fashions) and think that the other questions are irrelevant, then it might well be us who end up as the truly irrelevant. (Noël Greig in a leaflet publicising the Gay Sweatshop Times Ten Festival)

This is not to say that there was a total lack of hope. During the Miners' Strike, 'Lesbians and Gays Support the Miners' was set up to show solidarity with that struggle and strong links were made with one particular mining village in Wales. In 1985 Gay Sweatshop itself organized a reading of *The Dear Love of Comrades* to raise money for the Strike Fund and an important lesson of the Strike was that it was possible to make new friends.

It was clear that if Gay Sweatshop was to start operating again it would need to respond to the challenges the eighties were presenting. A new core group was needed to generate new work and to formulate policies. The company had been set up as a limited company with directors who worked together as a collective. When these founding members left in the late seventies membership of the collective became open to everyone who joined the company. In the end this proved to be an unwieldy way of running things. As we have seen, by 1981 the only two remaining directors were Philip Timmins and Noël and so when the company started again Martin Humphries and Kate Owen were asked to go onto the management as directors and a few months later I joined them. This obviously put Kate into a difficult position as the only woman on the management. The piece of work which had relaunched the company was male-focused and Kate had been the only woman working on it. Kate agreed to join providing that more women were brought onto the management at a later date. The company policy had always been that at least fifty per cent of the work should be created by lesbians; Kate was given an assurance that this would continue. Accordingly Sue Frumin was commissioned to write a new play – *Raising the Wreck*, and another woman, Tierl Thompson, joined the management to administrate the tour.

Raising the Wreck was to have a multi-racial cast. We were very aware of the fact that we were an all-white group and that in general over the years there had been few contributions from Black lesbians and gay men. The new initiatives to combat racism and to create equal opportunities (such as the GLC policies) had developed out of the Anti-Nazi League and the whole anti-racism struggle in the late seventies of which Gay Sweatshop and the Gay movement had been a part. However, as Angela Stewart-Park points out, *Iceberg* did not examine racism. At the time it must have seemed that it was enough to look at our own experiences as white lesbians and gay men. By 1984 this was no longer good enough. Theatre continued to be dominated by white people and there were still relatively few representations of Black people in plays and films. As far as Black lesbians and gay men working in theatre were concerned many of them obviously found it problematic to come out because it would mean facing up to double oppression. Added to this was the fact that as Black people their main support would come from their families and their communities where homosexuality might not be an acceptable choice.

With the company's tenth birthday approaching there was considerable discussion about how it should be celebrated. Kate suggested a festival, to be called Gay Sweatshop Times Ten, which would allow the company to broaden its scope and to work with more people than its programme of Arts Council funded projects usually allowed. A whole range of work could be given a platform without the usual pressure of being a major project. In effect it was a constructive way of responding to the new equal opportunities initiatives by seeing how they could enrich the company's work. Leaflets were sent out asking people to submit plays. Those chosen were to be given staged rehearsed readings over a three-week period at the Drill Hall in October 1985. The emphasis would be on looking at the present and the future in the light of the recent past. A special Festival Committee was set up to read these scripts and to help with programming special events – such as disability workshops, poetry readings, a Black lesbian writing evening etc. There was tremendous enthusiasm for the project but a lack of adequate funding. (An application had been made to the GLC and it did eventually come through after the festival was over). All-in-all ninety six plays were submitted and, after much discussion, seventeen were chosen and the writers were put in contact with a director. The subjects covered included gay teachers, the problems facing young lesbians and gays, lesbian custody, hidden disabilities, the experiences of Black lesbians, gay people's relationships with their families and AIDS. There were also performances of *Raising the Wreck* and of shows by visiting companies both from this country and the States as well as the poetry events, the workshops, the music in the bar and the grand finale cabaret. The sheer volume and scope of the work was quite astounding.

The huge success of the Gay Sweatshop Times Ten Festival showed that the company could be doing an unlimited number of plays each year if it had the funding and the resources. On the strength of it Greater London Arts awarded an annual grant which enabled us to employ an administrator (for the previous few years much of this had been done by Noël and other members of the management on a voluntary basis) and rent an office (Noël's basement was becoming cramped and inconvenient!) Most importantly, the festival was a seed-bed for future work; many of the plays read at the festival went on to be fully produced either under the auspices of Gay Sweatshop – *Julie, Skin Deep, More, Compromised Immunity* – or by other companies – *Chiaroscuro* by Theatre of Black Women, *A Quiet End* at Offstage by the group of people who had read it at the Festival, and *Boy* by Outcast Theatre under

Finding Room on the Agenda for Love lvii

the name *For Crying Out Loud*. Through the Festival the company came into contact with many new people which meant that there was a much bigger pool to choose from when looking for actors, directors and writers for future plays. All of the company's next three productions came out of the festival either directly (*Compromised Immunity*) or indirectly (*This Island's Mine* and *Twice Over*). It was particularly heartening to see lesbians and gay men coming together in this way to produce culture about our lives. Noël's fears about the Gay movement making itself irrelevant proved to be unfounded because we were able to begin to make links between different forms of oppression. We were also able to respond to the grief and suffering caused by AIDS in a positive way. This meant that the movement found a new cohesiveness and a unity in adversity which had been so lacking in the early part of this decade.

Immunity and Humanity

As part of its 1985 tour *Poppies* was booked to perform in The Taliesin Theatre at the University of Swansea. When the cleaners at the theatre heard about the performance they went to the theatre manager to express their alarm about the company's visit and their fear of contracting AIDS through clearing up afterwards. This response was, no doubt, fuelled to some extent by homophobia and prejudice but its principle cause was the hysteria and ignorance promoted irresponsibly by the media with headlines about 'the gay plague'. The theatre manager at The Taliesin responded to the cleaners' worries by leaking the story to the press in the mistaken belief that any publicity is good publicity. He allowed himself to be photographed in a white overall holding rubber gloves and bleach which he claimed he had issued to the cleaners to allay their fears. This meant that there were more headlines both in the local press and in the national tabloids which served to add to the paranoia and ignorance about the disease: *Gays put Mrs Mopps in a Sweat Over Aids* read *The Sun*. In the event the University's medical officer and the union representative were able to talk to the cleaners about the reality of how AIDS is contracted and the performances went ahead without incident. The reviewer in the *South Wales Evening Post* wrote:

> What a shame it would be if the only lasting impression Gay Sweatshop left on Swansea was the hysterical AIDS scare, for at The Taliesin last night they proved themselves to be one of Britain's best minor touring companies with important things to say about love, jealousy and aggression . . . I doubt Gay Sweatshop will forget Swansea. Let's hope the city will remember them for this charming and witty play.

What this brought forcefully home to the company was the extent of the ignorance and fear about the epidemic. Fear itself has been the main obstacle encountered by those trying to present the truth about AIDS because it stops people at risk from finding out about the real dangers and how to avoid them and encourages them instead to ignore the disease in the hope that it will go away. The tabloid press far from helping the situation merely used AIDS as an opportunity for more verbal queerbashing. Bigots and self-appointed moral arbiters called it divine retribution for perversion and sin (blithely ignoring the fact that lesbians are the lowest risk group) and there were politicians who went on television and recommended that homosexuals should be rounded up and put in camps. The fact that gay people are not protected in law against discrimination meant that they could say this with impunity. The government itself was slow to respond to the crisis and to learn from the experience of people fighting the spread of AIDS in the States. One can't help thinking that this was because they, too, believed that it was a gay plague. Many lives were needlessly lost. When it was realized that it wasn't just 'junkies and queers' who were at risk a government campaign was launched but in 1985 it was voluntary organizations from within the Gay Community such as the Terrence Higgins Trust who were leading the struggle against the epidemic.

Within the Gay Community there was considerable debate and disagreement about how best to respond. For a while it seemed as if all the advances made over the past twenty years were about to be swept away on a tide of illiberalism. The Gay Liberation movement of the early seventies now stood accused of promoting promiscuity and casual sex and of bringing the disease down on gay men. It looked as if all attempts to find alternative ways of relating and loving were to be dismissed as an aberration of 'the permissive society'. A major American play on the subject, Larry Kramer's *The Normal Heart*, presented in the West End, reinforced this view by showing the spokesperson for the early Gay movement unable to cope with the changes in sexual behaviour that AIDS was making necessary. In a very disturbing scene, he has a nervous breakdown and leaves the stage an emotional wreck. It was clear that any contribution that Gay Sweatshop was to make to the whole debate would need to be presented with thought and caution.

This explains why, when Andy Kirby sent *Compromised Immunity* to the Gay Sweatshop Times Ten Festival Committee, there was considerable disagreement about it. One reservation was that it seemed to suggest that once the disease was contracted then death was inevitable. At this point very little was known about how effectively the course of the disease could be halted or even reversed by treatments and alternative medicine. As far as people who are body positive (i.e. have antibodies which denote that they have come into contact with the AIDS virus) are concerned there are still no reliable statistics about the likelihood of them developing full-blown AIDS. At the start of the play Gerry is very bitter and in the final stages of the illness. All his attempts to fight it have failed. On the other hand through his relationship with Peter, the nurse, and the young gay men, Iain, he comes to realize that there are still things that he can do and still people he can help. The tension between living with AIDS and preparing to die with dignity is one which still causes debate.

A second reservation about the play was that it showed Gerry cut off from gay friends and his ex-lover; some people found this unduly pessimistic especially as in the earlier versions Gerry re-established contact with his old friends by going to the gay club with Peter. Given the state of his health, this had seemed implausible and was changed.

In the very first draft that Gay Sweatshop received the play was a two-hander which meant that many of the other relationships were described or narrated – this made it very wordy and static. The first feedback given to the writer was that he should write in some of the other characters. However the two female characters which were then included were very minor and not particularly positive or strong – Marie was portrayed as being on the lookout for a good husband and very prejudiced about AIDS and Miss Coates was also quite unsympathetic. It would have been very difficult to justify doing a male-focused play with two potentially negative female characters and so this was another area of concern.

There were also practical reasons which made the play difficult to evaluate – it was

Andy's first play and was densely printed on very wide computer paper which meant that by the time the reader reached the end of one line it was difficult to find the beginning of the next. For this reason alone other theatre companies might well have sent the play back unread. But with scrupulous care the company helped Andy to develop the script and it was included in the Festival programme.

Robert Hale had been asked to direct and it was cast from actors known to Gay Sweatshop including Richard Sandells and Peter Shorey who had been in the second production of *Poppies*. Together that group of people helped Andy to cut the play and shape some of the characters and scenes. Particular attention was paid to Marie as Pip Stephenson who was reading that character felt very strongly that her feelings about Peter should be more ambivalent and her response to AIDS more complex. The play was read on a Sunday afternoon in the bar at the Drill Hall. Alan Pope had been asked to chair a discussion at which Tony Whitehead of the Terrence Higgins Trust (THT) was to talk. By this time Tony, like many others, had given years of energy and emotional commitment to that organization. The play struck chords for him in the way that it showed people coping with AIDS and caring for the dying. He was very moved by the reading and found it difficult to speak afterwards which was a tribute to the play more eloquent than words.

I have described some of the reservations about the script but the readers decided that its strengths outweighed them. However I don't think anyone had anticipated the emotional impact of the relationship between the young heterosexual male nurse and the older gay man dying of AIDS. This central conceit is very simple but very effective and allows the writer to say things about Gerry's anger and bitterness and about straight society's response to gayness and AIDS. It also allows him to show a relationship develop between two men which, although it is not a sexual one, is nonetheless tender, emotional and loving.

After the reading at the Drill Hall there were requests that the company should come and read it at the THT conference, at the CHE Winter Fair, at the Leicester Haymarket and at the Nottingham Festival. It was clear that the play was very much in demand. In the Spring of 1986 Richard Sandells spoke to Noël about the possibility of staging a full production of the play during Gay Pride Week. Gay Sweatshop was about to make an application for funding for another project and so it seemed unlikely that it would be possible to get Arts Council backing for the play especially as this would require booking an out of London tour. Richard undertook to do the fundraising to enable the play to be presented on a profit-share basis as a Gay Sweatshop Times Ten production. If it had not been for his energy and determination the play would not have been produced; he wrote countless letters to people involved in theatre, to trades unions and political figures and to friends of the company and managed to raise £7,000 – a quite remarkable achievement. Robert was unable to direct the play and so I was asked to do it and a cast was found based largely on the original one for the reading. Tony Reeves who designed many of the company's early posters (*Mister X, Indiscreet, As Time Goes By, Dear Love of Comrades*) was brought in as poster and set designer. With him I made the decision to try to maintain some of the flavour of the reading by keeping all the characters on stage all the time. This helped to create ensemble playing and to give the feeling that the play came from the whole company. It also meant that the audience was aware of the other characters and of the world outside the hospital. The production opened in the heat of summer in the tiny studio at the Albany Empire. Performances at the Oval House and later at the Drill Hall followed and by this time it was clear that the production should also be seen out of London. At this point Richard Sandells joined the management and enlisted the support of people in the theatrical profession and friends in persuading the Arts Council to give the production enough touring subsidy to enable it to be re-rehearsed and taken out on tour.

The reading of *Compromised Immunity* took place in October 1985, it was then rehearsed for four weeks for the Albany and the Oval in the summer of 1986, and for another week for the Drill Hall that autumn. The touring production had a cast change and so there was another three-week rehearsal period in April 1987. This gradual evolution of the play and the production gave the company the opportunity to help Andy refine the writing and the actors the chance to develop their characterizations – for me as the director it was a very satisfying experience even though it sometimes felt as if I would be directing the play for the rest of my life!

The tour was a long one for Gay Sweatshop and allowed us to play in venues that didn't usually book the company such as the more prestigious studio theatres. We sometimes ran for half or even whole weeks – a luxury compared with the usual one and two night stands. Without a doubt this happened partly because of the subject-matter and it does seem a sad reflection that some venues have only booked Gay Sweatshop when we were doing an AIDS play. Over the years the company has acquired a following all over the country from amongst the Gay Community and heterosexuals but it is still difficult to persuade theatre programmers that this is the case and that the work is not just for a narrow minority. Nevertheless *Compromised Immunity* brought new audiences in to see the company – at the Leicester Haymarket tickets were sold out for the week before we arrived and the 'normal' theatregoing audience flocked to see the play. Throughout the tour the show played to packed houses, receiving critical acclaim and often standing ovations and it was especially interesting to note that many people from the nursing profession came to see the show and wrote to the company afterwards to express their gratitude.

Throughout the years Gay Sweatshop has received countless letters of support and thanks from audience members who have been moved or changed by the experience of seeing one of the shows. *Compromised Immunity* was no exception. One letter in particular demonstrates the warmth with which the play was received and the profound effect it had:

Dear Gay Sweatshop,
On Friday I saw a performance of your production of *Compromised Immunity* at the Gardner Centre, University of Sussex. Four weeks ago my brother died of AIDS and I would like to thank you for the immense amount of support I felt from the play. I have always believed in the power of theatre to enable people to share and understand experiences whatever their starting point. I felt that the play enabled people who had no knowledge of AIDs to acquire an understanding of its impact while providing encouragement, optimism and support for people like myself who are all too familiar with it. The play was very realistic, tragic, comic, and utterly believable and compared well with *The Normal Heart* which swamped the issue by resorting to political drama and intrigue. It was also an excellent play at the level of showing how people cope with death and demonstrated, as my brother demonstrated, that one can fight for a good life right up to the very end.

I would be grateful if you could tell me how I can get hold of a copy of the script as I would like to pass it on to the nurses who looked after my brother.

Please give my thanks to the company and I wish you every success with this and all your work.

Pretended Families

This Island's Mine was written with the help of an Arts Council writing bursary and it was not my intention whilst I was writing it that it should be produced by Gay Sweatshop. I wanted to write a play about refugees that centred on a large old house that I knew in West Hampstead. Some of the characters were already in my head: an elderly Jewish woman, the ghost of a White Russian Princess, a gay man who also lives in the house and a very old cat. I very much wanted to look at exiles and make links between them and people who feel like exiles in their own country. I had also been reading Dickens and was fascinated by the way he uses coincidence and chance to make links between different people's stories and lives which resonate thematically with each other and build up a picture of a whole society. My ambition was to write something which went some way to creating a similar impression of eighties Britain. I wanted to include a wide range of characters who did not, at first glance, have anything in common such as a young West Indian actor and an elderly Jewish refugee. This desire to make links arose out of conversations while we were planning and programming the Gay Sweatshop Times Ten Festival which is why the play sprang indirectly from it. I also knew that the play would include elements of my life and people I had met since I had moved to London and become involved in Gay Sweatshop. In the end the play was to explore the idea of families and how we create alternative families for ourselves based not on blood ties but on a community of interest and ideas – pretended families if you like.

I began work on the play in 1985 at the height of the AIDS hysteria and it was unavoidable that this should inform the mood of the play. Indeed it was responsible for the theme of exile. I was beginning to feel that I no longer belonged in a Britain increasingly hostile to everything I believed in. I began work on the play almost without realizing that this was what I was doing: I wrote some poems about a young man sacked from his job in a restaurant because he was gay and because, according to his employer, he posed a health risk. Just such a case had been reported in *Gay Times* in 1985 and my attention was drawn to it because it happened in Barnstaple – my home town. The style of these poems was far removed from any conventional dramatic form but I realized that it would allow me to create a whole kaleidoscope of characters and stories – their thoughts, hopes, dreams and memories. I would also be able to incorporate all my ideas about exile and the people in the house in West Hampstead. I was very sceptical about whether what I was writing would constitute a play. It seemed that it would be impossible to stage because it seemed such an extreme form of narrative theatre.

In 1980 and 1981 I had worked as an actor with Mike Alfreds and Shared Experience. The philosophy of that company complemented the philosophy of

Gay Sweatshop. For Mike, the essence of theatre was actors in a space telling a story to an audience. Just as the identification of the Gay Sweatshop actors with the characters makes for a stronger, more direct relationship with the audience, so Mike's approach in his early work meant that direct contact with the audience was not impeded by technical effects. In the company's first production, *Arabian Nights*, he had dispensed with set, props, lighting effects, costume and instead threw the emphasis on the actor's skills. There was a revival of *Arabian Nights* in 1981 in which I took part. In this play the company had developed a style where the actors spoke directly to the audience acting the story out at the same time. (Elements of this style were subsequently adopted by the RSC when they performed *Nicholas Nickleby*). It was a difficult technique to learn but in performance I found it very exciting and liberating – if you could make people believe they were seeing an Arabian prince or a white stallion through the use of your voice, your body and words then it seemed that this was creating illusion which was truly magical.

When I left Shared Experience in 1981 I sat down and tried to write a one-man show that used the techniques I had learned. I was keen to write something autobiographical about North Devon and about my own experiences growing up in that environment. I used a narrator and characters, created with the help of masks, who told their own stories. The show was called *Telling Tales* and when I was writing it I was convinced that it would be of little interest to anyone but myself because it felt so personal. It was performed at the Oval House as part of the Gay Pride Week celebrations in 1982 and the response was such that it was revived on a number of occasions and became a Gay Sweatshop production when the company was resurrected in 1983.

As the actor who left drama school in 1977 my ambitions did not include being a writer and I had little understanding of what the writing process was about. I remember in some early rehearsals for *As Time Goes By* being shocked and dismayed that Noël and Drew sat down with myself and Philip Timmins to re-write the Edward Carpenter scene. Until then I had thought that writers were somehow omniscient figures whose work was sacrosanct. Through working with Gay Sweatshop I came to value the way theatre could be used to communicate ideas and experiences and slowly I began to accept a less élitist view of the creative process – the example of people like Drew and Noël was crucial in this change. Gay Sweatshop allowed me to develop both as a director and as a writer and I was encouraged in this particularly by Noël because he believed that it was important to find your own voice and to believe in your own potential – as an actor it is often difficult to do this because you rarely have much control over the work. When Noël read *This Island's Mine* in 1986 he strongly recommended that Gay Sweatshop should produce it. It was given an initial reading during the Gay Sweatshop Times Twelve Festival at the Oval House in 1987. This second festival was a sequel to Times Ten and allowed the company to continue to develop the processes started in 1985. From the reading it was clear that the play had resonances for audiences even without the political events of the following months.

The reading of the play took place at a time when Margaret Thatcher's government was about to be re-elected for a third term. They had already abolished the GLC and the next targets for attack were the ILEA and the Labour-controlled boroughs. Section 28 began its life as an amendment to the Local Government Bill and it was introduced towards the end of the committee stage in December 1987. Whilst it was under consideration it was called at different times Clause 27, 28 and 29 becoming a section when it passed into law. For the purposes of clarity I will refer to it

Finding Room on the Agenda for Love lxiii

throughout as Section 28. It seeks to prevent councils from funding lesbian and gay organizations by making illegal what it calls the promotion of homosexuality by local authorities. It was also attempting to stop any presentation of positive images of homosexuality in schools and any discussion of alternative living – such as where children are brought up by a lesbian couple; this it refers to as a 'pretended family'. There is also concern that local authorities which provide counselling services for lesbians and gays could be liable to prosecution because of Section 28. Reactionary politicians have always been the first to attack any measure which tries to prevent discrimination against lesbians and gay men and it was no exaggeration when opponents of the section called it a bigots' charter.

Just a few months before Section 28 was first introduced Gay Sweatshop had hit trouble with a local authority – in Devon. *Compromised Immunity* had been booked to perform at the Exeter and Devon Arts Centre. There had already been trouble earlier in the year when the gay cabaret group The Insinuendos had performed at the Centre. When Gay Sweatshop's visit was announced a Conservative on the city council tried to get the Arts Centre's grant suspended. It was Dublin all over again only this time AIDS was exploited to make explicit and sinister links between homosexuality and sickness. The councillor argued that the Arts Centre should be a family venue and that there was a danger that young people could wander into the building and come into contact with homosexuality and AIDS and somehow contract both! In the city council no one party had a majority and on this occasion the Alliance voted with Labour and the motion was defeated. However another councillor took the matter to the county council which was Tory controlled and which also funded the Arts Centre. In the end a £10,000 subsidy was cut.

This caused a huge political battle in the county which came to a head on the eve of the General Election. The company arrived in Exeter and gave a press conference and interviews on local TV. Once again the effect of the opposition to the company was that support was rallied and the Arts Centre had to hire a bigger venue. The Arts Centre's grant was not recovered and a community outreach post was lost but the campaign had politicized whole sections of the community. 200 people attended the play that night and, in a questionnaire which they were asked to complete afterwards, unanimously endorsed the booking of the company. I hope this goes some way to qualifying the rather negative picture I have given of my home county and its inhabitants. The audience that night gave *Compromised Immunity* one of the warmest and most enthusiastic receptions of the whole tour.

When Section 28 was given its first reading the Gay movement was caught unawares. In very little time a campaign was mounted to draw attention to the discriminatory nature of the legislation which ended with lesbians abseiling into the Lords and handcuffing themselves to Sue Lawley's desk during the 'Six O'clock News'. Gay Sweatshop was aware that the section could have a drastic effect on the arts and on lesbian and gay culture but, more importantly, the company was aware how censorship could shock liberal-minded members of the Establishment into realizing just how dangerous the legislation could be. The company called a meeting at the Drill Hall just after Christmas and the Arts Lobby was set up. This proved to be a very effective way of opposing the section and drew many influential figures into the campaign who were vociferous in expressing their concern. The press conference at The Playhouse organized by the Arts Lobby and Ian McKellen was one of its greatest achievements. At the press conference prominent figures from the Arts pledged their support of the campaign and their abhorrence of the prejudice behind the legislation.

When *This Island's Mine* opened it was held up as an example of the kind of initiative which the government was trying to censor. The government tried to assure opponents of the section that it would not affect the arts but the backbenchers who introduced it had obviously done so in a spirit of censorship. When Tony Banks MP had asked a question during the first reading in the Commons about how it might be used to stop the work of Gay Sweatshop he was greeted with a barrage of ridicule and jeers at the very mention of the company's name. There is no doubt that Section 28 gave the play an added significance which meant that critics who had never before come to see the company reviewed the production. Once again the high artistic standards were praised and the response from audiences and critics are perhaps best summed up by the review in *The Listener*:

> With Clause 28 lumbering towards the Statute Book, Gay Sweatshop find themselves at the very front of the frontline, missiles of prejudice whistling around their ears. So you might have expected the group's latest show to adopt an introspective, angry or didactic stance – or a touch of chauvinism, at least. But *This Island's Mine* written and directed by Philip Osment, is the mellowest, most warm-hearted and sagely contemplative new play I've seen in many months. For an example of 'ghetto' theatre, its heterosexual characters are remarkably three-dimensional. And far from blindly thumping a militant tub, the play poses awkward questions about the loyalties of the oppressed.

In *The Times* the critic drew attention to another threat presented by the Clause:

> The really pernicious effects of Clause 28 will not be that a play as resonant and richly patterned as this by Philip Osment may find it hard to discover venues out of London, though for all we know it may. The danger will come when discouraged authors practise self-censorship and turn their creativity into other channels.

Section 28 marks an attempt to turn back the clock. Ever since the 1967 Sexual Offences Act was passed there have been those who have sought to ignore it. This was illustrated in 1978 when the Charity Commissioners refused to grant Gay Sweatshop charitable status. An assistant Commissioner explained that it was refused because homosexual acts are 'regarded in law as immoral and contrary to public policy because they are a deviation from normal sexual behaviour.' An editorial in *The Guardian* at the time urged them to think again:

> By continuing to interpret the 1967 Act in a fashion which helps to attach obloquy to conduct rendered legal by its enactment, some members of the judiciary have chosen to place themselves at variance with a body of clerical, medical, academic and intellectual opinion which had urged the full implementation of the Act.

The Charity Commissioners did eventually accept and endorse a second application in 1986 and the company became a registered charity in recognition of its educational work. The proposers of Section 28 would seem to want to return to the pre-1967 days when EM Forster felt unable to publish *Maurice* because its happy ending seemed to recommend crime or even to promote homosexuality.

Whilst Section 28 was going through Parliament, Gay Sweatshop made an application to the Arts Council for *Twice Over* which we were particularly keen to present to younger audiences. The Council awarded a grant in spite of the uncertainty about how the section might affect bookings. Almost all of the company's venues receive local authority funding. There have always been venues that have been scared or reticent about taking Gay Sweatshop shows but, as yet, the new law does not seem to have caused theatre programmers to censor themselves for fear of prosecution. This is, of course, very difficult to monitor and in the event of a test case with an unfavourable outcome it could still happen. However the tour of *Twice Over* went ahead without incident.

The company met Jackie Kay when her first play *Chiaroscuro* was read at the Gay Sweatshop Times Ten Festival. At this time she had already established a reputation as a poet. *Chiaroscuro* was written in a highly poetic form which was very original. It dealt with responses to lesbianism of four Black or mixed race women and it tackled head-on the idea that only white feminists are lesbians. The play was breaking new ground both in style and content and the company was very keen to work with Jackie in the future.

Twice Over was commissioned by Theatre Centre, one of the country's leading schools touring companies. The play had the support of many members of Theatre Centre but it caused considerable debate within that company because other members were uncertain about aspects of some of the characters. The fact that it showed both an Irish woman and a young black woman responding badly to the idea of lesbianism raised objections and there were worries about how the play would be received in schools. In the event they did not produce the play but Noël who had now left Sweatshop and was writer in residence at Theatre Centre suggested that Gay Sweatshop give it a staged rehearsed reading at the Gay Sweatshop Times Twelve Festival in 1987. Sally Aprahamian who had helped Jackie to develop the script at Theatre Centre directed.

In researching the play Jackie talked to young women and girls about their perceptions of lesbians – many of which are expressed in the play by Sharon and Evaki. One thing that struck her most forcefully is that lesbians were seen as being young. When she asked if a Granny could be gay the young women expressed shock and even disgust. So she decided to examine this response. Gay Sweatshop had never done a play which successfully explored a relationship between two older women. The tenderness and love that Cora and Maeve have for each other made the play moving and poignant.

Like *Compromised Immunity*, *Twice Over* has a very strong central conceit. When Evaki finds the letter from Maeve to her Gran, and the diaries recording their relationship, it propels her onto a course of confrontation with Maeve. Evaki's dilemma is whether to accept this new Cora that she has discovered and Maeve's dilemma is whether to to keep silent or to accept that she can only mourn Cora properly if she is able to talk to someone about their love. Secrecy is a thread that runs through the whole play as every character has something to hide.

Jackie re-worked the play in consultation with members of Gay Sweatshop and with Nona Shepphard, the director. Originally one character, Jean, was a teacher and much of the action took place in the classroom as it was intended to be performed in schools. Taking the play out of the school and making Jean a workmate of Maeve and Cora allowed Jackie to concentrate on the personal lives of the characters. It also allowed her to develop the theme of friendship between the two sets of characters – the older women and the schoolgirls.

The company also encouraged Jackie to include extracts from Cora's diaries and to develop the sensual side of her relationship with Maeve. The fact that the play was not to be performed solely to young people made this possible. And so the description of their first date was included and references to the sexual side of their relationship.

One of the problems the play poses to a director and designer is the use of monologues and the number of locations. This was solved in the Gay Sweatshop production by creating a set where each character has her own space – Jean sits crocheting in her chair in the works canteen, Tash is in her bedroom painting, Sharon is locked in the toilet, Maeve sits fretting at home and Cora had what was almost a throne on a rostrum at the back and in the centre. Kate's design also allowed for a grave which was set in the middle of the stage and out of which Cora's belongings could be taken.

Twice Over was a significant production for Gay Sweatshop for a number of reasons. It was the company's first play by a Black writer and the mixed race cast of characters flowed naturally from the writing. This meant that the policies which inspired the Gay Sweatshop Times Ten Festival had to some degree paid off. The play also strengthened the company's profile with regard to women's work. It was as popular and highly regarded as previous men's and mixed shows had been. Lastly it went out on tour just after Section 28 had been introduced onto the Statute Book and drew an audience that needed to be heartened and encouraged. Lesbians and gay men were under attack. We were being told that the rights that had been so slowly gained over the past years were privileges that could be withdrawn and that our relationships had no validity and were based on pretence. During the tour people travelled miles to packed-out performances in Sheffield, Bradford and Bristol and the play took on a significance that made the atmosphere in the theatre both emotionally charged and celebratory. At the beginning of the play we see Maeve excluded from Cora's family and unable to share her grief. At the end she is given her rightful place amongst the mourners and Evaki has learnt that the ties of blood and marriage are not always the strongest or most important.

Epilogue

Drew Griffiths once said, 'If the aims and objectives of Gay Sweatshop are ever achieved, we will have done ourselves out of a job.' Certainly Gay Sweatshop is needed in 1989 as much as in 1974 and in some ways this could be seen as a failure. Prevailing attitudes still make it difficult for two women or two men to kiss on stage without an issue being made of it. It is hard for gay characters to be introduced casually into plays and films. In light entertainment gays and lesbians are still used as an excuse for cheap laughs. Homosexuality is still not respectable.

On the other hand a whole generation of young lesbians and gay men have grown up knowing that they have their own culture. They have had some access to images of people like themselves. Angela Stewart-Park remembers that the only book that she could find when she was coming out was *The Well of Loneliness*. Now our history has been written about, plays are published, films and television programmes are made. It is heartening to see programmes like the recent *Out on Tuesday* series shown on Channel Four. Gay people are now presenting culture about our lives with a new assurance which is without any trace of apology. This confidence arises out of a shared awareness of our worth that the AIDS crisis and Section 28 have only made stronger.

In the face of all this Gay Sweatshop goes from strength to strength. There is now a third generation of people running the company. (Philip Timmins left the management in 1986, Martin Humphries and Noël left in 1987, Kate Owen, Tierl Thompson and myself all left in 1988.) The new group will bring new priorities and new ideas but will continue to be influenced by the traditions that have given the

Finding Room on the Agenda for Love lxvii

company its unique identity.

There are many directions in which the company could go. Some of the people I interviewed feel that it should have a venue, others that it should do more youth work and should try to provide a training for lesbian and gay performers, others that it should be producing large-scale celebratory events. But it is impossible to see into the future – who could have predicted the advent of AIDS ten years ago or foreseen the way that the Peace movement and anti-racism would inform the company's work? What is certain is that how the company fares in the nineties is very dependent on funding.

At the time of writing the company still does not receive revenue funding from the Arts Council. This seems incredible given the sheer volume and quality of the work produced over the last fourteen years. The Arts Council is currently encouraging their clients to seek out other forms of sponsorship. This is difficult enough for companies that are much more prestigious and much less controversial. It is hard to imagine that commercial companies will find kudos in sponsoring Gay Sweatshop. The company provides a forum for lesbian and gay artists to work together and to respond to broader political debates and activities. Without adequate Arts Council subsidy there is no guarantee that there will be an ongoing thread of work from these artists in this country.

In talking about Gay Sweatshop and its work the word that crops up most frequently is 'love'. When the company was set up homosexual love was still 'the love that dare not speak its name'; Nancy talks about the quantity of love there was within the group in spite of the arguments and the difficulties; Alan feels that Gay Sweatshop's work at its best has a special quality that is 'to do with love'; a key moment in *The Dear Love of Comrades* is when Carpenter tells the Labour Party Official to ask the committee if they can find a place on the agenda for love.

This love springs out of an ideology of compassion. It stops the work becoming chauvinistic and keeps it humane and generous. It prevents legitimate anger from turning to bitterness. It is a mighty weapon against oppression.

Sometimes it is difficult to keep faith with such an ideology, especially when the work is undervalued or dismissed, when disagreements and anger cause strife within the company, when political battles are lost and our rights are taken away. At such times it is not always possible to see the value of what we are doing here and now. The struggle seems in vain. But it is important to remember that ideas do not die and that we cannot always predict how they will affect the future. The lives and work of people like Edward Carpenter provide us with very tangible grounds for hope when it might be easy to despair and so I will leave the last word to him:

Think not that the love thou enterst into today is for a few months or years:
    The little seed set now must lie quiet before it will germinate, and many alternations of sunshine and shower descend upon it before it become even a small plant.
    When a thousand years have passed, come thou again. And Behold! a mighty tree that no storms can shake.

Love does not end with this life or any number of lives; the form that thou seekest lies hidden under wrapping after wrapping;
    Nevertheless it shall at length appear – more wondrous far than aught thou hast imagined.

Therefore leave time: do not like a child pull thy flower up by the roots to see if it is growing;

Even though thou be old and near the grave there is plenty of time.

('When a Thousand Years have Passed' in *Towards Democracy*, Part Three)

The original poster for the Almost Free season (1975)

The companies of *Any Woman Can* and *Mister X:* Dublin (1976)
Back: Philip Howells, Tim Barwick
Middle: Helen Barnaby, Julie Parker, Nancy Diuguid, Sara Hardy, Alan Pope, Bob Stratton *Front:* Jill Posener, Gordon MacDonald, Drew Griffiths

Drew Griffiths as the New York Drag Queen in *As Time Goes By* (1977-78)

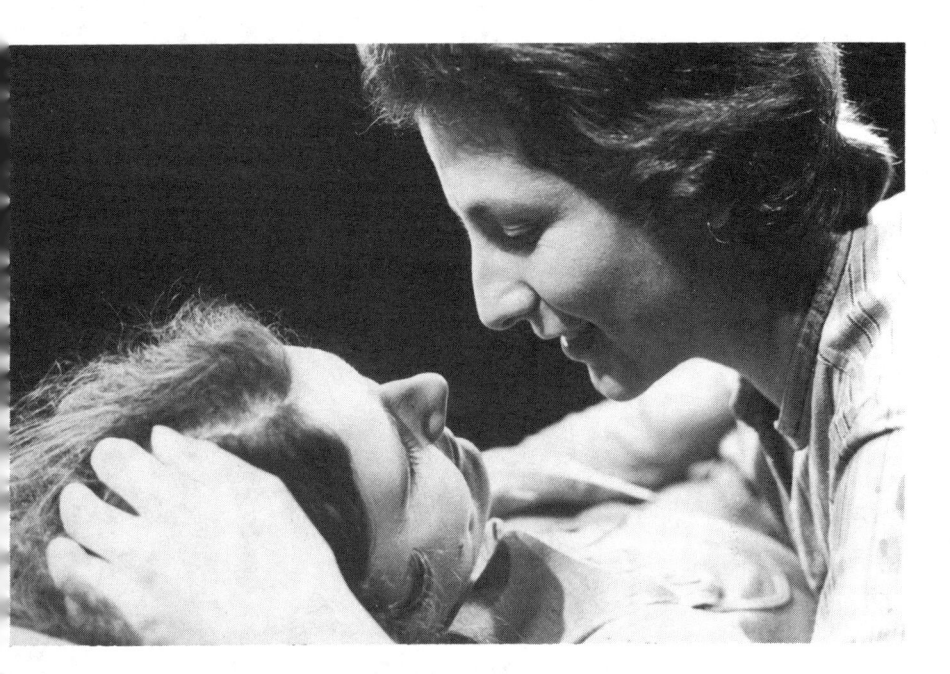

Sara Hardy and Nancy Diuguid in *Any Woman Can* (1976)

Poster for *Care and Control* (1977)

George Hukin (Stephen Hatton) confronts Edward Carpenter (Noël Greig) in *The Dear Love of Comrades* (1979)

Edward Carpenter (Noël Greig), Frank Simpson (Ray Batchelor) and George Merril (Peter Glancey) in *The Dear Love of Comrades* (1979)

The Gay Sweatshop Times Ten Festival committee (1985)
Left to right: Back: Bernardine Evaristo, Martin Humphries, Tierl Thompson *Middle:* Philip Timmins
Front: Philip Osment, Diane Biondo, Kate Owen, Noël Greig

Peter Shorey and Gordon MacDonald as the Mouldy Heads
in the second production of *Poppies* (1985)

Peter Dennett (Richard Sandells) and Gerry (Peter Shorey)
in *Compromised Immunity* (1986-87)

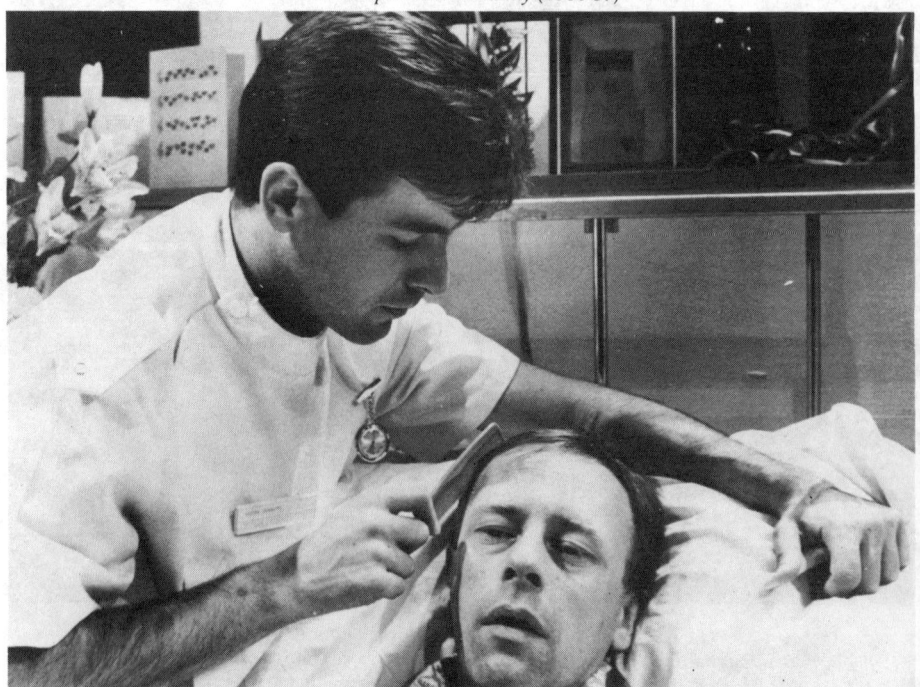

Selwyn (Trevor Ferguson) and Mark (Richard Sandells)
in *This Island's Mine* (1988)

Mme Irina (Diane Hall) eating her truffles watched by
Luise (Margaret Robertson) in *This Island's Mine* (1988)

Cora (Pamela Lane) and Evaki (Adjoa Andoh) in *Twice Over* (1988)

Maeve (Mary Ellen Ray) and Cora (Pamela Lane) in *Twice Over* (1988)

The Dear Love of Comrades

A play with songs

Noël Greig

The Dear Love of Comrades received its first performance at the Oval House Theatre, London on 8 March 1979. The company for the original Gay Sweatshop production was as follows:

E M Forster; Fred Charles	
Frank Simpson; Fisher-Unwin	Ray Batchelor
George Merril	Peter Glancy
Edward Carpenter	Noël Greig
George Hukin	Stephen Hatton
George Adams	Philip Timmins
Accompanist	Alex Harding

Directed by Nancy Diuguid
Set, Costume, Lighting Design Paul Dart
Music by Alex Harding
Haircuts Robin
Administration Gean Wilton

The words and music of the song 'England Arise' were written by Edward Carpenter. The words to 'One Night As I Lay Sleeping' were written by Drew Griffiths.

The play is set in and around Sheffield, and in London, between 1891 and 1898. The major political events affecting the lives of the characters have been shown in accurate chronological order (the Walsall anarchists' trial, the founding of the Independent Labour Party, the Oscar Wilde trial); in other areas there has been some sacrifice of total academic accuracy, in order to retain dramatic clarity.

Author's Note

The Dear Love of Comrades is about Edward Carpenter, one of the leading lights of the early socialist movement in Britain. His open declaration of his homosexuality challenged this movement to take a stand for gay rights, in the same way as feminists of the time, with whom Carpenter was closely associated, fought to make women's liberation a central issue. After decades of oblivion, Carpenter's life and work is now being rediscovered.

An original music score by Alex Harding, which accompanies all productions, is available from the author's agent.

Act One

To one side of the acting area, a Victorian piano. At the other, a radio on a small table, circa 1940s.

Lights up on **Carpenter, Hukin, Adams** *and* **Merril.**

Song: 'The Body Electric'

All I sing the body electric
I sing of the light that flows
From the flesh of those that I love

I sing the body electric
I sing of the flame that glows
In the blood of those that I love

Those who defile the living
Are the same as those who defile the dead;
Those who corrupt their own bodies
Conceal themselves

Therefore:
I sing the body electric
I sing the body electric
I sing the body electric.

Lights dim, but not out. Spot on radio. **Hukin** *and* **Adams** *lie on the ground. They are reading a letter.* **Merril** *kneels on the ground at some distance. He carries a small posy of flowers.* **Carpenter** *crouches, looking out.*

Announcer's Voice This is the BBC Home Service. Book Talk. This week the author and critic E. M. Forster speaks on the life and work of Edward Carpenter.

Adams *gets paper, ink and pen and returns to* **Hukin. Merril** *places flowers on ground.*

Forster's Voice One hundred years ago, on August 29th 1844, Edward Carpenter was born, and I want to talk about him. Do you know the name Edward Carpenter? It is being forgotten, partly because he was a pioneer, and his work has passed into the common stock. He was a good man, certainly an unusual one.

Carpenter *cups his hands and calls out.*

Carpenter Hello!

The piano echoes him.

Adams (*to* **Hukin**) Not 'dear Edward', call him Ted.

Hukin Oooh, you! (*Screws up first bit of paper.*)

Adams You're not applying for a job, you know.

Hukin I've got one. Your secretary. (*Begins again, with mock deliberation.*) 'Sheffield, March 1891. Dear *Edward* . . .'

Forster *appears. He stands near the radio.*

Forster In 1944, when I spoke on the wireless, the end of the bloodletting seemed close and, to socialists, the dawn of a new era seemed imminent. So I chose to recollect a man to whom such a movement owed so much. I talked of his political work in Sheffield; his writings on democracy, his love of India, his farm . . .

He is looking at **Hukin** *and* **Adams.**

Hukin (*reads over what he's written*) 'We sang your songs in the pub last night, loud enough for them to be heard in Calcutta. So if you didn't catch them you must have been in Bombay.'

Adams Tell him the spuds've done well.

Hukin He won't be interested in spuds.

Adams Tell him they've made a profit.

Hukin (*shoves paper at him*) Do it yourself, I'm not writing a letter to India about spuds.

Carpenter (*cups hands*) Edward Carpenter!

The piano echoes him.

Forster He was also a homosexual,

although I did not announce this fact over the airwaves. How could I admire in someone else a quality that I loathed in myself?

Merril (*to the ground*) I feel so lonely now. Why did you have to? Why did you have to go and leave me? Mam, Mam?

He places flowers on the ground.

Forster It was while visiting Edward that something occurred that was to spark in me an intense awareness of my own nature. I have George Merril to thank for that. He showed me that . . . well, to put it quite simply, he pinched my bottom.

Hukin *grabs the letter and gets up. He is chased by* **Adams**, *who tries to get it off him. They are laughing.*

Hukin You cheeky sod!

Adams (*grabs*) Give it here, I've not done.

Hukin (*reads*) 'George and Fannie must be very pleased with the new bed you've bought them, because they're never out of it.' It's a letter not a scandal rag. It's my turn now.

He lies down and writes. **Adams** *lies on his back with his head in his hands.*

Adams Ask him if he's seen a jungle.

Hukin I wish there were a jungle near Sheffield, you could get away from nosey-bloody-parkers like you!

Carpenter (*cups hands*) I love men!

The piano echoes him.

Forster But the electric shock that entered my spine did not reach my brain. I drew a veil between myself and the world.

Carpenter (*with piano*) The sun, the moon and the stars, the grass, the water that flows around the earth, and the light of heaven. To you, greetings!

Hukin (*reads*) 'Goodbye, and be back soon. We'll drum up a party and declare the New Age officially open. Your loving friends George E. Hukin . . . (*Passes letter to* **Adams** *who writes.*)

Adams . . . and George Adams.

Forster In short, I didn't really like myself.

Merril She's dead now.

Carpenter I'm alive, I'm alive, I'm alive.

Forster *watches during the song. He exits at the end. The other characters move into the station.*

Song: 'And Heaven Cannot Be'

All And heaven cannot be
The gods are dead and we are free
There's nothing more to know
Than the universe can show

And heaven's just a story
Nothing less there is no glory
There's nothing but the stars
The universe is ours.

April 1891. Totley station. Late afternoon.

Adams *and* **Hukin** *are waiting.* **Carpenter** *emerges through the smoke. He has a greatcoat, hat and two bags. They all meet and embrace.* **Hukin** *takes a bag and* **Carpenter** *puts an arm around him. They start to leave.* **Merril** *is leaning against a wall. He smiles.* **Carpenter** *says something to the other two and gives second bag to* **Adams**, *who looks annoyed.* **Hukin** *puts arm around him and they move away.*

Carpenter I wanted to say goodbye.

Merril We never said hello.

Carpenter You smiled at me on the train.

Merril I couldn't get any further. I'm a bit shy.

Carpenter (*extends hand*) Hello then.

Merril Hello. (*Extends hand. He has a bit of paper.*) Oh. That's my address. It's for you. I scribbled it down.

Carpenter Would you like me to come and see you?

Merril I'm in most days. I'm a layabout. Will you come?

Carpenter Probably.

Merril Good. (*Starts to go.*) I'll see you then, Edward.

Carpenter How d'you know my name?

Merril My secret!

Carpenter Tell me!

Merril I will. In bed. (*Exits.*)

Adams Twelve months away and he chases a stranger.

Hukin Perhaps he knows him.

Adams Does he heck.

Hukin Perhaps it doesn't matter. (*Crosses to* **Carpenter**, *leaving* **Adams** *to carry both bags.*)

Adams Porter and servant, that's all I am.

A pub. The same evening

Song: 'Chandeliers'.

Merril (*sings*) She said goodbye to the chandeliers
To follow her gypsy lover;
Bade farewell to the coach and pair
And her bed with the silken cover.

Spoken, piano under.

I was that close to the Prince of Wales once (*Holds out hand.*), *that* close. Tranby Croft. He'd all these chaps with him, frock-coats, tall hats, flowers in their buttonholes. One of them dawdled behind after – such a good looker too – and he smiled at me. So I went up to him and he asked me to come and meet him that night. So I did. He brought me some grapes to eat, and we saw each other every day after that. He'd leave a bunch of violets outside his window on the ground floor, and a little bit of paper twisted amongst them saying where to meet. He said he didn't care for the shooting and the cards, but he did long for some love and affection from someone like me, only it was impossible in his situation. He gave me his address when they left. But I lost it. I knew it wasn't possible.

Sings

She rode with him gladly over the hills
His Romany ways to follow;
Danced barefoot on the hillside green
And slept in the leafy hollow.

Millthorpe. Later the same evening.

Adams (*shuts the accounts book*) That's that done.

The other two look up.

Carpenter Do we have the pleasure of your company, now?

Hukin He's going to sulk for days.

Carpenter Well, he won't get his present till I see a smile.

Adams (*thawing a bit*) Here we go, wheedle wheedle wheedle.

Carpenter Just a little one, George, don't overdo it.

Adams *forces a smile.*

Carpenter Talk about cracking ice.

Hukin And talking about presents... (*Gets up and picks up a bunch of daffodils.*) ...I picked them on the way back from the station.

Adams We were trying to fill in the time...

Hukin (**thrusts them at Carpenter**) Welcome home! When there's yellow daffs in a green vase I know spring has sprung. Now let's see what you've got us.

Carpenter (*opens a bag. Brings out gifts*) Well. That's yours (*Hands one to* **Adams**.) I hope they fit. I got them in Bombay, so I can't change them if they don't. (*To* **Hukin**.) Yours might need taking in a bit.

Adams *has a pair of Indian sandals.* **Hukin** *has a long linen garment.*

Hukin It's a nightshirt.

Carpenter It's not a nightshirt.

Hukin Well, I'm not wearing it down the pub. I'll wear it in bed. When I've got visitors.

Adams (*has put on sandals*) They fit! I shall use these as a pattern. They'd sell down the market.

Hukin He'd put a price tag on anything.

Adams I've been making sandals all year. They go well

Carpenter (*another package to* **Adams**) That's for Lucy. Tell her to wear it next time she's up here. (*To* **Hukin**.) And that's Fannie's. I hope she likes the colour. And don't open them yourselves.

Hukin Now tell us about it. What was the best bit?

Adams Did you get to ride on an elephant?

Carpenter I think I liked Calcutta best.

Hukin Why?

Carpenter I met a couple of railway clerks there.

Adams You can meet railway clerks at Sheffield station.

Carpenter Not if you want to visit an opium den with them.

Hukin You didn't!

Carpenter I did. I met them after work, and they took me down an alley and up some back stairs. They knocked on a door, and someone had a squint at us through a peephole. You can only get in if you're with locals. Then you go into a room, with cushions on the floor, and very dim lights, and there's people sitting and lying around smoking.

Adams Sounds sordid to me.

Carpenter It's very pleasant.

Hukin What does it do?

Carpenter It calms you down.

Hukin Have you got any with you?

Carpenter No.

Adams Good. Because you won't have any time for lolling around on cushions now, you've got a farm to run (*He opens the books.*) and it's being run like it should, now.

Hukin You're making a profit now, Ted.

Carpenter Oh, yes?

Adams You were chucking money away like it had no end. But as you'll see, you've a proper system now, so you'd better keep it up.

Carpenter I'll look at them tomorrow, George.

Adams I'll come up and check them over now and then. You need a business manager.

Carpenter But, I'm not in business, George.

Adams You could be.

Carpenter I don't want to be . . .

Adams That is if you stopped playing at being a farmer and started growing for profit.

Carpenter I don't want to grow for profit, I want to grow for use. Anything left over we'll take and sell at the market, but I'm not turning this place into an industry.

Adams (*points at page*) Now, if you lay down two acres for strawberries, 'stead of just one . . .

Carpenter To hell with that, I don't need two.

Adams You need a roof over your head.

Carpenter I don't want to talk about it. I'll talk about in the morning.

Hukin *has kept out of this. He has picked up the flowers and has looked at them. He goes to the drawer in the table. He gets out a hammer. He looks at it and looks at the flowers.*

Adams (*now angry*) I don't know how much money you shelled out on your jaunt to the East, but you might thank a friend for making sure you've got a roof over your head to come back to.

Carpenter All right! We'll turn it into a factory farm. Then we'll hire labour at dirt-cheap prices and live off the profits.

Adams If you'd spent your life working week in, week out, scraping the pence together, you'd not be so high and mighty about a few pounds profit.

Hukin *starts to hit each stem off the daffodils with the hammer. They don't notice at first.*

Carpenter There's no need to shout.

Adams It's you that's being unreasonable.

A huge whack from **Hukin**. *The others stare in disbelief. He looks up innocently.*

Hukin It's scientific.

The others look at each other. **Adams** *shrugs. They look back.*

Hukin I read it in a book. When you cut the stems, the sap seals over. Like a scab when you've cut yourself. So when you put them in water, it can't get up the stems. So they die. But, if you follow *my* method, you squash the ends, they can drink the water, and they live longer. Good eh?

He gives another bash.

Hukin This lot'll be fresh all week now.

Another bash. He holds them up and sniffs them.

Carpenter (*grins at* **Adams**) Now there's an idea, George. Wrap them in damp paper, take them to the market, they'd stay fresh all week. You'd make a fortune.

Adams I might just, an' all. Just to spite you. I'll be back tomorrow, we'll go over those books, and you'll not get out of it. (*To* **Hukin**.) Coming, George . . . ?

Carpenter (*to* **Hukin**) Stay a bit longer.

Adams (*to* **Hukin**) George?

Hukin (*uncertain*) Well . . .

Adams No matter, I'll sing to myself on the way. (*To* **Carpenter**.) I'm not jealous of your trips abroad, Ted; so don't start having a go at me for making sure you've a roof over your head to come back to.

Carpenter *puts out a hand. They kiss.*
Adams *goes.*

Hukin George is right. You do need help with this place.

Carpenter I thought about that while I was away.

Hukin Then you should've said something.

Carpenter He's the wrong person.

Hukin He's the person who's helped you.

Carpenter Not the right one. Listen. Why don't you and Fannie move in here? You're right, I can't manage on my own, and I don't want to. I want to share this place with people I love.

Hukin Edward, I work with six other men. It's taken us years to set up on our own. I'm not walking out on them now.

Carpenter But George, it's such an

opportunity. Are you going to spend the rest of your life grinding razors? You're wasting your youth.

Hukin I'm free. I don't work for anyone else, I work for myself.

Carpenter You'd be working for yourself here. It's yours, take it.

Hukin I don't want a gift.

Carpenter You're being selfish, think of Fannie. She loves it out here. It'd be the best thing in the world for her.

Hukin Then you'd better talk to her.

Carpenter Tell her what I've said.

Hukin It's your idea, you ask her.

Carpenter We'll both talk to her. We'll get up early in the morning and walk back to town together.

Hukin I can't stay, Ted.

Carpenter Oh – you're not going to leave me on my own. Not on my first night back.

Hukin I told Fannie I'd be back.

Carpenter But she never minded before. She was never jealous when we slept together.

Hukin And she wouldn't be jealous if I stayed tonight.

Carpenter Then stay.

Hukin Ted, I made a decision, while you were away . . . I've my own life to lead.

Carpenter I don't want to be on my own tonight.

Hukin You could've asked the boy back.

Carpenter I didn't want the boy, I wanted you. All right, I'll admit it. I spoke to him to make you jealous.

Hukin You've no need to make me jealous, I'll always love you.

Carpenter Not in the way that I want.

Hukin In the way that I can. I've learnt that from you.

Carpenter It's very easy for you to say that, you've got a wife waiting for you.

Hukin No. A friend. Fannie and I try to practise what you preach, and it isn't easy.

Piano.

Carpenter I never said it was.

Song: The Dear Love of Comrades.

Both There's so much I had to say
Of the year I've/he's been away

Carpenter Of the temples and the tribes
Of the poverty and the bribes

Hukin Of the riots and the fights
Of the pickets and the strikes

Carpenter English rich and Asian poor

Hukin Of the government and law

Both You fool you've lost a loyal friend
You'd better face the fact you've got yourself to blame –
You still feel love but try to see best go your way
And discard all the pain

But we can't help remembering the dear love of comrades
When George and George and Edward agreed Utopia

And we can't help hoping still the dear love of comrades will
Help George and George and Edward to find
The road that leads, the road that leads
To Utopia.

Hukin *leaves.* **Carpenter** *watches as he goes.*

May 1891. The riverbank.

Fred Charles *enters. He looks around, satisfied that he has found the perfect spot for a picnic. He whistles to someone.* **Hukin**

enters with a hamper. He sets it down on a blanket. **Adams** *enters with an easel and painting equipment.* **Charles** *squats downstage and sings quietly to himself. They are bare-footed, carrying their shoes.*

Charles (*sings*) England arise, the long, long night is over,
Faint in the East, behold the dawn appear;
Out of your evil dream of toil and sorrow
Arise, oh England, for the day is here.

Hukin I still don't see why we couldn't have stayed on the other bank, my feet are frozen.

Adams It's a better view.

Hukin (*looking at feet*) They're bright blue.

Adams *is setting up his easel and throughout the scene paints.*

Charles He's right about the view.

Hukin Well, I shall go back over the bridge. I'm not risking life and limb twice in one day.

Carpenter *comes over to them, with trousers rolled up. He goes and looks at what* **Adams** *is painting.*

Adams Not till it's done, buzz off!

Carpenter *wanders over to the food, reaches out.* **Hukin** *slaps his hand.*

Hukin Not till it's ready.

He carries on arranging food and sorting it out. **Carpenter** *squats next to* **Charles**. *He picks up a stone and throws it.*

Carpenter I could never make them bounce.

Charles (*throws one*) Easy. Have another go.

Carpenter (*sits back*) When I was a child I'd go down to the beach at Brighton and throw stones at the sea. It never worked, they never bounced.

Charles You didn't try hard enough.

Carpenter So, I just sat there and dreamt about desert islands.

Charles (*throws another*) We'll have a competition.

Carpenter Definitely not.

Charles Why not?

Carpenter I don't like losing. It's my nature.

Charles Change your nature.

Carpenter Ah! But your nature depends upon your circumstances.

Charles I thought you'd come back from India a mystic; I hope you've not come back a cynic.

Carpenter I could never be a cynic, Fred. Not with people like you in the world.

Hukin (*calls*) Grub up!

Charles Well, I'm glad you've not ended your days in a monastery in the Himalayas.

Carpenter It did cross my mind. But, I don't think I could cope with the chastity. I think you'd be more suited. You'd have no difficulty with the poverty vows.

Hukin (*calls*) D'you want it or don't you?

Carpenter Fred Charles! The only man who can keep alive on cups of tea and talk of the revolution.

They cross to the others.

Hukin Cheese and pickle, cheese and cucumber or cheese and tomato?

Charles Cucumber and pickle.

Adams Trust an anarchist to upset the menu.

Charles No God, no master and no one dictating my diet.

Carpenter Talking of which.

Charles What? My diet?

Carpenter No. Banners, anarchist ones.

Charles Did you like it?

Hukin He made it.

Adams Edward, will you sit down. You're blocking the view.

Carpenter Oh, I'm terribly sorry, Monsieur Monet.

He sits. Takes a sandwich.

Charles We're going to lead the Mayday parade with it.

Carpenter I know. I heard.

Charles And you don't approve?

Carpenter The Socialist Society's always led the parade. It's traditional.

Charles But anarchists don't believe in tradition.

Hukin (*looking in the hamper*) Where's the ham?

Carpenter Fred. If you put yourself outside the movement, you'll be picked off like bottles on a wall.

Charles Stay inside, and we'll end up on back benches in frock-coats. There's the government threatening to use troops to break up strikes, and there's people calling themselves socialists talking votes and reform.

Hukin Ted, did you see the ham? I was sure we'd packed it.

Carpenter Stay inside! Look what's happening in America, in France . . . the moment you put yourself outside the mainstream the police'll pounce.

Hukin Edward Carpenter, where's that ham?

Carpenter You don't need ham.

Hukin It was on the kitchen table when you were . . . You left it out!

Carpenter It's bad for your system.

Hukin *My* system likes it.

Carpenter Meat makes you bad-tempered.

Hukin (*exasperated*) You make me bad-tempered. (*To* **Charles**.) He's a tyrant.

Charles Typical socialist. Starts out wanting the best for us all, ends up telling us what's best for us.

Hukin Vegetables! Now we'll all end up farting.

Charles Anyway, I'm leaving Sheffield.

A pause. They all look at him.

Carpenter You can't leave us, Fred.

Charles (*shrugs*) There's no work here, anyway.

Carpenter We need you. We have to stick together.

Charles You've been away a twelvemonth, Ted. It's all changing.

A pause. **Hukin** *breaks the silence.*

Hukin Who's for the last tomato?

Charles Ta.

Hukin *throws it to him.* **Charles** *misses it. He picks it up and rubs it on his sleeve.* **Carpenter** *puts his hand on his arm.*

Carpenter Excuse me, my good man. Did I see you pick up that tomato? And an exploding tomato at that. Manufactured at great expense by Her Majesty's government, although that fact will not be mentioned in court. What do you have to say in your defence?

Charles It's a plant.

Carpenter (*quietly*) But they'll never believe you.

All of a sudden, **Hukin** *jumps up and starts to stamp the ground with one foot.*

Hukin Get off get off get off!

Adams I told him to wear a hat.

The Dear Love of Comrades

Hukin The butter. They're in the butter.

They look at the food.

Carpenter Ants.

Hukin Little blighters (*Stamps.*)

Carpenter Poor ants.

Hukin They bit me!

Carpenter You didn't have to commit a massacre.

Hukin Here we go, 'all life is sacred'.

Charles It is.

Hukin Just you stick up for me, I did for you just now.

Charles I don't believe in party discipline.

Hukin Well, you can't side with him. He's an authoritarian posing as a socialist, you just said so.

Carpenter I refuse to compromise my principles as a vegetarian.

Hukin And I refuse to share my food with a load of greedy ants.

Carpenter There's some men in India who'd not even step on an ant.

Hukin Don't be daft. How could they?

Carpenter They'd carry switches of grass with them, and they'd brush the ground, so as not to tread on an insect and kill it.

Hukin They'd never get to work on time.

Carpenter Holy men.

Hukin What's holy in sweeping up ants?

Carpenter All life is equal.

Hukin Creepy-crawlies too?

Charles What if a house was burning down, and one of the insect-brushers was going along his way, then he sees it..

Hukin Help! Help! The house is on fire and the baby's at home.

Charles What would you do?

Carpenter Flatten the ants to save the baby.

Adams Quite right.

Carpenter But that's because I'm a Christian.

Hukin You're an atheist!

Carpenter I'm a socialist who doesn't believe in God.

Hukin Then you're not a Christian.

Carpenter As long as socialists see the world as something for men and women to plunder, then there is no hope for socialism. Who's to say that a human baby has more value than an ant?

Hukin It has.

Carpenter In cash value? Socialism's just another form of Christianity. 'We shall inherit the earth.'

Charles Perhaps you should bring this up at one of the meetings.

Carpenter Why not? I think it's just as important as who works what hours and how much is earned by who.

Charles So we talk about ants while people are starving?

Adams (*concentrating on his painting*) I agree with Fred.

They look at him. He does not look up.

Adams If socialism's not practical then what's the purpose? It's like art.

They all look at each other. He looks up.

Adams (*quite serious*) I don't paint in the romantic tradition. I'm interested in showing what *is*.

Charles People can see that for themselves. You must show them how to change it.

Carpenter Wrong! You must show them how it *could* be.

They are moving towards **Adams**. **Hukin** *stays where he is.*

Adams You can't invent something that doesn't exist.

Carpenter It's called imagination.

Charles True imagination can only come from the philosophy of anarchy; it's the greatest act of imagination to imagine what's there not being there.

Carpenter It's a greater act of imagination to put something in its place.

Charles And that's the seeds of tyranny.

Adams (*to* **Carpenter**) Ted. Will you just go and stand over there. I need a figure.

Carpenter (*moves downstage*) Here?

Charles Getting back to the baby . . .

Adams Lie down as if you're dead.

Carpenter What about the baby? (*Lies down.*)

Charles If you put the baby's life over the ant's life, you're a socialist tainted with Christianity; but, if you spare the ants and let the baby burn, what are you then?

Hukin Splitting hairs.

Carpenter My loyalties are with the baby.

Adams (*to* **Carpenter**) Don't move.

Carpenter But the insect-men in India might see it differently. Who's to say who's right?

Hukin I'm right, and I'd put a stop to them.

Carpenter That's imperialism.

Hukin It's human decency.

Carpenter It's called spreading civilization.

Adams Edward, keep still.

Carpenter It starts with telling people to stop doing something, and finishes with killing them if they don't. Can I get up, the ground's damp?

Adams Nearly done.

Charles This is just like one of the Sheffield meetings. All jaw and no do.

Hukin He's right, Ted.

Carpenter The unity of differences. That's our strength. Once we start splitting off, we're done for.

Charles We're done for if we don't. That's why I'm leaving Sheffield. I want to be with people who I can trust.

Hukin Fred . . .

Charles Not you. Not any of you. But I must work with other anarchists.

Adams There. (*He's finished. They all crowd round.*)

Hukin It doesn't look like Ted.

Charles It doesn't look like anything.

Carpenter It looks like a corpse.

Adams It is. It's called 'The Miner's Day Off'. Edward's the miner.

Carpenter I thought you weren't a romantic.

Adams It goes with another one I've done, called 'The Miner at Work'. People'll look at it and make the connection.

Charles But will it make them *do* anything?

Adams It might make them vote in the right direction.

They all look at him. He packs his paints.

Adams I agree with Edward. We do need a party that unites us all under one banner. And we're going to have one. And it's going to be a party of elected representatives! (*He leaves.*)

Piano in.

Carpenter I didn't quite mean that.

Charles I'm glad to hear it.

Carpenter Though it's not to be sniffed at.

Charles You won't be pinned down, will you?

Hukin Ouch. They're back. (*He gets up.*) But, just in case I'm accused of being a Christian imperialist, I'll leave them the rest of the butter and find another spot. (*They leave.*)

Song: 'God Came to Sheffield'

Charles God came to Sheffield Saturday
He met a woman in the street,
She said 'I've got no boots to wear,
My clothes are worn, I've nowt to eat'.
God pointed to a nearby church
And said 'Go in and pray,
Let your immortal longings lead
You from your fleshly greed today'.

But if the poor are often virtuous
Then that's the worse for them,
What's the point in virtually starving?

The master sitting in the pew
Remarked upon the woman's feet,
'They're stinking dirty, sir', she said,
'From muck and mud on that there street'.

He took his wallet from his coat
And offered her some hope,
'Go out' he muttered, 'get yourself
A pennyworth of good clean soap'.

But if the poor are often grateful
Then that is their hard luck
For what's the point in gracefully starving?

There'll be no virtue in the poor
Until they show their lack of grace;
Despatch the master up to Heaven, and
Tell God to go to the other place.

October 1891. **Merril**'s *house.*

Merril *is sitting on a chair.* **Carpenter** *stands with his coat on.*

Merril It took you long enough to come and see me.

Carpenter I know. I'm sorry.

Merril Don't be. I've got by.

Carpenter I've been busy.

Merril So've I. I've had three jobs and lost three jobs since we met.

Carpenter You didn't like the work?

Merril You can't meet anyone stuck at a factory bench. Sit down if you like.

Carpenter D'you live here alone?

Merril Since Mam died. Is your Mam dead?

Carpenter Yes.

Merril D'you get lonely?

Carpenter I've got friends.

Merril Edward?

Carpenter Yes?

Merril Aren't you going to ask me?

Carpenter What?

Merril Don't say you've forgotten. Edward.

Carpenter Oh, yes. All right.

Merril All right. (*Gets up.*) Come on.

Carpenter Where?

Merril To where I said I'd tell you.

Carpenter Tell me now.

Merril (*sits*) All right, I'll let you out of your agony, since it's dead obvious you've thought about nothing else for the past three months. Behind the slaughterhouse.

Carpenter What?

Merril You were on a platform making a speech. About the unemployment I think. That's why I went. I thought it might teach me a thing or two.

Carpenter Did it?

Merril No. But, I liked the look of you, so I found out your name. So I did learn something. It was a couple of years back. (*Pause.*) Will you stay?

Carpenter Oh, I don't know. I've found out what I want now, haven't I?

Merril (*can't sum him up. A pause*) Well, it's too late for you to walk back now. (*Looks at* **Carpenter***'s sandals.*) 'Specially in those things.

Carpenter They're fine.

Merril They're daft.

Carpenter They're sandals.

Merril Well, you won't catch me in them.

Carpenter I'll give you some.

Merril I'll stick to my clogs, they're the only thing for cobblestones.

Carpenter What about when you're out on the moors?

Merril I don't like the moors, they're draughty.

Carpenter You prefer to be stuck in the smoke?

Merril (*crossing to a table on which is a bottle and a glass*) I get lost in the country. If you get lost in town you can ask a bobby. Here. (*Hands* **Carpenter** *some wine.*) There's only half left. I was keeping it for when you came, but I gave you up for good and made a start. It's homemade.

Carpenter Aren't you having any?

Merril After you. There's only one glass. I chucked the other at a mouse. The mouse got away and the glass got bust.

Carpenter Then I'll drink to the mouse.

He drinks. **Merril** *watches him..*

Merril Sandals!

Carpenter The only thing for walking. Clogs!

Merril The only thing for *dancing*!

He does a short but very expert clog dance. **Carpenter** *applauds.*

Carpenter You should go on the stage.

Merril I sing too, down the pubs. You can come and listen one night.

Carpenter Try and stop me.

Merril Good. Well, I'm ready.

Carpenter For some wine?

Merril For the seducing.

Carpenter The what?

Merril You can start doing it.

Carpenter I'm not going to seduce you.

Merril You've got to.

Carpenter Why?

Merril You're older'n me, so you must take the lead.

Carpenter Well, if I'm the 'older seducer', what does that make you?

Merril Bloody impatient.

Carpenter I've no intention of seducing you.

Merril But I'm all ready for it.

Carpenter But 'seducing' implies that I'm forcing my will on you. I don't want to do that.

Merril You won't, I promise. Now, give us that wine.

He takes the glass and drinks some. He does not swallow it but kisses **Carpenter**.

October 1891. Sheffield station

Hukin *and* **Charles.**

Charles I promise to write.

Hukin I'm sorry to see you go.

Charles I shall be more useful in Walsall. There's a strong anarchist group there.

Hukin (*hands him some money*) I did some overtime this week.

Charles I've more than I need, George.

Hukin You've never had a penny before you gave it away to the first beggar you saw.

Charles I've a French pal in London. He sent me the fare.

Hukin Till you've found work then.

Charles I've a job in the foundry, I shall be all right.

Jody It's only half a crown. I don't need it.

Charles Send it to the *Sheffield Anarchist*.

Hukin Take it.

November 1891. A pub. Evening.

Loud music. **Carpenter** *and* **Merril** *are drinking.* **Merril** *brings in some beer.*

Merril (*bit drunk*) Edward, sit up, you'll get round shoulders.

Carpenter (*bit drunk. Sits up*) That's how my parents sat. Very proper. I thought they were just like the sofas they sat on, all stuffed full of horse-hair.

Merril Sofas! You should be so lucky.

Carpenter I decided to run away, to a desert island. Got it all planned. I'd saw the legs off the dining table and sail there, live in a hut. Eat pineapples and never wear clothes.

Merril Your poor old Mam. She'd miss you.

Carpenter She'd miss the table.

Merril It's a daft idea, an island. You'd get lonely.

Carpenter Oh, no. There'd be lots of us there. Hundreds and hundreds of Uranians.

Merril Who?

Carpenter S'people like us.

Merril (*ponders on the word*) Uranians? Me Mam used to call that being a Mary-Ann. I just used to call it pleasant. She'd say 'watch out George lad, you'll turn into one of them Mary-Anns'. Mind you, she never complained at all the washing and sewing and cleaning and cooking I did for her.

Carpenter Did she know?

Merril Course she did. But she told me not to let me Dad know. He used to knock us about. He was a goods-engine driver till he got blinded in one eye. They gave him a few quid and got rid of him, so he took a full-time job as a first-class bastard. In the evenings he had a part-time job as a drunk. Is your dad dead?

Carpenter Both.

Merril So we're a couple of orphans.

Carpenter (*solemn*) You'd not need parents in Urania.

Piano in.

Merril I'd miss me Mam anywhere. (*Crosses two fingers.*) We were like *that*.

Song: 'One Night As I Lay Sleeping'

Merril One night as I lay sleeping I heard somebody swear
So up from bed I rose and tiptoed down the stair.
What a sight did greet me, what d'you think that I saw there?

Me drunken dad upon his knees, his bum up in the air
(And he was saying) God, dear God, what've I done with it?
I could've spent the bloody thing and had some fun with it
But it's fallen from me pocket, she'll give me a rocket
Got to find it or I'm going to be undone with it.

(*spoken*) You see, he'd come in legless, dropped a whole half-sovereign, couldn't find it. It was down the floorboards. So I had an idea.

(*sings*) I picked up the fire irons
And gave them quite a clout,
Thought to wake me Mam up
But like a light she's out;
'Mrs Denvers taken worse,
She needs you' I did shout,
So down she comes and sees t'find
I got from the drunken lout.

(And she said)
Lad, well done, the things I'll do with it
Buy a blanket and a pair
Of pants for you with it;
I'll buy us both a mock-chop
Get me clothes out of the pop-shop
There won't be 'a' pence left when I am through with it.

(*spoken*) When he came in next night he ranted on and on about how he knew we knew, and where was it?

(*sings*) At first we ignored him
And pretended not to hear,
Then says me Mam 'In any case
You'd've spent it all on beer'.
'Tell me where it is,' he said,
'Or I'll clout you round the ear'
So she pointed round the room and said,
'It's theer and it's theer and it's theer'.

(She told him)
Look, mean sod, look what I've done with it
I've fed and clothed your wife
And starving son with it;
And with Christmas getting closer
I paid the rent 'n grocer
Bought the boy a pair of trousers
And some cotton blouses,
So I hope that makes you wiser
Serves you right you rotten miser,
So shut your bloody trap and let's have done with it.

Carpenter *applauds at the end of the song.*

Millthorpe. Dawn the next day.

Hukin *enters. He has no shirt under his jacket.* **Adams** *holds a lamp. He has been stitching sandals.*

Adams Six o'clock in the morning's a funny time to be visiting.

Hukin Fred Charles has been arrested.

Adams Refusing to pay his rent again.

Hukin It's not rent, it's bombs.

Adams Don't be daft, he'd not chuck a bloody bomb. George, I'm whacked, I was up till two stitching.

Hukin I read it in a London paper last night.

Adams Well, you've got the wrong bloke. Fred Charles we know's in Walsall.

Hukin It's him I tell you. We must find Edward.

Adams Well, you'll not find *him*, up at this hour, and if he is the pubs have been open all night.

Hukin We'll get him up.

Adams You're sure it's Fred?

Hukin Fred Charles. Walsall. Bombs. I'll tell you on the way.

Merril's *house. That morning.*

Loud knocking. **Merril** *enters, wearing only a shirt. He yawns.*

Merril Hold your horses!

Adams *and* **Hukin** *enter.*

Merril It's a bit early.

Hukin Is he up?

Merril Still snoring.

Hukin I'll tip him out. (*Exits.*)

Merril He won't thank you. (*Yawns.*) Oooh I'm parched. We'd a night of it. I'll put the kettle on. What's up?

Adams Someone's been arrested.

Merril I got myself arrested once, for being legless on New Year's Eve. They put me in for the night, but I was too far gone.

Carpenter *enters with* **Hukin**. *He has not finished dressing.*

Adams I'm beginning to feel overdressed!

Carpenter You're right. It's bad: 'The police are acting on information from a certain Monsieur Coulon and have evidence of a widespread bomb conspiracy throughout the country.' There's Fred, and some others, I can't make out who they are...

Hukin What shall we do?

Carpenter We'll need a defence committee. The police obviously are going to have a field day.

Adams It'll be swarming with detectives.

Carpenter We can speak to the people who know him and while we're gone you (*To* **Hukin**.) can fix up a meeting for tomorrow night.

Hukin Look, I think I'd rather go myself, I'd like to find out what's happened to Fred.

Adams Let me go, George. It's important to me.

Hukin (*after a pause*) All right.

Adams Well, that's that fixed then.

Carpenter (*looking up from the paper*) I should like a bite to eat first.

Adams Let's find out the times of the trains first, we can eat near the station.

Merril (*enters with teapot*) Tea up.

Carpenter Oh, George...

Adams Come on...

Carpenter I've... got to go away for the day... I'll see you tomorrow.

Adams Bye...

Outside the house.

Adams We'll need to raise money.

Carpenter I'm going to London in a couple of weeks, I'll fix up a meeting. And there's a solicitor there I know, I'm sure he'll handle the case. It's going to be a long business, George.

Adams We can do it... together.

Carpenter It won't be a part-time job.

Adams I'm ready for it. And while you're away I'll go and stay at Millthorpe. There's bound to be a lot of correspondence over all this. I can keep tabs on that, and keep an eye on the farm.

Carpenter Ask George Merril to lend a hand, he's not working.

Adams Oh, Ted, I'm so happy. At last we're doing something together again. Give us a hug. (**Carpenter** *does so.*) And you can give me a kiss. (**Carpenter** *gives him a chaste peck.*) There's no need to be shy. (*He pulls* **Carpenter** *towards him and gives him a full kiss.*)

Back in the house.

Merril Aren't you going too?

Hukin Er... No.

Merril Would you like a cup of tea?

Hukin That'd be nice.

Merril Where's your shirt?

Hukin I forgot it, I was in a hurry.

Merril I'll fetch you one of Edward's.

Hukin Don't bother.

Merril No bother. You'll catch your death running around like that.

He goes. **Hukin** *follows him upstairs.*

February 1892. A prison.

Fred Charles *in convict costume seated at a table.* **Carpenter** *reads from a newspaper cutting.*

Carpenter (*reads*) 'Fred Charles, you have been found guilty that between August 1891 and January 1892, you did conspire with others to obtain or control explosives. I would remind you that no part of the sentence passed is because you are an anarchist. I am aware that it is from the philosophy of anarchy that such acts can flow. I do not feel that this is the time to deal lightly with such acts.' Ten years.

Carpenter *crosses to the table.*

Charles There's a man in my cell with me. He said, 'Do it bit by bit, take it easy, and you'll come out the other end. Take it day by day.' He shared his tobacco with me. He robbed twenty pounds. He's in for twenty years.

Carpenter I take the blame, Fred. I hired the wrong man to defend you. He bungled it but I hired him.

Charles We play chess. He's got a whole set of pieces, made from chewed bread, and a board scratched out on the floor with a nail. He's won every game yet, but I'm learning.

Carpenter (*not giving up*) We are going to appeal. I promise you, Fred, we'll do better.

Charles (*refusing to be drawn in*) I'm learning all the time in here. It's full of poor people who got fed up being poor; they've got their own language. Do you know what 'smatter-hauling' is?

Carpenter Fred...

Charles It means stealing handkerchiefs. 'Doing a little soft' means passing bad notes. The man in my cell had a friend who got hung for that. Hanging's called 'topping'.

Carpenter Do you not want to talk about the last few months, the trial?

Charles That's over. This is my life now.

Carpenter We'll get the sentence reduced.

Charles I got confused with all the new words he taught me; but when I talked, he got confused. He didn't know what a capitalist was and I didn't know what a 'finnie' was. A 'finnie' is a five pound note and you can get fourteen years for taking one. I said a capitalist was someone who takes fistfuls of 'finnies' off people every day and gets a knighthood at the end. I'm not sure if he understood.

Carpenter Then I'll talk. You needn't reply. When I took the solicitor on, I'd no idea he'd make such a mess of it, but by that time we were stuck with him, and the press had already convicted you. I know the whole thing was set up by the police, that they'd not a shred of real evidence against you. But, given the press hysteria, given the bombs that went off in Paris while the trial was on, given there was no way you'd be found not guilty, I truly believed we should go for the lowest sentence possible. And the only way to do that was not to provoke the police. It could only have done you harm.

Charles (*some anger creeping in*) We recite poetry to each other. He knows some, and so do I. Some of it's yours. I quote from things I've read and remembered. Some of that is yours. There's one in particular he likes. I thought of it during the trial: 'Perhaps there is no better mark of the social degradation of the times than the appearance of that crawling phenomenon in question, the police'. My friend likes that one.

Carpenter (*takes the package*) George Merril made some cakes. I hope they let you keep them. (*Smiles.*) You can give them all away.

Charles The whole anarchist movement's been identified with bombs and indiscriminate slaughter.

Carpenter (*softly*) I wanted you to be free. I didn't want you to waste your youth in prison.

Charles I'd have done twenty, forty years, and done it gladly, if the police had been shown up. If *someone* had stood up and said – shouted – in that courtroom that they were the real conspirators.

Carpenter (*after a pause*) Do you want us to continue?

Charles If you like.

Carpenter The defence committee still stands.

Charles You know where to find me.

Carpenter Fred. Don't be bitter.

Charles 'Mild-mannered Fred'? Well, I've proved one thing. Human nature can change. That should give us cause for optimism.

Voice Off Time's up.

Charles You were right you see. I did end up in a monastery. A kind of one.

October 1892. **Merril**'s *house.*

Merril *enters. He holds a letter.* **Carpenter** *moves into the space.*

Merril I've got it.

Carpenter What?

Merril The job.

Carpenter Oh, well done.

Merril 'Dear Sir, this is to confirm your appointment' – appointment, eh? I've been hired and I've been fired, but I've never been appointed – 'as general assistant on the *Sheffield Telegraph*, to start next Monday'. As soon as I get my first wage-packet we'll do the town.

Carpenter We won't.

Merril Why not?

Carpenter I shall be in London.

Merril Put it off.

Carpenter It's too important.

Merril What's more important than a piss-up on my first payday?

Carpenter I've got to see my publishers. Let's celebrate tonight instead.

Merril Oh, all right. Where? The 'King's Head'?

Carpenter Or bed?

Merril I've only just had my tea.

Carpenter Don't you like doing it on a full stomach?

Merril I've hardly seen you these past three months.

Carpenter You can see all of me. Come upstairs.

Merril Lucy Adams says her George might as well be married to you for all the time she gets with him.

Carpenter Is she jealous of me?

Merril She said you were made for each other.

Carpenter The perfect couple?

Merril Just what you need. He'd run your life like a clockwork engine.

Breakfast at eight, accounts at nine, brisk walk, lunch . . .

Carpenter Two till five no less than a thousand words on political economy . . .

Merril Tea on the dot, committee meeting in the evening, straight home, no pub, straight to bed . . .

Carpenter And?

Merril I give up. I can't imagine George Adams doing it. I'll ask Lucy.

Carpenter Perhaps she won't tell you.

Merril And perhaps she tells me more than you realize.

Carpenter Such as?

Merril Such as *her* George has been angling to move into your place at Millthorpe, but he's afraid *your* George'd put a stop to it.

Carpenter Would you?

Merril It's up to you.

Carpenter I do need someone up there with me.

Merril Someone you can rely on?

Carpenter He knows how the place runs.

Merril So he's the one you need then.

Carpenter He's got the lock and the stock. It only seems sensible to give him the barrel.

Merril Yes. I suppose you've got no choice in the matter.

Carpenter What does Lucy think? Has George spoken to her?

Merril (*lightly*) Oh, I don't think he'd be interested in her opinion. (*Pause.*) What's it to be? Bed or beer?

Carpenter You choose.

Merril I'll leave it to you. I'm not very good at making decisions.

Sheffield station. The same week.

Hukin *carries a bag.* **Adams** *has a piece of paper.*

Adams I am a Parliamentary Committee.

Hukin (*laughing*) You don't look like one.

Adams Use your imagination.

Hukin You are a Parliamentary Committee.

Adams And I am going to question you very closely on the subject of conditions in the razor-grinding trade.

Hukin It'll all end up in a filing cabinet.

Adams Committee's not a dirty word. I'm not saying it'll work miracles, but if it's there, use it.

Hukin You sound more like Edward Carpenter every day.

Adams That's because we understand each other's minds.

Hukin I'll go to London, and I'll speak to the Committee, and I'll learn every answer off by heart if that's what you and Edward want.

Adams Thank you.

Hukin On one condition.

Adams What condition?

Hukin You do something for me.

Adams What's that?

Hukin Keep an eye on George Merril while we're gone.

Adams I'm not a baby-minder; and I don't think Lucy'd want to bother.

Hukin She likes him.

Adams I reckon she might tolerate him.

Hukin He wants to be friends. If you're going to move to Millthorpe you'll have to learn to get on with George Merril.

Adams Perhaps when Lucy and I are there Edward won't need to spend all his time pubbing it with Merril. He'll have a settled home with people he loves. It'll be a new start for us all.

Hukin Then make a new start with George. Trust him. I do.

Adams I've noticed. And I don't. I was worried he'd try to wheedle his way into Millthorpe. He'd've turned the place into a saloon bar in next to no time.

Carpenter *enters with bag. He gives a package to* **Hukin**.

Carpenter George . . . from George, for the journey.

Adams When will you be back?

Carpenter Couple of weeks.

Hukin I'll send you a postcard of Buckingham Palace.

Adams Send it to Millthorpe then.

Carpenter So you've decided.

Adams Why wait?

Carpenter And Lucy?

Adams She's packing.

Carpenter (*to* **Hukin**) Do you know your speech?

Adams He ought to, number of times I made him go over it.

Hukin We made a bargain, didn't we George?

Adams Oh, aye. (*Quickly.*) Now, which bedroom shall we take, Ted?

Carpenter You and Lucy decide.

Adams We'll take the big one at the back, then.

Hukin Come on, we'll miss it. (*Looks for train.*)

Adams (*puts arm round* **Carpenter**) I'm so happy, Ted. It's what I've always wanted. We can help each other.

Carpenter Will you go and see George Merril? He gets lonely.

Adams It's going to be a busy time.

Hukin (*mock-worried*) Oh, Ted. I hope I can remember that speech.

Adams (*glances at* **Hukin**) But if that's what you want.

Hukin Come *on*.

Carpenter *and* **Hukin** *leave* **Adams**.

Song: 'Three at Millthorpe'

Adams I've listed all the options
Weighed the cons against the pros,
Checked them off against objections
Should Merril interpose;
Now with all the figures balanced
In a debit-credit style,
The sum is the conclusion
That I've wanted all the while.

We'll live as three at Millthorpe,
Contented be at Millthorpe
Respectably at Millthorpe
Ted, Lucy, me.

I've calculated losses,
What's to win and what's to gain,
Made a personal investment,
Hope there's interest to claim;
And now that there's a contract,
A bargain of true friends,
We can truly count the blessings
That time and patience sends.

I, she and he at Millthorpe,
Triangularly at Millthorpe,
Who'd disagree with Millthorpe?
That's all they'll see.

The train. Immediately following.

Carpenter *opens the sandwiches. He hands some to* **Hukin**, *who munches.*

Carpenter Well, thank you, George Merril!

Hukin What's up?

Carpenter They're all meat. He knows I don't like meat. Are yours meat?

Hukin Beef.

Carpenter I shall just have to starve.

Hukin Just as well. You're putting on weight.

Carpenter I am not! I'm as slim as I was at eighteen. (*But he looks at his tummy nonetheless.*)

Hukin (*nods at* **Carpenter**'s *sandwich*) Don't you want it?

Carpenter I wouldn't touch it.

Hukin Good. (*Takes it.*)

Carpenter Dead flesh!

Hukin You wear sandals.

Carpenter What?

Hukin (*munching*) That's flesh ripped off the backs of dead animals; so why be so hoity-toity?

Carpenter It's not that simple. If socialists . . .

Hukin Oooh you, you've always got to have the last bloody word. Now shut up and let me enjoy my grub in peace.

Carpenter *grins. He gets out some manuscripts.*

Carpenter I'll feed my thoughts if I can't feed my belly.

Hukin Read to me.

Carpenter No. I've got to check the text.

Hukin Well, read it while you're checking it. I like your poetry.

Carpenter It's prose.

Hukin Prose'll do. What's it about?

Carpenter Sex.

Hukin How to do it? They'll never print that.

Carpenter Different forms of sex. You know, George . . .

Hukin Well, they certainly won't print it.

Carpenter They've said they will.

Hukin You'll land yourself in prison.

He looks at the manuscript. Skims through it.

Hukin (*skimming*) 'The Sex Passion' . . . 'The Intermediate Sex' . . . 'Jealousy' . . . you've got the lot here.

Carpenter Read it.

Hukin Oh, I don't know . . .

Carpenter Read the chapter on Jealousy.

Hukin I don't want to disturb you. I mean, your work.

Carpenter You won't. I'd like you to read it. Read it out aloud. It'll help me.

Hukin (*reads*) 'One must distinguish two kinds of jealousy. The first arises perhaps from the real uniqueness of the relationship between two persons. This kind of jealousy seems in a sense natural.' Perhaps I'll wait for the book to come out . . .

Carpenter (*has his arm around him*) Go on. I wrote it for you.

Hukin (*reads*) 'The feeling of jealousy may in time, equally naturally, die away; and may do so without damaging the intimacy and uniqueness of the alliance.'

Carpenter And it has.

Hukin (*ploughing on*) 'The other type of jealousy rests on the sense of property. This kind of jealousy, seen in a husband who is furious at the idea of his wife disposing with her body because he considers it to be *his* property, is the product of immediate social conditions. And is in that sense artificial. Though probably not as heart-rending as the other, it is often passionately felt, and lasts on like a chronic disease . . .'

Carpenter George, I haven't been entirely honest in getting you to come to London with me. I want to help you with your union work of course, but I did have other motives. You see, I have changed. I feel I can live up to my own theories now. I don't want to own you.

Hukin (*not looking up*) Edward.

Carpenter George.

Hukin I slept with George Merril.

A silence.

Hukin That night you went to Walsall?

A silence.

Hukin Do you mind?

Carpenter (*of course he does*) Of course not.

Carpenter *takes the manuscript.* **Hukin** *takes a bite. A train whistle is heard.*

Three weeks later. Millthorpe. Night

Merril *drunk.* **Adams** *irate.*

Merril Edward! Edward! 'I came to see my true love and lie with her all night, but the ale I'd supped had all but put my passion quite to flight.' Eddie! Come out! Whoops-a-daisy. I've come to see you, so come and get me, or I'll be in the ditch all night.

Adams Hey!

Merril Eddie!

Adams Clear off!

Merril I've come to see you.

Adams You're tight.

Merril I've come home, Edward.

Adams This isn't your home and I'm not Edward!

Merril Who're you?

Adams George.

Merril Let us in.

Adams Go back to Sheffield!

Merril It's too far.

Adams Then sleep in the ditch and be late for work.

Merril I've lost my job.

Adams Drunk again, I suppose.

Merril No. Because I'm a Uranian.

Adams What?

Merril I pinched the editor's bum.

Adams You'll get yourself in trouble one of these days.

Merril I can't pay the rent. I am in trouble!

Adams Expect Edward to come to the rescue this time? Well don't.

Merril Let us in.

Adams This isn't a hotel.

Merril It's Edward's home.

Adams And it's mine as well, and we're quite contented without drunken louts like you disturbing us!

Merril *Eddie!*

Adams He's not here now. Be quiet or you'll wake the neighbours. Leave Edward alone, he doesn't need you, he said so. So you won't be seeing him or the inside of this house tonight or any other night.

Merril He never said so!

Adams I'm sorry George.

Merril Then sod off, the lot of you! (*Turns to go.*) Here, ditchy ditchy ditch.

January 1983. A church hall in Bradford.

Frank Simpson *on platform.* **Adams** *in the audience.*

Simpson Ladies and Gentlemen. I give you the new year and the new party. Let 1893 be remembered by the working folk of this land as the start of a great journey. Let us hope that the separate desires and objectives that gave rise to the many socialist organizations of the '80s, will now find their true place in the Independent Labour Party. Let us take our ideas and energies into the mainstream of British politics. Let us working people of this land, and their elected representatives, demand and receive the respect that is their due. I think it is fitting that we should conclude by singing the song that is perhaps best known to all of us who have marched and demonstrated and picketed these past two decades. It was written by one without whose work we would not be meeting here in Bradford tonight. Let us hope that his faith will not be betrayed.(*Music in.*) His name is Edward Carpenter. The song is 'England Arise'.

Song: 'England Arise'

Simpson England arise, the long, long night is over,
Faint in the East, behold the dawn appear;
Out of your evil dream of toil and sorrow
Arise, oh England, for the day is here.

Immediately after. The train from Bradford to Sheffield.

Adams *seated.* **Simpson** *enters in a rush.* *Piano: 'England Arise'*

Voice Bradford to Sheffield, calling at Wakefield and Dewsbury.

Adams You just made it.

Simpson I sometimes wish the railways weren't so punctual.

Adams (*peering at him, then a big smile as he extends his hand*) Put it there!

Simpson Beg pardon?

Adams I saw you on the platform.

Simpson At the station?

Adams At the meeting.

Simpson (*beams*) You were there?

Adams Cheering my bloody head off, I was.

They shake hands violently.

Adams This could be the biggest thing that's ever happened.

Simpson Since the French Revolution!

Adams And better, because it's here to stay. I'm George Adams. I'm from Sheffield.

Simpson I'm Frank Simpson. Prospective candidate for Chester le Street.

Adams It's an honour.

They shake hands again, and again with vigour.

Simpson We set a lot of store on Sheffield.

Adams You've a lot of friends there.

Simpson And we'll not let them down.

Adams You do know Edward Carpenter lives near Sheffield, of course.

Simpson I've corresponded with him often. I've read his books, listened to his speeches, but I've never met him.

Adams (*a bit important*) Well, you're speaking to his best friend.

Simpson (*impressed*) You don't say?

Adams True as I sit here.

Simpson *shakes* **Adams'** *hand again.*

Simpson I'd give the world to meet him.

Adams You shall meet him tonight, if you wish.

Simpson I could break my journey...

Adams He'll be dying to know how things went.

Simpson I thought he'd be there.

Adams Extended lecture tour; he's been half round the country in the past year.

Simpson But he's back now?

Adams This very night.

Simpson I'll come.

Adams It'll be an historical occasion.

Simpson You've made my day.

They shake again.

Adams (*takes a couple of bottles out of bag*) I got a bit of comfort for the journey. We'll drink a toast.

Simpson To the railways!

Adams To the railways!

Simpson Communications! If we get to Westminster, we'll give part thanks to speed of communication these days.

Adams And when we get there, we'll do away with First, Second and Third Class, eh?

That same evening. Sheffield station.

Hukin *sees* **Carpenter**. *Crosses to him.*

Carpenter No more trains for me for the year. No more lecture tours. No more committees. I shall put my feet up in a chair and write poetry.

Hukin Did you get my letter? The one to Newcastle?

Carpenter They changed the venue to Glasgow.

Hukin Have you heard from George Merril?

Carpenter Not even a Christmas card, so I hope he's got a good excuse.

Adams *and* **Simpson** *enter.*

Adams (*crosses to them*) There's someone I should like you to meet, Ted.

Carpenter I'm tired, George.

Adams He's a candidate. Frank Simpson. I met him in Bradford.

Carpenter Tomorrow. I want to see George Merril tonight.

Adams You won't be seeing him tonight.

Carpenter Yes, I will. He's expecting me.

Adams He's left.

Carpenter Left?

Adams Today. George knows.

Hukin That's why I wrote to Newcastle, to tell you what was happening.

Carpenter What *is* happening?

Adams He's gone to Blastow. He's got a job at the spa.

Carpenter He's working for the newspaper.

Adams He got the sack. He decided to move. He'd nowhere to live.

Carpenter He could've stayed at Millthorpe.

Adams He didn't seem interested.

Carpenter (*to* **Hukin**) Why didn't you stop him?

Hukin He wouldn't listen to me, he'd made up his mind.

Adams He's just unreliable. You're better off without him, Ted.

Carpenter I want to know what's been going on. (*To* **Hukin**.) I want to know what was in that letter.

Hukin (*to* **Carpenter**, *aside*) I can't, not with *George* here.

Carpenter Oh, I'm beginning to understand.

Hukin No, not that . . .

Carpenter *turns away.*

Hukin (*to* **Adams**) I wanted to see Edward on my own.

Adams It's important he meets Frank tonight, he's leaving tomorrow.

Hukin And George Merril left today,

that's more important!

Adams He'll get over George Merril. I said it'd be a new start for us all. I waited while he mooned over you. I kept the farm going while he was in India. I stuck to my sandal-making while he chased Merril. I listened while you all talked about your political beliefs. But, I was the only one to do anything practical about it. Well, his personal life is sorted out now...

Hukin You mean you've sorted it out!

Adams I'm right. I've made the connections.

Hukin *crosses to* **Carpenter.**

Hukin Edward...

Carpenter *brushes him aside and crosses to* **Adams.**

Carpenter Did he leave an address?

Adams He just said he'd be in touch.

Merril *enters with a small suitcase upstage.*

Carpenter When?

Adams He was vague.

Hukin *sees* **Merril** *and crosses to him. The music for* England Arise *plays over the following dumbshow.* **Fred Charles** *is seen, in prison garb, and joins in singing with* **Simpson.**

During song: 1. **Merril** *and* **Hukin** *talk.* 2. **Carpenter** *and* **Adams** *talk.* 3. **Hukin** *and* **Merril** *embrace.* 4. **Adams** *sees them.* 5. **Carpenter** *turns and sees them.* 6. **Merril** *goes towards* **Carpenter.** 7. **Carpenter** *turns away.* 8. **Merril** *gives* **Hukin** *a letter and leaves.* 9. **Hukin** *brings letter down to* **Carpenter.** 10. **Carpenter** *brushes him aside and leaves.* 11. **Hukin** *looks at* **Adams.**

Song: 'England Arise' (continued).

Simpson
Charles } From your fields and hills
hark the answer swells
Arise, oh England, for the day is here.

Forth then ye dreamers, dear as any lovers,
Comrades in danger, poverty and scorn,
Mighty in faith of freedom we discover
Angels refreshed in joy's new rising sun;
Come and swell the song
Silent now so long
England is risen and the day is here.

Act Two

June 1893. Millthorpe, Sheffield, Blastow and Cambridge respectively.

Adams *is stitching.* **Hukin** *is reading,* **Merril** *is polishing some silverware,* **Carpenter** *is cleaning some shoes. They each pick up a letter and read it.*

Song: 'Letters Song'

All Please forgive the delay
I have meant to reply
I'm amazed how the days seem to fly;
I intend every night
To make sure that I write
It's alarming how time passes by.

But I'd not like to cause you to worry
So I'll jot down the best of my news;
It's been done in a bit of a hurry
So my handwriting please to excuse.

Carpenter *speaks his letter to* **Merril.** *The other two continue with their activities.* **Merril** *continues working but does not listen.*

Carpenter 'Cambridge, June '93. Dear George. I am sending this letter to Millthorpe, and hope that George Adams will see you and pass it on. As soon as I know your address in Blastow I will send direct. I could not settle to poetry-writing after your departure, and have a heavy round of public speaking. Sometimes I curse the railway system . . .'

He goes back to polishing his shoes.

Merril 'Blastow, June 1893. Dear Eddie. I cannot bear this silence, and I've no one to talk to here. Mrs D, who runs the hotel, keeps me at it all day, polishing and scrubbing, and I live in a draughty old room at the top. But she's not a bad sort, and it's better than being in a factory. I shall walk over to Millthorpe with this, and ask George Adams to post it on if the snow lets up. it's a four-mile trek, which shows how much I want to be in touch.'

He goes back to the silverware.

Adams 'Millthorpe, July 1893. Dear Edward. Please send instructions as to the west roof. The slates need fixing, and the damp patch in your room is getting bigger. I'm enclosing a letter from Frank Simpson. He wants you to speak on "Private Property and its Origins" for the ILP next month and needs to know if you can do it. Very little otherwise.'

He goes back to stitching.

Hukin 'Sheffield, July 1893. Dear Ted . . .'

Adams (*looks up*) P.S., Lucy had a miscarriage.

Hukin '. . . Fannie and I are looking after Lucy till she gets better. She'd no one to talk to, with George out in the fields all day and at his sandal-making all night.'

Merril 'I wish you'd send just a note . . .'

Hukin 'P.S. Enclosed are a couple of letters to you that have been waiting at Millthorpe. Lucy brought them over with her.'

Song: 'Letters' (continued)

All (*read letters*) Please forgive the delay
I have meant to reply
I'm amazed how the time seems to fly,
I intend every night
To make sure that I write
It's alarming how time passes by.

Merril 'Blastow, April 1894. Dear Eddie. It was so lovely to see you, and so sad that you were gone again so soon. After we said goodbye, I walked back here over the moors, singing all the way, but have now got a face-ache for my pains. I thought about you all last night, dear, just when I was feeling sleepy, and wished I was in your arms.'

Carpenter (*to* **Adams**) 'Norwich, June '94. Dear George. As to my shares in the Pennsylvania Railway Company, please tell them I wish to sell half. That should buy us a new cart and horse beside...'

Hukin 'Sheffield. July 1894. Dear Edward. We all four sat up till two in the morning playing cards. George Adams got very sulky when Lucy and Fannie said they were going to pay George Merril a visit at Blastow...'

Carpenter (*to* **Hukin**) 'Bristol, November '94. Dear George. It's really too bad of George and George not to be friends. I wish you could make them patch it up. I want us all to spend Christmas together, and no quarrels...'

Merril '... if you get me a ring, can it be a twisted one, or a snake shape, but not in *silver*. The measurement of my finger is two-and- a-half inches round. George Hukin sends his love. By the way, the measurement means *inside* the ring...'

Adams 'Millthorpe. December. Dear Ted. Poor George Hukin, he's been in bed with a bad cold all this week, ever since walking over to Blastow in a near blizzard...'

Carpenter (*to* **Merril**) 'Cardiff, December '94. I *shan't* be home for Christmas, as there's a big meeting here and they want me to talk on the subject of marriage.'

Merril Oh!

Adams Ted!

Hukin We've just bought the biggest turkey in Sheffield!

Song: 'Letters' (continued)

All I'm reading between the lines you write
All the messages left unspoken;
I can hear in the space between the words
Promises that are broken.

Hukin But dear Edward,

Merril dear Eddie,

Adams dear Ted,

All Love from George and I really do care.

Carpenter Dear George Hukin, George Merril and George Adams
I'm here, but would rather be there.

All But I'd not like to cause you to worry
So I'll jot down the best of my news;
It's been done in a bit of a hurry
So my handwriting please to excuse.

Carpenter (*to* **Merril**). 'Oxford, March 1895. Dear George. I'm sorry our last time together was so short...'

Hukin 'Dear Edward. I went to one of the meetings in the town, but it was all talk of blood and vengeance on the capitalists, or death on the scaffold. I don't want to die on the scaffold...'

Adams 'Nine of the chicks are flourishing, all fat and fine...'

Merril 'Promise me that as soon as you come back from London, you'll stay for a while...'

Carpenter 'London, April 1895. I was shouted at by someone in the street the other day. I was wearing a coloured cravat. Someone yelled 'there goes an Oscar!' All the men have cut their hair, as well, and you rarely see a flower in a buttonhole.

All (*sing*) But I'd not like to cause you to worry
So I'll jot down the best of my news;
It's been done in a bit of a hurry
So my handwriting please to excuse.

Carpenter *completes dressing. He is in evening dress. He puts a flower in his buttonhole.*

May 1895, London. A private dining-room.

At the table are **Fisher-Unwin** *and* **Carpenter** *both in evening dress. They have just eaten.* **Unwin** *smokes a cigar.*

Unwin How is Lady Daubeny?

Carpenter My sister is in the best of health.

Unwin She must be pleased to have you in town.

Carpenter We miss each other.

Unwin You are missed. You shouldn't bury yourself out there in the wilds.

Carpenter My home is open. Visitors are welcome.

Unwin But it's so far from civilization.

Carpenter It's four miles from Sheffield.

Unwin That's not civilization, that's a smoke-stack!

Carpenter (*picks up a knife*) It's where your cutlery comes from.

Unwin That's no reason to live there.

Carpenter Let's say I . . . like the atmosphere.

Unwin Factory smoke?

Carpenter Not in Millthorpe.

Unwin Ah yes. Millthorpe. You've put Millthorpe on the map, Edward.

Carpenter It was there before I was, and it'll be there when I'm gone.

Unwin All things shall pass? Come on, Edward, admit it, you're playing a game.

Carpenter What game?

Unwin Or perhaps you're just being very sensible?

Carpenter Well, make up your mind.

Unwin All right. You are playing a sensible game. Did you ever meet Oscar Wilde?

Carpenter No.

Unwin A pity.

Carpenter For who?

Unwin Both of you. He could've shown you how to write material that would sell commercially, and you could have shown him how to have working-class-type boys and not get caught.

Carpenter You're trying to make me angry, aren't you?

Unwin I'm just trying to sum you up.

Carpenter I thought you were a publisher. I didn't realize you were a psychologist.

Unwin I keep in step with science, as well as literature.

Carpenter Which is why you are prepared to publish scientific literature.

Unwin As long as it sells.

Carpenter Do you think my book will sell?

Unwin Oh, yes. We'd make a lot of money . . . .

Carpenter Good!

Unwin Till the court case.

Carpenter What?

Unwin (*waves his question aside*) Never mind, never mind, there's plenty of time to talk business.

Carpenter It's the only reason I'm in London.

Unwin You mean you're not looking forward to the opera tonight? There can't be much opera in Sheffield.

Carpenter I don't miss it.

Unwin Too busy with the working-class boys?

Carpenter You are trying to annoy me, aren't you?

Unwin I'm just interested. I'm interested to know how a man from a good background, a comfortable background, can bury himself in the wilds, surround himself with people who he has very little in common with and maintain that he is happy. How can you be satisfied?

Carpenter I'm not. I'm very unsatisfied that I have to come and dress up like a dummy in a tailor's window, and make conversation about the opera in order to get a book published. I don't like London. I like Yorkshire. I'm bored in London. If you'd not been so evasive about the contract, if we could've signed and been done with weeks ago, I'd be back digging the fields this very moment, and much happier for it.

Unwin I heard a very interesting story this morning...

Carpenter Now I am going to get angry...

Unwin (*rides over him*) It's about a bank. In Liverpool.

Carpenter Money... That's all you can think about.

Unwin And sex...

Carpenter If it makes money...

Unwin And politics.

Carpenter Money, politics and sex! If only we could get rid of the first two, we might get the third one right.

Unwin But you're not living in your dream world at Millthorpe now, Edward, and if you want to print what you have to say about sex, you'd better listen to what politics and money have to say.

Carpenter Liverpool...

Unwin Thank you! There's a bank just closed down in Liverpool.

Carpenter Banks often do close down.

Unwin Not because Oscar Wilde has been thrown into prison. You see, after the trial, when the panic set in, and the boat-train to Dover was packed with English gentlemen who wished to avoid notoriety, this bank was forced to close its doors, because every single employee had been and packed his bags and got on the boat-train himself. Because every man jack of them didn't want to end up in the Scrubs with Oscar. Now, don't you think that's extraordinary?

Carpenter I think it extraordinary that we can have a society where such people can only show their presence by running away. Why didn't they close the bank and say they'd not open the doors again until Wilde had been let out?

Unwin Perhaps because they didn't have a country cottage where they could carry on as they liked and not have to worry.

Carpenter Well, I shan't be on the boat-train. And I shan't be in Berlin or Paris or Amsterdam when *Love's Coming of Age* is in the bookshops.

Unwin You won't need to be.

Carpenter I shall be in Millthorpe.

Unwin (*quietly*) You want the book published, don't you?

Carpenter More than anything in the world.

Unwin (*takes out contract*) Here's the contract.

Carpenter That's all I'm here for.

Unwin On one condition.

Carpenter What condition?

Unwin The chapter on 'Homogenic Love' is omitted.

Pause.

Carpenter The book is about all forms of love.

Unwin Oscar Wilde is in prison. I have no intention of joining him there.

Carpenter *All* forms of love. You agreed on the draft.

Unwin There have been changes in the social atmosphere...

Carpenter You mean that politics have intruded.

Unwin I mean I'm not prepared to risk money on a book that would lead to a court case. I've investors to think of.

Carpenter Is that what it comes down to?

Unwin Investors are very important, Edward. You'd not manage that Utopia of yours in Yorkshire without stocks and shares, so don't attack me for protecting my own business. Here's the contract. I'll publish without the chapter. There's no way that you can alter my mind; I drew up the contract and I'm very well protected. Well?

Carpenter You cannot do this!

Unwin Easily. There is a clause in the contract that says if any part of the manuscript has been published before, I can refuse to print it under my own press. The chapter on 'Homogenic Love' *was* printed by the Manchester Labour Press . . .

Carpenter For *private* circulation!

Unwin I'm *still* covered . . .

Carpenter You bastard!

Unwin I thought you'd given up swear-words, along with alcohol, tobacco and opera. Don't let's have a shouting match, Edward. I'll print, but only without the chapter.

Carpenter Please. Please print. Wilde is in prison. That's why we *must* print!

Unwin No.

Carpenter Workers don't strike when the wages are high. They show their strength when they're under attack.

Unwin And they have mass support. Who would you have? The socialists? What support did they give to Wilde?

Carpenter Someone has to speak out. Someone has to make a shout.

Unwin Not at my expense. It's your choice, Edward. Stop living in a cloud-cuckoo land.

Carpenter Perhaps that's next door to Utopia.

Dim out. **Carpenter** *comes down to spot.*

Song: 'The Literary Pages'

Carpenter In the literary pages
Of the better class of press
They reviewed today a volume
That aroused some interest
By a writer of distinction
With progressive-minded views
With ability to challenge
In a style that will amuse.

The Times was quite enchanted
By his bold and witty fervour
And made clear that it hoped
His writing would go further
His desire for social justice
Was a theme to be admired
And a subject to which many
Striving writers had aspired.

In conclusion they advised him
Not to go beyond the pale
Since such radical pretensions
Couldn't guarantee a sale
If he watered down his content,
Concentrated on his form
Then the poor would feed his conscience
And the rich would keep him warm.

They exit.

May 1895. The Blastow Hydro. A health baths. **Merril** *and* **Hukin.**

Hukin *watches as* **Merril** *pours steaming water into a bowl.*

Merril Sit down. Take that jacket off, and that scarf.

Hukin *does as he is told.*

Merril (*puts basin in front of him*) Now,

stick your head over that.

Hukin Oh George, it's nothing.

Merril Don't 'oh, George' me and do as I say. Me Mam swore by a balsam bath for a chill. I shall give you another in the morning.

Hukin (*popping up*) Oh, I shall have to get back today.

Merril Get back! (**Hukin** *does so.*) If you think I'm letting you trek four miles over the moors in this weather and in your state, you've got another think coming.

Hukin I only came to deliver your present.

Merril And I'm not sending you back to Fannie with pneumonia. She'd murder me. *Deep* breaths. You must get the fumes right into your lungs.

Hukin *breathes in. Coughs.*

Merril Where is it?

Hukin What?

Merril My present.

Hukin Jacket pocket.

Merril *fishes a book out of* **Hukin***'s pocket.*

Merril Oh!

Hukin What's up?

Merril I thought it'd be something else. (*Opens it.*) He's not even inscribed it. (*Takes out a note that is in the book.*) He says he's back next week.

Hukin George, I'm suffocating.

Merril All right, you can come out. (*Flicking through book.*) I don't think I shall get through this. Still, I shall give it a try. At least I'll have something to occupy me when I get to bed at nights.

Hukin Do you get bored?

Merril I like waiting at table, but the cleaning tires me. Mrs D's standards are ever so high. But I like her. She gets testy when the guests get on at her. They come here for their health and the waters, and lie about in the baths all day, and nearly all of them catch colds. You can do that for free by walking on the moors without a top-coat. How're you feeling?

Hukin You're right. It's a cold.

Merril *puts his own head over the steam bath.*

Merril When I was little, I'd pretend I'd a cold coming on, so Mam'd give me a balsam bath. I loved it. I used to think I was invisible.

He pops out. Looks at the note that was in the book.

Merril Next Tuesday!

Hukin Do you miss him?

Merril More than he thinks. I wish . . .

Hukin What?

Merril Nothing. (*Looks at the book.*) I shall never understand this. I'm not educated enough for politics.

Hukin I've seen you run into a church and shout at the vicar in the middle of his sermon.

Merril That's just me being drunk. I don't like priests. I mean, organized things. Unions. Books like this. (*He yawns.*)

Hukin You'd've liked it in the early days. We'd cycle out to the mining villages, and speak on socialism from a pile of rocks or a wall. Other days, we'd walk round town handing out leaflets. Edward and I used to sit up till all hours writing them, then take them round to the printers the next day.

Merril (*half asleep*) You used to stay with him, didn't you?

Hukin Yes.

Merril He told me.

Hukin It was too late for him to get back one night. Though I seem to remember all we did that time was to fall straight asleep.

Merril *is asleep with his head on the table.* **Hukin** *looks at him.*

Song: 'Dear Edward' (gentle entry).

Hukin Dear Edward, I hope you don't mind,
Dear Fannie, don't think me unkind,
Dear George said 'stay here for the night'
And the way that I'm feeling, I might.

But I wonder what Fannie is doing?
And who she might be with tonight;
Should I hurry back home
To make sure she's alone?
Yes I will, no I won't, well I might.

Dear Edward, please don't criticize,
Dear Fannie, I'm telling no lies,
Dear George needs a friend he can hold,
So I'll not lay the blame on a cold.

But I wonder how Edward will take it?
So would it be better to go?
To avoid hurting Ted
I'll avoid George's bed!
Yes I will, no I won't, I don't know.

Dear Edward, I trust you'll forgive
Dear Fannie, I'll trust who you're with,
Dear George needs us all in his way,
So I'll love you and leave you and stay.

Same. The following week.

Carpenter *enters.* **Merril** *jumps up and runs across to him. A pause. They look at each other. Then* **Merril** *snatches* **Carpenter***'s hat and runs off.* **Carpenter** *chases him.* **Merril** *runs and sits at the table and pretends to be writing.* **Carpenter** *comes up to him.* **Merril** *pretends not to notice him.*

Carpenter Can I have my hat back, please?

Merril What hat?

Carpenter The hat on your head.

Merril You can't have this hat. This hat is my hat.

Carpenter You're a liar and a thief.

Merril I'm a famous writer and I need this hat to stop all my brains popping out of my ears. Now buzz off. I've three books and an article to get through by supper, and supper's always on the dot in this house.

Carpenter (*playing the game*) Can I sit and watch?

Merril You might learn a thing or two.

Carpenter How do you start?

Merril You think up a subject. You choose.

Carpenter Love.

Merril Don't believe in it. Work.

Carpenter That's boring.

Merril I know. That's why I'm a writer.

Carpenter That *isn't* boring?

Merril Well, it's not as boring as scrubbing the floors of a spa hotel in Blastow and living in a draughty room at the top of the building; and never getting to see your friends because it's a four-mile walk over the moors and in any case they're usually in London when you get there.

Carpenter Someone you know?

Merril The hero of my book.

Carpenter Oh. It's a story.

Merril Yes. I haven't worked out the ending yet. You can give me some ideas.

Carpenter Where are we?

Merril Well, our hero, George, has just finished his week's work and has run four miles over the hills to see his friend. I've called his friend Edward, after me. But, like every other week, Edward, if he's there at all, is sitting scribbling at his desk.

Carpenter Sounds like a very busy man . . .

Merril And hardly has the time of day for poor George . . .

Carpenter That's not fair!

Merril That's how George sees it.

Carpenter Then George must be a very selfish man.

Merril I beg your pardon, but he's very unselfish and caring and kind and loving, and he gets ignored all the time by Edward's friends . . .

Carpenter Not true!

Merril Well, some of them; and generally he feels like he's getting in the way.

Carpenter Well, he isn't.

Merril (*snappy*) Yes, he is, it's in the book. Now, put yourself in George's place. What would you do?

Carpenter Get a job nearer Edward.

Merril He can't, there isn't one.

Carpenter Live with Edward and walk to work.

Merril Four miles and back every day! I told you Edward was selfish.

Carpenter No, he's not.

Merril Yes, you are . . . I mean he is. You want to hear what other folk have got to say about him?

Carpenter Who?

Merril His present cleaner, for a start.

Carpenter He hasn't got a cleaner!

Merril Exactly! He thinks he's got a nice little set-up where all the work's shared. But he's got a free cleaner, cook and bottle-washer and her name's Lucy and he takes her for granted, just like he takes George for granted.

Carpenter I don't think I'll buy your book.

Merril You won't get a chance anyway.

Carpenter Why not?

Merril Too risky. They'll not publish.

Carpenter Perhaps you could water it down.

Merril To suit them?

Carpenter *turns away.*

Merril Should I carry on?

Carpenter With your book?

Merril Perhaps I've lost heart.

Carpenter I'll help you.

Merril Do you want me to?

Carpenter Let's try. What happens next? In the book you're writing?

Merril I'm not sure. Edward's come home and George has come to see him. If you were George, what would you say?

Carpenter I'd say this George loves you, Edward.

Merril And this Edward loves you, George.

They kiss. **Adams** *enters.*

Merril The chapter ends when the gaoler appears. Bye, Eddie. See you, George.

Millthorpe. 1895.

Song: Seasons

All And the seasons go round and round and round
It's in the nature of the world to change
But the cycle of love and friendship's
Not so easy to arrange. Arrange. Arrange.
It's not so easy to arrange.

Carpenter October Eighteen

Ninety-Five,
Dear Sir, I do declare
That your attitudes on Ireland
Are not ones I care to share.

Adams December, Ted, I'll interrupt,
We need to plant more trees,
Plus, give me advance warning
When George Merril's coming, please.

Carpenter Jan of Ninety-Six,
Home Rule for Ireland I'm defending!
And George, I suggest,
Your manners need mending.

Adams Feb and March and late April,
Frost has been severe.

Carpenter Just like my temper
If you don't make friends with George
this year.

All And the seasons go round and
round and round
It's in the nature of the world to change,
But the cycle of love and friendship's
Not so easy to arrange. Arrange.
Arrange.
It's not so easy to arrange.

Adams Summer, Autumn, Ninety-Six,
You've been asked to go and speak
At the local branch committee
Of the ILP next week.

Carpenter Christmas, and George
Merril
Will be spending it with us
So calculate for extra food,
George, and don't make a fuss.

Adams Feb of Ninety-Seven,
You're to talk on dockers' wages,
And Ted, I'm feeling lonely,
You've not talked to me for ages.

Carpenter Autumn, Winter, Spring and
Summer,
Politics and cultivation.

Adams Take a lesson from the crops,
Put your lovers in rotation.

All And the seasons go round and
round and round
It's in the nature of the world to change,
But the cycle of love and friendship's
Not so easy to arrange. Arrange.
Arrange.
It's not so easy to arrange.

*July 1896. On the road to Millthorpe.
Midday.*

Frank Simpson *is standing with a suitcase.
He is looking at a piece of paper and repeating
some instructions.*

Simpson 'Left outside the station . . .
follow the road to the mill
. . . cross the stream . . . . (*Looks up and
around him.*) . . . then take the track
alongside the spinney till you come to a
gate.' (*He looks up.*) Track to the left or
track to the right, that's what I'd like to
know. (*He goes over his route in his mind
again, obviously lost.*)

Merril *enters. He's just walked over the
moors.*

Merril You're lost, aren't you?

Simpson I'm used to street names, not
spinneys and streams and tracks.

Merril Where're you going?

Simpson Millthorpe.

Merril You're miles off.

Simpson I've followed instructions.

Merril Well, tear 'em up and listen here.
You go down that slope, through that
gate, cross over the road and through
the farmyards. You'll come to a church.
The Millthorpe road's the other side of
the church. Turn left at the gravestone
in the shape of three angels. Half an
hour at a brisk pace.

Simpson Most grateful.

Merril I'd keep you company, but I'm
off for a swim. Tara.

He runs off. **Simpson** *smiles after him. Picks
up case and trudges on.*

Millthorpe. The garden. Later that afternoon.

Carpenter *is sitting in a garden-chair reading.* **Adams** *comes in with a bowl of strawberries and cream.*

Adams Like a treat?

Carpenter What?

Adams Guess.

Carpenter Give up.

Adams Go on.

Carpenter I don't know where to start.

Adams Start with the time of year.

Carpenter July –

Adams What happens in July?

Carpenter July the fourteenth . . . Got it! Fall of the Bastille, anniversary of . . .

Adams Wrong.

Carpenter Still, we could celebrate it.

Adams With my treat! (*Gives* **Carpenter** *the bowl.*)

Carpenter Strawberries!

Adams Best crop to date. Go on.

Carpenter *has one.*

Adams Well?

Carpenter Delicious. Here's to Liberty, (*Eats one.*), Equality, (*Eats one.*) and Fraternity. (*Puts one in* **Adams'** *mouth.*)

Simpson *appears. He looks hot.*

Simpson Here I am. Better late than never.

Adams *and* **Carpenter** *look up.*

Simpson Give me avenues and alleyways any day.

Adams (*to* **Carpenter**) I was going to tell you . . .

Carpenter After the strawberries?

Simpson (*comes over*) Strawberries? Very nice. Your own?

Adams I'll get you some, Frank.

Simpson A long cool drink's what I need.

Adams I'll see what there is. (*He goes.*)

Simpson When George wrote and asked me up I thought I'd have to refuse. But then the conference in London was cancelled, and I thought, why not? A weekend away from the stresses and strains. I could've done without the trek, but I've got to admit, it's a charming spot. I'm feeling calmer already.

Carpenter It's the atmosphere.

Simpson I'd've been tramping around all night if I'd not met a local lad. He was just off for a swim, happy as a lark and not a care in the world. If I'd've been a few years younger I'd've joined him.

Adams *comes out.*

Adams There's some tea on the brew. Are you coming in, or shall I bring it out?

Carpenter Frank?

Simpson Tea in the garden at Millthorpe. It sounds like Paradise come true.

Adams *goes to get the tea.*

Simpson It's always been my wish to come here. It's famous, you know. You've set an example. The simplification of life. I want to see everything: the fields, the workshop, the hut at the bottom of the garden where you write. That's famous, you know, that hut.

Adams (*carries plate of sandwiches*) Tuck in. I'll get the tea.

Simpson No, you won't, I will. I know all the work's shared here, so don't treat me as a guest. I'll muck in with the rest of you. (*He goes.*)

A pause.

Carpenter Well?

Adams I was going to tell you.

Carpenter We'd agreed to have no more guests till the autumn.

Adams I forgot, Ted. I'm sorry.

Carpenter I've not seen George Merril for two months. I wanted to spend the weekend with him. Not with Frank Simpson.

Adams Well, he's here now. A year back I promised to be friends with George Merril. I've done that as best I can. So you return the favour and be nice to Frank Simpson. Is that a bargain?

Carpenter I'll be on my best behaviour.

Hukin *enters.*

Hukin (*out of breath*) Sorry I'm late.

Adams What are you doing here?

Hukin What are *you* doing here? You're supposed to be in Sheffield with Lucy, she's expecting you this evening.

Adams Something cropped up.

Hukin Well, she'll not thank you, you're going to the social evening with me and Fannie.

Adams So why are you here?

Hukin (*points to* **Carpenter**) He asked me. Here's the letter.

Adams Did he now?

Hukin Said he had to talk to me.

Adams I thought you wanted a quiet weekend with George, Ted.

Carpenter And it seems like you should really be in Sheffield, George.

Hukin And I'd like to know why I've been summoned to Millthorpe, Edward?

Simpson *comes out with a tray of tea.*

Simpson Tea up!

Carpenter *walks away.*

The garden. Later the same day.

Simpson *is in the middle of a conversation with* **Hukin** *and* **Adams**. **Hukin** *is bored and is glancing through the book* **Carpenter** *was reading. It is* Love's Coming of Age.

Simpson It's all within our reach now. Better wages, better conditions, better housing, better schools. If we just get the confidence of the voter, we can sail into the twentieth century with a Labour party in the House of Commons. (*He takes a bite of cake.*) Did your wife make this?

Adams I made it.

Simpson You're married, aren't you?

Adams Yes.

Simpson Will I have the pleasure?

Adams She's in Sheffield.

Simpson Had a tiff?

Hukin I'll go and find Ted.

Simpson (*to* **Hukin**) Where's he gone?

Hukin To meet someone. (*He goes.*)

Simpson We'll be quite a crowd here soon. I hope there's enough beds. (*Picks up the book, sees what it is. Looks at* **Adams**.) You were . . . you did understand what I meant in the letter, didn't you, George?

Adams Yes.

Simpson And you thought it was . . . reasonable?

Adams Oh, yes. I'll support you.

Simpson I'd rather do it in a friendly way.

Immediately following.

Merril *is sunbathing by the river.* **Carpenter** *kneels and kisses him.* **Merril** *wakes, and pulls at* **Carpenter**'s *shirt.*

Merril Take them off.

Carpenter It's a bit near the house.

Merril Go on.

Carpenter *takes off his shirt.*

Merril I like your nipples, they're like berries. Are they poisonous?

Carpenter Suck one and see.

Merril *does so. We hear* **Hukin**'*s voice.*

Hukin Ted! Ted!

Merril It's George! Over here!

Carpenter I wanted to talk to you alone first . . .

Merril We can talk alone in bed. (**Hukin** *has entered.*) Hullo, George, come and give us a hug.

Hukin Ted, it's not good enough. Sending mysterious notes saying to see you, then ignoring me when I get here.

Carpenter I wanted to talk to you on your own.

Merril Edward, stop repeating yourself.

Hukin Well, you can talk to us together.

Carpenter I don't *want* to talk to you together, I want to talk to you separately.

Hukin What about?

Carpenter It's personal.

Merril *and* **Hukin** *look at each other.*

The garden.

Simpson *is talking.* **Adams** *is sharpening a scythe.*

Simpson (*shows* **Adams** *a picture he's taken from his wallet*) There she is.

Adams (*looks briefly*) Lovely smile.

Simpson That was taken before a big 'do' in Huddersfield last Mayday. I bought her the dress specially for the occasion. Paris design. Does your wife dance?

Adams We've dances in Sheffield.

Simpson Mine loves to dance, she can keep going till dawn. I can never understand that. She'll sit around the house for days on end, complaining of headaches, then get her to dance and she's like a clockwork toy that won't run down.

Adams (*looks again*) Yes. A real china doll.

Simpson That's how I think of her. I tell her, she's lucky now. When we had the shop to run ourselves she'd never a moment to herself, but now we've got staff she can take it easy. I tell her, 'Once we're in power, there'll be no women slaving on the benches any more, they'll be back in the home where they're needed.' Does your wife work?

Adams We share all the work here.

Simpson Good. Of course. And just because I'm lucky enough to make sure mine doesn't have to go out, I don't want you to think I treat her like a paid servant; I lend a hand whenever I'm there, and when I'm not I get a girl in.

Adams (*he's looking at the scythe*) That's that done.

He gets up. **Carpenter** *comes on, followed by* **Hukin.**

Hukin Edward, you're not being reasonable.

Carpenter *stops and turns round.*

Carpenter And you and George Merril have been less than honest.

Simpson George Merril. That name rings a bell.

Adams I'm going to cut the hedge.

Simpson Where've you been, Edward?

Carpenter A little light work in the fields.

Simpson I hope my visit's not interrupted your routine?

Carpenter No. We've decided that the

weekend is another bourgeois institution, designed as a recuperation period for those unfortunate enough to have to exhaust themselves labouring all week. At Millthorpe we make no such artificial divisions. (*To* **Adams**.) Do we, George?

Adams I'll cut the hedge. (*He goes.*)

Hukin Ted. I'd like to speak to you alone.

Carpenter Excuse me, George, I've my guest to attend to.

Simpson As I said, treat me as part of the family. Just ignore me. I'll take a look at the vegetables before the light goes. (*He goes.*)

Hukin You've upset George Merril!

Carpenter You and George Merril have upset me.

Hukin Because we've seen each other a couple of times without you there?

Carpenter Behind my back!

Hukin Shall we ask your permission next time?

Carpenter I just need to know where I stand.

Hukin Is that why you asked me up here?

Carpenter I thought you'd be here earlier.

Hukin Before George Merril arrived?

Carpenter Though perhaps you'd've both preferred me not to be here.

Hukin And perhaps you could've come to see *me*. I feel like I've been summoned to court.

Carpenter I couldn't because I thought George Adams and Lucy were going to Sheffield this weekend. Frank Simpson turned up, George Adams stayed, you arrived late and George Merril arrived early.

Simpson (*runs in*) Edward! There's a half-naked man walking across your potatoes!

The garden. That evening.

Merril *darns a sock.* **Adams** *is sketching.* **Carpenter** *reads to* **Hukin**. *Piano 'Dear Love' theme.*

Carpenter To lie all night beside the loved one – how lovely,
To hold in one's arms something so precious,
So beautiful;
Dear head and hair and lips and limbs that shrine
Eternity;
Through scent and sense and breath and touch and
Love – forgetting all but this one, all but this one.

Simpson I'm out of my depth. Two hours ago they were like cat and dog.

Adams You have friends don't you? Friends always row.

Simpson I have . . . differences . . . with men that I work with . . . in the party.

Adams (*to* **Hukin**) George, can you move over a bit, you're blocking Ted.

Simpson It's like they were married. I don't know to put it quite. Petty.

Adams Petty?

Simpson Trivial.

Adams How?

Simpson Well . . . like my wife when she says I don't understand her. She went mad when I said I was coming here. She didn't understand when I said it was important.

Adams She could've come.

Simpson She'd've been bored surrounded by men.

Adams I'll . . . go and make up the beds.

Simpson I'll help you.

Adams No, I'd rather do it on my own. I can think.

Adams *gets up and leaves.*

Merril (*has pricked his finger*) Ouch!

Carpenter George, put it away, you'll ruin your eyes in this light.

Merril Ooh, it's drawn blood.

Carpenter *sucks his finger for him.* **Hukin** *sees that* **Simpson** *is on his own. Puts the book down and crosses and sits near him.*

Hukin Are you cold, Frank?

Simpson A bit. I'm not used to being outside. But I like it. I like the quiet.

Hukin I'm sorry you got caught in the middle, earlier.

Simpson It all happened too fast for me. The boy turning up again, and then turning out to be Edward's . . . well, his . . .

Hukin What?

Simpson I'm confused.

Hukin Why?

Simpson Well, I know about Edward, of course. I know the way he is, and I know that's none of my business. But, I can't help feeling it's not right. It's like a husband and wife.

Hukin You mean, it's not right to be a husband and a wife?

Simpson If you're a man and a woman, it is.

Hukin How do you know they are a husband and a wife?

Simpson He's darning his socks for him.

Hukin He'd darn your socks if you asked him.

Simpson Well, I wouldn't. It wouldn't be right.

Hukin A couple of years back, I was ill for three months. I couldn't go to work. We'd three new men with us, the place was in chaos, and the books were in a mess. Fannie took over from me. I didn't lift a finger for three months, and when I started going out for walks, people'd say 'Good morning, Mrs Hukin', and 'How's your hubby doing at the works?'

Simpson They just couldn't see you'd got a partnership. She did it because she wanted to do it.

Hukin That's why George is doing the darning. He wants to.

Simpson Then he shouldn't. It's . . . it doesn't seem right. I mean, if he was a woman, and he knew that's his job . . . but it isn't his job . . .

Hukin Then he's made a free choice.

Simpson To make a fool of himself.

Hukin Why a fool?

Simpson Look. This may be old-fashioned, but the world is divided into men and women. Now, if there's men who want to . . . well, be like Edward, fair enough. But to stop being men in the process, well it . . . unsettles me.

Merril *has by this time passed the sewing on to* **Carpenter** *and is reading the book himself.* **Adams** *comes out.*

Adams I've made up a bed in the spare room, Frank. You'll have to sleep on the sofa, George. (*He goes.*)

Merril *yawns and gets up. Takes sewing off* **Carpenter.**

Merril Give it here, I'll finish it off inside. (*He goes.*)

Hukin *crosses to* **Carpenter**. *Picks up the book.*

Hukin I'll take this to read in bed.

Carpenter *looks up.*

Hukin I mean, on the *sofa!*

He goes. **Carpenter** *and* **Simpson** *look at each other.*

Carpenter Would you like to go to bed, Frank?

Simpson (*not sure of the implications*) Oh, Er . . . well, I don't know . . .

Carpenter Don't worry, it wasn't an invitation.

Simpson Oh no, that never crossed my mind.

Carpenter Really? It did cross mine.

Simpson But the lad . . .

Carpenter You think he'd be jealous if you and I . . . ?

Simpson *My* wife'd be, if I . . .

Carpenter But, he's not my wife . . .

Simpson But, he's your . . .

Carpenter What?

Simpson I don't know the word.

Carpenter Perhaps we don't need one.

Simpson I wish there was one.

Carpenter Why?

Simpson Words make sense of the world. You know where you stand when you put a word to something.

Carpenter Frank. Let me tell you a story. It starts on a beach in Brighton, when I was a little boy. Sitting there dreaming about islands. Even after I'd left Brighton, when I was a student at Cambridge, I had the same dreams. When I went into the Church, when I left the Church and became a teacher, I'd still have visions of coconut groves and white beaches. But it was only when I came North, to Sheffield, that I knew it wasn't an island that I wanted; but to be with other men in ways that the world didn't allow. Women that I knew, women who were beginning to rebel against men, said 'good! you want to stop being a *man*'. I didn't mention the sexual aspect, and I wonder how that would've affected their reaction. Then I began to meet men, working men from the town, who were not afraid to show genuine affection for each other, to kiss each other. I was, to put it mildly, staggered.

What was considered 'unmanly' in polite society, was allowed by people who, I had been brought up to believe, were a lower race. Brutes and animals with no human feeling. And yet, I found love. Not an abstract notion, or an old man in the sky, but an active force. The island wasn't necessary. I knew I had to throw my lot in with them, because if a new order and vision of the world was possible, it could only start here. Yes, yes, I know they'd been brutalized by the machine and the factory; the husbands beat the wives and the mothers joined with the fathers to beat the children. But, there were some hearts and some minds that still lived.

Pause. **Simpson** *gets up.*

Simpson I'm tired. Can we talk tomorrow?

Carpenter *picks up the lantern. Very little light now.*

Carpenter There's more blankets in the chest of drawers if you get cold. There's books by your bed if you want to read. I'm afraid they're all written by myself.

Simpson I'm always interested in your books, Edward.

He goes. **Adams** *comes up.*

Adams Edward, I spoiled the weekend. I'm sorry.

Carpenter I'm sorry I shouted at you earlier, George. We have our ups and downs, but I know where I stand with you.

Adams *goes.* **Hukin** *comes up.*

Carpenter I've behaved like a spoilt child, George. I apologize.

Hukin Edward, Fannie and me have got a marriage certificate. We try not to let that affect our lives together. You can never have one. So don't start acting as if you'd like one.

He goes. **Merril** *comes up.*

Merril Here's that daft map George Adams sent Frank. Can't make head nor tail of it.

Carpenter *looks at it. Sees that it's on the back of a letter.*

Carpenter 'Dear Frank . . .'

Merril You shouldn't read other folks' letters.

Carpenter 'Dear Frank. If the party is worried about Edward's books on sex, please take my advice and don't send a letter, but get someone here to talk to him, preferably yourself. I'm sure, like myself, he has the best interests of the ILP at heart, and will listen to what you have to say . . .'

Merril What's that?

Carpenter Who knows? A storm in a teacup or a cloud on the horizon.

Merril The trouble with you is you never say what you mean.

Carpenter Let's go to bed.

Merril That's clear enough.

Merril *blows out the candle.*

Adams *alone.*

Adams The feet went up the stairs. I listened to them. In the kitchen George Hukin was talking to me about overcoming our personal problems, supporting each other in difficulties. I agree with him, said I would try, but all the time I was imagining what was happening above me, above my head, in the room above where we sat. I wished I could see through the ceiling.

George realized how late it was, finished his tea and left. I was at the foot of the stairs. I took of my shoes and lifted my foot on to the first step. It didn't creak, neither did the second one. I kept really close to the wall, moving slowly, slyly, until I reached the landing. His room was at the far end. I crept towards it. I was halfway down the corridor when I heard the first sound: springs creaked as the weight was shifted and there was a murmur. It might have been a word but I wasn't close enough to hear. I continued, each step slower and more deliberate than the last. The floor did not betray me and I got to the door.

The sounds from the room were more distinct now but I didn't pay the full attention as I had to get in position first. I bent my knees and started to lower myself. The rustle of clothes against your body can be so loud when every ounce of concentration is channelled into your ears. But at last I was crouching, breathing as silently as possible and listening. Listening. Sheets rumpled and pulled, rolled on, slid on, lay on. Growls, murmurs, sighs, breath catching in the throat. Hands roughly or gently or urgently stroking flesh. And the bed responding as the positions alter. I can't see them but I can imagine what they're doing. I imagine . . . I imagine . . .
I imagine it's me, there with him. My body with his, his hands on me, his lips on mine, his voice in my ear, my voice saying 'Edward, Edward, please now, Edward, yes . . . I've waited, I've waited . . . yes . . . Edward, please, I've waited so long . . . I've wanted you . . . but now, Edward, please, I love you'.

When the sounds stopped I stayed there for about an hour, and then found I could hardly stand. I went to bed. I imagined Lucy lying next to me, pretending to sleep as usual, with me beside her, pretending not to hear her crying. In the morning I heard them in the kitchen and I heard the back door open and close. They'd gone. I got up and went into Edward's bedroom; I looked at the bed, it was just as they'd left it. I took a step nearer and the bottom sheet came into view. It was all creased and crumpled. I went a bit nearer.

Sheets. How different they look when they're washed and fresh. How smooth they look when they're ironed. So unlike this one. (*He reaches out.*) I could take it and wash it for him, he'd appreciate that. I could strip the bed and wash the sheets because look . . . (*He has an imagined sheet in his hand.*) Look, this one is dirty, this one is soiled. It's stained, why it's even damp. You can smell, it isn't clean, I can smell it I can . . (*He sinks his face into the imagined sheets.*)

Carpenter *enters.*

Adams I was going to wash them.

Silence. **Adams** *crosses to* **Carpenter** *and embraces him. There is no response.* **Adams** *exits.* **Merril** *enters with a clothes line.*

Merril Grab this.

They tie up the line. It crosses the stage.
Merril *exits.* **Carpenter** *takes out the letter to* **Simpson** *and glances at it. He puts it away as* **Simpson** *enters.*

Simpson The simplification of life! You don't know how lucky you are, Edward.

Merril *reappears with a basket of wet sheets. He has a mouthful of pegs. He and* **Carpenter** *start to hang them.*

Simpson Get up in the morning, smell fresh air, eat fresh food that you've grown yourself . . .

Carpenter There's the other side, of course.

Simpson What side?

Carpenter You can get out of touch with the real world.

Simpson Ah, yes. It had crossed my mind.

Carpenter There's all sorts of cranky ideas about. Food-faddism, Nudism, Telepathy, Psychology, Friendship with the animals, Free love.

Simpson Where's the prop?

Carpenter In the outhouse.

Merril *goes to get it.*

Carpenter (*holds sheet out to* **Simpson**). Would you mind?

They hang a sheet.

Carpenter I suppose the sight of two men hanging out the washing would seem a bit odd to some people.

Simpson It wasn't odd when I was a kid. My dad used to do the washing. But, you're right, it's a dying tradition.

Carpenter Except at Millthorpe!

Merril *re-enters.*

Merril He cut the hedge!

Carpenter Who?

Merril George Adams. (*To* **Simpson**.) Now the neighbours'll see in. Nosey-parkers. I came and stayed when George and Lucy went to Morecambe last year. I was in the bedroom, and I could hear them in the lane below: 'who scrubbed that?' and 'who polished that?' It was two of them squinting into the kitchen window. So I popped my head out and said, 'I did'. One of them said she wished I was her husband. I'd not the heart to tell her I was spoken for.

Carpenter You're not.

Merril I am.

Carpenter You're free to do as you choose.

Merril I know. And I choose to be 'spoken for!

Carpenter George, I don't want to own you.

Merril You don't.

Carpenter Or be owned.

Merril (*to* **Simpson**) He means he likes a bit on the side.

Carpenter I mean we're not married.

Merril Ta for telling me.

Carpenter Then don't act as if we are.

Merril (*stops*) Did you object to me washing this lot?

Carpenter No.

Merril Did you *make* me wash this lot?

Carpenter No.

Merril Did I *mind* washing this lot?

Carpenter No.

Merril Then don't talk to me about acting married. (*To* **Simpson**.) Now if him or George'd done the washing, we'd've not heard the end of it for a week. Lucy says I'm the only one round here who can pick up a broom without it being a political gesture. Here, (*Gives* **Simpson** *a sheet.*) you can finish off, and I'll go and make breakfast. (*To* **Carpenter**.) 'Cos I *want* to.

He goes. **Simpson** *stands with the sheet.*

Simpson I read your books last night, Edward.

Carpenter I know why you're here, Frank.

Pause. **Adams** *enters with a case. He is half hidden by the sheets. The other two do not notice him.*

Simpson George told you?

Carpenter We've no secrets here, Frank.

Simpson I'm here on behalf of the party. A certain section of it. I'm not speaking for myself.

Carpenter Where do you stand?

Simpson We need votes.

Carpenter And a pamphlet on the position of the homosexual in this country today won't get votes?

Simpson It's not the time for such matters.

Carpenter Get the bread, then think about the butter?

Simpson We just want you to go easy on the sexual thing.

Carpenter Is this a final decision?

Simpson There's other matters. Your opinion is highly respected. You gave a fine speech at Scarborough, last May.

Carpenter On the subject of state censorship.

Simpson We're just putting out feelers, Edward.

Carpenter But, you have to report back to the committee?

Simpson Tell me what I'm to say.

Merril (*off*) Grub up!

Adams *goes.*

Carpenter Ask them if they could find a place on the agenda for Love.

A pause.

Simpson I shall catch the next train. Thank you for your kind hospitality. (*He takes* Love's Coming of Age *out of his pocket.*) Oh, I er . . .

Carpenter *takes it. They shake hands and* **Simpson** *goes in the direction of the kitchen.* **Carpenter** *flicks through the book.*

Carpenter (*reads*) 'Perhaps it will only be for a society more fully grown than ours to understand the wealth and variety of affectional possibilities which it has within itself.'

Hukin *enters. He gives* **Carpenter** *a note. He reads it.*

Carpenter He's a good man, Frank.

Hukin A bit of a stuff-shirt now he's got a back bench in mind.

Carpenter He'll be as good as his word. (*Glances at note.*) I suppose this means Lucy won't be back.

Hukin She'd already decided. She told us yesterday. (*Looks at* **Carpenter**.) Still. You could always get another married couple in.

Carpenter George?

Hukin (*softly*) Edward, George Merril wants to live here. When I went to see him the other weekend, he told me.

Carpenter No!

Hukin Why?

Carpenter It's impossible!

Hukin Yes, I suppose you're right. You'd probably both end up in prison.

Carpenter I didn't mean that.

Hukin You mean George Merril hasn't got a wife?

Carpenter What difference would that make?

Hukin You never wanted me and Fannie to move in here. You wanted George Hukin and his *wife*.

Carpenter Two people I loved!

Hukin One man you loved, plus an insurance for respectability.

Carpenter All right! So he moves in! Splendid! George and Lucy, George and Fannie, Edward and George.

Simpson *crosses the stage with a case. Pauses and exits.*

Hukin Very well, Edward. Sit and write your books; about a world where there's no such thing as a couple; where marriage doesn't exist; where there's no jealousy and no guilt; where it isn't a crime to love your own sex. Write till there's not a scrap of paper left and the ink's run dry. One day it might all come true, but there's people living here now who'll thank you much more for doing the *one thing* that you're not supposed to do. Which is to be homosexual. Not think and write and talk about it, but be it. In whatever way you can. And, something else. You won't be thanked for it and you won't be remembered for it. But, you might be loved for it.

Carpenter I'm afraid, George.

Hukin I've waited years for you to say that.

Carpenter Why?

Hukin Because I've sometimes thought it's all been a bit of scientific research for you. With us under the microscope. You were so much cleverer than us. And, you could always pack your bags and go. We couldn't. We've got to live with what we've learnt from you.

Carpenter Are you afraid?

Hukin Ever since I first saw you. Standing on a platform, making a speech. I fell in love with you. The world didn't seem very safe any more.

They kiss.

Hukin It's only a razor-grinder's advice.

He goes. A pause. **Merril** *enters. He has a frying-pan in his hand.*

Merril Where is everyone?

Carpenter They've all left.

Merril They might've said. All of them?

Carpenter We're on our own.

Merril Well, they've missed a good breakfast. Come on Eddie, I'm starving.

He goes. **Carpenter** *follows him.*

August 1944. On the radio

Forster's Voice As for his socialism, I wonder if it would be recognized as such by people of the left today. For he was not interested in organization or efficiency or party discipline. He was not really interested in industrialization, though he loved the industrial workers individually.

Forster *is standing by the radio.*

Forster Edward Carpenter and George Merril lived together for thirty years. At first, Carpenter found himself abandoned by many of his old friends, whose distaste for the new arrangement at Millthorpe expressed itself in doubts as to whether the housework would get done without a woman there.

But, gradually, new visitors arrived and the house became a place of pilgrimage for those of us who had not yet found the courage to declare ourselves to a hostile world. Some stayed and lived with Edward and George. This aroused further disgust. But, the world became too busy with wars and revolutions and social progress to be bothered with the cranky old fellow and his menage. Therefore, I had only a slight pang of conscience when I did not declare, from the safety of a BBC studio, that Edward Carpenter had been . . . but, then, had been lucky.

If only, I said, the world had allowed me to become an optimist, I might not have become a cynic.

Carpenter As a child I'd sit on the shore and dream. Now that I am on the shore of human life, I find that I dream practically the same dreams.

Song: 'The Body Electric' finale

All Those who defile the living
Are the same as those who defile the dead;
Those who corrupt their own bodies
Conceal themselves

Therefore:
I sing the body electric
I sing
I sing
I sing the body electric.

THE BODY ELECTRIC

(Based on a poem by Walt Whitman)

Music: Alex Harding
Lyric: Noël Greig

♩ = 108

G+C

1st time / 2nd time

1. I sing the bo - dy e -
   sing the bo - dy e -

lec - tric I sing of the light that flows ____ from the
lec - tric I sing of the flame that glows ____ in the

flesh _____ of those that I love
blood _____ of those that I love

1st time | 2nd time

2. I

Those who defile the li-ving are the same as those who de-file the dead. Those who cor-rupt their own bo-dies con-ceal themselves

50

therefore I sing the bo-dy e-lec-tric I sing the bo-dy e-lec-tric I sing
I sing I sing the bo-dy e-lec-tric

C   G   C   G   F

C   F   C

molto dim.

Compromised Immunity

Andy Kirby

'Neither blame nor guilt is a useful response to an epidemic.'
Dennis Altman

Compromised Immunity was first performed as a staged reading at the Drill Hall Arts Centre on 20 October 1985 as part of the Gay Sweatshop Times Ten Festival. This was under the direction of Robert Hale with the cast as: Richard Sandells, Lennie St Luce, Pip Stephenson, Peter Shorey, Nigel Hughes, Alan Hooker and Peter Seton. The play subsequently opened as a Gay Sweatshop Times Ten production on 3 July 1985 at the Albany Empire, Deptford with the following cast:

Peter Dennett *aged 22*	Richard Sandells
Miss Coates *aged 43*	Madeline Blakeney
Marie *aged 20*	Pip Stephenson
Gerry Grimond *aged 36*	Peter Shorey
Hugh Emmerson *aged 32*	David Benedict
Roy	Alan Hooker
Ian Edwards *aged 18*	Duncan Alexander

Directed by Philip Osment
Designed by Tony Reeves
Lighting design Matt Shadder
Costumes Caroline Burgess
Stage management Janet Cantrell and Terri Ford
Poster design Tony Reeves
Fundraising Richard Sandells
Photos David Benedict

The first production of the play in its present form opened as a Gay Sweatshop production at the Leicester Haymarket on 28 April 1987 with the same director and designers but with Sarah McNair as **Miss Coates** and with the role of Roy cut.

Time: September and October 1985
Place: Isolation Room at the East London Teaching Hospital

Author's Note

I wrote **Compromised Immunity** in anger, sorrow and hope at the AIDS health crisis. Anger at what needed to be done and was not being done. Sorrow at the passing of friends, of lovers and of illusions. (The seventies were a good time to grow up gay and complacent about being gay.) Hope that from suffering we grow in self-knowledge and spirit. That hope was justified, but only because I kept faith with the anger and the sorrow. This play is dedicated to those living – in any sense – with AIDS.

'Black March' is reproduced by permission of the estate of Stevie Smith.

Portion of *Tales of the City* by Armistead Maupin, © 1978 by the Chronicle Publishing Company. Reprinted by permission of the author.

All characters and locations in this work are fictitious, any resemblance to actual persons or places is purely coincidental.

Act One

Scene One

A Lecture Theatre.

Peter Er, good evening, Dr Morley, ladies, gentlemen. You were actually supposed to be watching a video this evening but... you've got me instead. My name's Peter Dennett, twenty-two years old. I'm a student nurse. It has a few advantages, some allowances and a room in a hostel which is better than some of the bedsits I've lived it, I can even take the unsocial hours. The pay's nothing to write home about, in fact it's barely enough to write home with. I wouldn't say that I have a vocation, but at least I have a career, and that's quite an achievement these days. Two years ago I came here. The East London Teaching Hospital, ELTH as we call it. National ELTH of course. I've had to do a series of six month stints in the various sections. I'd done Obstetrics, Paediatrics, and was nearing the end of my time on Avard Wing, the Terminal Ward, known to us as Terminal One. Terminal Two, by the way, is the Mortuary. Anyway I'd just come back from two weeks at Tring Residential Nursing College.

Scene Two

A hospital corridor.

Coates Hello there Peter. How was the course?

Peter I know a lot more about pharmacology now Miss Coates, can tell my uppers from my downers. How have things been here?

Coates Short staffed as usual and every bed in the hospital's filled.

Peter All hands to the stomach-pumps eh? Sorry. About my transfer Miss Coates...

Coates I was going to mention that. You'll be moving out of Avard in a few weeks won't you? I think I can get you into one of the operating theatres.

Peter That'd be good.

Coates I'll look into it and come back to you nearer the time. Right now you'd better get changed. Oh, and there's a new man in the Isolation Room. Grimond, a transfer from St Andrew's. AIDS. Our first. We took him on as a favour.

Peter Haven't we got enough troubles of our own?

Coates They've got more than they can cope with so they're farming out some of the less complicated ones. This time we're scratching their back but it'll even out. Where was I?

Peter AIDS. Homosexual is he?

Coates I believe so. But then considering the alternatives are mainly drug-related or haemophiliac we've got off fairly lightly. Anyway we're not used to these cases here so Dr Hillman says we should adopt full isolation precautions, until we're more familiar with the routine. So for the time being it's gloves, mask and sterilization. You do know about AIDS?

Peter I read the papers, yes. I know all about AIDS. How do long do they give him?

Coates A couple of months. It's hard to tell. Believe me it makes staff planning impossible!

Peter Maybe I should hurry him up a bit. Sorry.

Coates Grimond is proving difficult though.

Coates Hostile. He's upset all the other nurses.

Peter So you call in the thick skin and penetrating wit of Peter Dennett.

Coates Your shift begins in ten minutes. (**Coates** *exits*.)

Peter I knew I should've stayed away.

Peter *is changing. His head is in his jumper when* **Marie** *enters.*

Marie Guess who?

Peter Marie! You look great.

Marie In C&A overalls!

Peter You look great in anything.

Marie Ugh! You had a shave? It's like kissing a hedgehog.

Peter I'm thinking of growing a beard. It'd give me a more masculine, rugged look.

Marie Ragged more like.

Peter I came over to see you last night.

Marie I was out wasn't I? Don't stay in every night on the off-chance of you dropping by.

Peter But you got my cards?

Marie Yes. Thanks.

Peter I missed you. Even missed this old place.

Marie It is run-down, isn't it. Can see now why you never encouraged me to visit.

Peter Well, now you've seen it. Though I've not got the time to give you the tour. Look, I'll see you tomorrow love. Unless you want to come round the hostel tonight.

Marie You know I can't stand that place Pete; so poky and walls so thin you can hear everything in the next room.

Peter They say you can count the orgasms four doors away.

Marie You should get a place of your own.

Peter We've been through all this before, you know I can't on my money. Unless you came in with me.

Marie There'll be time enough if we get married.

Peter What do you mean 'if'? There's no other woman.

Marie Well that's hardly reason enough is it?

Peter How's work?

Marie Another sale. Summer Reductions, Autumn Clearance. The mugs fall for it every time. How are things here?

Peter Same as usual.

Marie You never tell me anything about your work.

Peter It'd only depress you; and me.

Marie But you spend more time here than you do with me.

Peter I could say the same about you and C&A. But it doesn't give me a burning curiosity about this year's trend in winter woollens.

Marie You know what I mean!

Peter There's another reason. This place is about dying. Trying to die. You can't make small talk out of that.

Marie You think I wouldn't understand!

Peter It's not that. Look, I must go or Sister'll kill me. See you tomorrow evening. (*They embrace and* **Marie** *exits*.) Now then, let me see... disposable gloves, disposable masks and a scrub up before I start. That'll make me look like a real nurse. Either that or Baron Frankenstein.

Scene Three

The Isolation Room a few minutes later. **Peter** *enters carrying* **Gerry***'s dinner on a tray. He is dressed for barrier nursing.* **Gerry** *is tapping on the window.*

Gerry The window won't open.

Peter It's not meant to. This is an Isolation Room. They don't even let us in if we don't know the password?

Gerry What is the password?

Peter Joke.

Gerry Very funny.

Peter I meant we have to control who comes in here.

Gerry And who goes out.

Peter Have you tried? The door's over there. You wouldn't if you knew what was good for you though.

Gerry Nothing is any good for me. That's why I'm here.

Peter Well come and eat your dinner. That's good for you.

Gerry Have I seen you before?

Peter I doubt it. I'm just back from a training course. Do I remind you of someone?

Gerry How can I tell with that mask? I sometimes wonder if I'll ever see another human face.

Peter Of course you will, but for the time being we have to keep you protected.

Gerry Or protect other people from me?

Peter No. But we have to keep you in a protected environment so as to avoid the risk of opportunistic infection until the specialists have decided what they can do for you.

Gerry They'd better hurry up.

Peter There's research being done. I've read all about in in the Nursing Times. The papers are full of stuff about AIDS.

Gerry I know! 'GAY PLAGUE KILLS PRIEST', 'CLUB BANS TWO IN GAY PLAGUE PANIC', 'MY DOOMED SON DIES IN GAY PLAGUE'. Doesn't something strike you about those headlines?

Peter Yeah, you've picked all the ones with 'gay' in the title.

Gerry No, I've picked all the ones with 'plague' in the title. And the significant thing is the way they put those two little words together. I wouldn't be at all surprised if 'they' brought back the pink triangle.

Peter The what?

Gerry The Pink (*Drawing it in the air with his finger.*) Tri-an-gle. The Nazis made the Jews wear yellow stars and the gays pink triangles. Who are you anyway?

Peter Me? Peter Dennett. They give me a badge to wear in case I forget. Not quite as distinctive as a pink triangle but it does the trick.

Gerry No I mean what are you? A therapist?

Peter A shrink? That's a good one. We'll have a right giggle over that one next time we're emptying the bedpans. No, I'm a nurse. They do recruit men, you know. The only real difference is that I don't get my bum pinched quite so often as the others.

Gerry You will now . . . About all I can do.

Peter Except make life hell for us.

Gerry What do you mean?

Peter It isn't only your sexual popularity that's gone downhill you know. In two days you've made yourself the most disliked person in the hospital which, considering the competition from the staff is quite an achievement. It's understandable though.

Gerry What is?

Peter Stands to reason. Homosexuals don't get on with women, sexual rivals you see. You're both after men.

Gerry So you don't get on with lesbians then?

Peter I don't even know any.

Gerry You work with at least two.

Peter Who?

Gerry My lips are sealed.

Peter I'm not, by the way.

Gerry A lesbian? Oh I didn't think for one minute –

Peter GAY!

Gerry Oh, I know. I think it was the crass insensitivity that gave you away.

Peter You don't seem particularly sensitive yourself. I just wanted to set the record –

Gerry Straight?

Peter Avoid any ambiguity.

Gerry I think you've achieved that all right. Though it's hard enough to tell if you're a man or a woman under all that ... protection. So, we have established our respective sexual identities, well that seems a good start for a deep and meaningful relationship. Did you come here just to pass the time of day?

Peter I told you, I've brought your dinner. Bit cold now. Meat pie, runner beans and potatoes with fruit salad to follow.

Gerry Not hungry.

Peter If you don't eat it we'll sedate you into submission and give you a suppository. Perhaps you'd prefer that. Don't take out your anger on me Mr Grimond. I warn you we have the technology!

Gerry It might help if you stopped pontificating about what gays are and are not and do and do not prefer.

Peter Only if you eat your dinner first. (*Pause.*)

Gerry All right. I understand. You're only doing your job, and it's not one that I envy. Ugh!

Peter What do you think of the new contract caterers then?

Gerry Is this the best they can do?

Peter No, but it's the most profitable.

Gerry What would happen if I discharged myself?

Peter Apart from the nursing staff breathing a collective sigh of relief you mean? We'd put someone else in here. Protected environments don't come cheap you know and there's plenty out there who'd live longer with the benefit of this place. The only reason you got it is that we're not used to AIDS cases, so we're taking no risks. (**Gerry** *resumes eating.*) Only you'd not be allowed to go. The Area Health Authority would take out a court order to keep you here.

Gerry So I'm a prisoner.

Peter You could call it protective custody. You'd be a potential risk to other people.

Gerry So much for my being protected! You know nothing about AIDS!

Peter Stick around and teach me then. And if you want my sympathy you'll have to start treating me like another human being. Imagine I'm gay if it makes it any easier.

Gerry It's just not fair!

Peter Do you think any of these people deserve to die? Viruses don't have a social conscience. Life isn't fair. But you're going to – you have an adverse prognosis and here we can give you as good care as many places and better than most.

Gerry You people will never actually tell me in so many words that I'm going to die. However I put the question, you always manage to create the general impression that I won't be around for very long, but without using anything as vulgar as a date . . .

Peter That's because we don't pretend to know. Well, I see you've finished your dinner.

Gerry No point. My symptoms include chronic weight loss.

Peter You're using those words in the clinical sense I take it?

Gerry I think I have a better idea of what's wrong with me than you do!

Peter What's wrong with you is temper.

Gerry I mean my symptomatology.

Peter Please don't use those long words. I only know what they mean when I've been swotting up for an exam.

Gerry I read all the medical journals you know.

Peter That's really going to impress the viruses isn't it. (*Picks up a gay magazine.*) Is this one of them?

Gerry I suppose you think that's funny?

Peter Where's your sense of humour? Look, why don't we pretend this never happened and try again later, eh? (**Peter** *exits.*)

Scene Four

The Isolation Room later the same day. **Gerry** *is writing his diary.*

Gerry 17 September. The end of my second day at the East London Teaching Hospital. There was a new nurse in today. A man. I think he means well, but then the people who really get your back up do. (**Gerry** *turns on the light.*) I've come to welcome the evening when I can't see out of the window. It's not an inspiring view. A few trees, a building site. I never used to feel this low. But then until now I've always had the consolation that, however painful the treatment was, one day I would leave. No treatment now, and no hope. Today I made this long list of all the people I'd ever known in my life; lovers, friends, relatives, colleagues, landlords, the lot; I was well into the hundreds before writer's cramp set in. Silly really! But it somehow seemed important to make some sort of pattern out of my thirty-six years. Better have a bath. (**Gerry** *puts diary away and removes dressing gown and pyjamas.*) I cultivated you like a garden. Look at you now, one invisible virus and you become blighted, a wasteland. Nothing to do except wait for the cancers. I needn't have bothered. Needn't have bothered about anything at all!

Peter *enters with sheets, forms, 'Nursing Times' and yellow rubbish bag.*

Peter My name's Peter Dennett. You must be Mr Grimond, how are you settling in?

Gerry We've been through all this before.

Peter I know. Didn't work out though did it? This is Take Two. What are you doing?

Gerry Going to have a bath.

Peter I'll see to that later. You might have an accident, you're weak.

Gerry Immunosuppressed.

Peter Weak.

Gerry You really don't like those

medical words do you?

Peter They're useful and necessary, but not so that patients can use them to distance themselves from their illnesses. Dressing gown?

Gerry Over there.

Peter I'll get it. Now sit down here while I change the sheets. Here, read this. There's an article here I thought might interest you, 'AIDS – the search for a cure'. Page 17. That'll cheer you up. I was reading it up in the medical library this afternoon. They've come a long way.

Gerry They've found what they think is the virus, well two viruses actually. Just like they used to think it was caused by poppers and then by semen and then –

Peter They're doing their best.

Gerry To get the next Nobel Prize! The National Institute of Health and the Pasteur Institute taking each other to court to patent their tests. And it's tests that bring the money in you know, not a vaccine. And as for a cure! There'll only be money for that when they realize that everyone's affected.

Peter It'll happen.

Gerry But when? They found cures for Lassa Fever and Legionnaire's disease soon enough, and with millions of government money. But this is different, AIDS is associated with junkies and queers so the first priority is a test so that the rest of you are safe.

Peter There's something in that. They'd soon find a cure for a disease that only Cabinet Ministers got.

Gerry They *are* the real disease. And expecting us to take seriously those prissy safe sex advertisements. I mean whose ever heard of 'rectal sex'? Of course there were no pictures, if the ads had actually been erotic someone might have read them.

Peter But at least the Health Department is publishing something. I mean that *must* be a step forward?

Gerry Sure they are, in papers which have distorted everything about gay people for years.

Peter Well that is something you lot have rather brought upon yourselves isn't it? I mean flaunting all those lapel badges and earrings and –

Gerry And all those wedding rings and pictures of children on office desks.

Peter You see what I'm getting at?

Gerry And you can't see what I'm getting at. I've never been allowed to just happen to be gay, always 'The Homosexual'.

Peter Come on, back into bed.

Gerry What for, the next batch of tests? There must be more of me in that laboratory than there is in this bed.

Peter Now there's something else I was supposed to do . . .

Gerry I presumed that you weren't here for the pleasure of my company.

Peter Your papers haven't come over from St Andrew's. There are a few things Sister wanted to get sorted out for the records. She was going to do it herself but –

Gerry Why use up two pairs of disposable gloves where one will do? Leave the form here and I'll fill it in. Unless you don't want me to touch it.

Peter There's no need to take unnecessary risks.

Gerry Or unnecessary precautions.

Peter Right, home address?

Gerry What's my room number?

Peter Pardon?

Gerry The number of this room.

Peter 501.

Gerry Room 501, Avard Wing, East London Teaching Hospital.

Peter I mean your permanent address.

Gerry Oh, so do I.

Peter But where were you before you came here?

Gerry Oh there was . . . somewhere. But there's no going back. I couldn't afford the mortgage while I was here, could I?

Peter Social services should have seen to that. So where will you go afterwards?

Gerry A small sub-basement, I expect. Come off it Peter Dennett! We both know where I'm going, unembalmed in a body-bag. Uncomfortable?

Peter Where there's life there's –

Gerry Death. I live from one day to the next. You're the one who keeps talking about the future.

Peter So, no permanent address.

Gerry No, but I'm sure if you write to me care of the East London Teaching Hospital the message will get through, not that anyone's tried. Which reminds me, could I have a telephone please?

Peter I'll have one sent in. It ought to stay in here for the time being.

Gerry Of course, wouldn't want any viruses travelling up the wires now would we?

Peter Next of kin?

Gerry Another cheerful thought for a Friday evening.

Peter Everyone who comes in here gets asked about their next of kin.

Gerry My mother I suppose, Mrs Pamela Grimond.

Peter Of?

Gerry 27 Ridley Road, Stafford, Staffs.

Peter Quite a long way to come and visit.

Gerry Which may be why she doesn't. Only it isn't. You know I haven't even thought about her for months. But she *is* my next of kin.

Peter Blood's thicker than water, eh?

Gerry And far more infectious.

Peter I know it's not my business Gerry, but have you thought about a will?

Gerry Frequently. But nobody ever leaves me anything. Oh you mean my will. What's the point. My worldly goods are contained within those two suitcases. I'd have to sell one to pay a solicitor, which would rather defeat the object of the exercise.

Peter Well, I think that's all we need to know for the minute.

Gerry Close my file and go onto the next one then?

Peter I could always stay and talk.

Gerry What's my ration? Half a pint of the milk of human kindness?

Peter I'd like to get to know you. Did you have – have you got a job? Or are you one of Maggie's millions?

Gerry Amenities Department of the Greater London Council.

Peter Oh.

Gerry At least I managed to outlive that.

Peter Some people recover.

Gerry Some people linger. None recover. This ward is for the no-hopers isn't it?

Peter Yes.

Gerry It's strange . . .

Peter Go on.

Gerry No, you've got better things to do. Go and talk to one of those other patients you mentioned. They might show you a bit of gratitude.

Peter I'd like to listen.

Gerry Tell me Peter, is that mask for my benefit or yours?

Peter You're the one at risk from opportunistic infections.

Gerry Dr Hillman said I've got that already.

Peter It would defeat the object of a protected environment if I took it off.

Gerry You know what I long for. An *un*protected environment. None of this will make any difference you know.

Peter You read too much for your own good.

Gerry Or for your peace of mind?

Peter All right, so the mask's for my benefit then. Do you want me to die?

Gerry Hang on, a minute ago you were waxing lyrical about my chances. You should know AIDS is one of the least infectious diseases in the world! We'd have to get into things for which I haven't the energy nor you the inclination for that to happen. Like blood transfusion between consenting adults.

Peter Why does it mean so much to you?

Gerry I can't talk to a guy whose face I've never seen. And I'd like to Peter, I've never been so lonely.

Peter You're our first AIDS case here, we're just being careful. If it makes that much of a difference. (**Peter** *removes the mask.*) Is that better?

Gerry And the gloves. You look as if you're about to advertize Domestos.

Peter (*removes gloves*) Well?

Gerry Good bone structure.

Peter Go on then, I'm listening.

Gerry About your bone structure, it's tempting.

Peter No. You know, what you were going to say before.

Gerry 'Why'd you do it?' my mam asked.

Peter Do what?

Gerry Go with a man. Not that it was the first time. Weren't seduction either, not on his part at least. Nothing fancy. A shot in the dark. Then I walked to Marsden Rock, thinking to myself. Stood on the beach for a while, skimmed some stones into the sea and beachcombed back to Roker, the Sunnyside Guest House. 'What did you do this afternoon?' my mam asked when I sat down to tea. So I told her. 'Why'd you do it?' she asked, as if it was something I'd done out of spite.

Peter And was that it?

Gerry That was the start of it. I'd simply decided to stop lying. Not come out in a blaze of nail varnish or anything like that. Didn't make things any easier of course, just simpler. I exorcized the guilt that afternoon on Whitburn Sands. The shame took much longer.

Peter I don't understand.

Gerry Guilt is how you feel about what you are. Shame is how you feel about how other people feel about what you are. I used to move every year so's I'd not have to worry about when the landlord would find out. It takes time to build up an immunity. Right up to the time I met Hughie I suppose. We'd been friends for about two years before we became lovers. And it lasted you know, five years. Not exclusively you understand – well you probably don't. But I'd been avoiding American accents like –

Peter – the Plague?

Gerry Precisely. Not that it made any difference of course. It's what you do that matters, not who you do it with. It started off like any old fever. Most venereal diseases feel venereal, I mean you start to notice them between the legs don't you?

Peter So I've read.

Gerry Well you've been lucky, or very self-controlled. Anyway this was what they now call ARC, AIDS-related complex, which doesn't usually develop into the full-blown syndrome. Hughie was very good about taking time off work to look after me, of course he couldn't tell them why. And then friends would come round with grapes – why is it always grapes? – and copies of 'Punch' they'd started reading on the bus and say how thankful I should be that it wasn't AIDS, because if it was you see I'd know. Went to St Edmund's for tests and I asked. (*Scottish accent.*) 'Too soon to tell' says this nice Scottish consultant, 'but you should avoid sharing razor blades until we're sure.' I never trust anyone who calls himself 'we'. The results came, two months later.

Peter It must have still been a shock.

Gerry It wasn't shock, it was anger. I was angry at the bloke who infected me, at the doctors for taking so long, and at myself, I suppose, for taking them so seriously. After that it became very noticeable.

Peter What did?

Gerry People stopped coming round for meals, even if Hughie was doing the cooking, rushed off before I had time to kiss them goodbye. Back at work they didn't even have the sensitivity to pretend. My desk had been discreetly moved to the other end of the room and I started being asked to make written reports rather than present them in person. Of course no-one actually mentioned AIDS because welfare records are confidential. So I took the easy way out and resigned. That's the real test of immunity. It took me years to build up a resistance to the way people treated me as gay and now that's as compromised as my physical immunity. Hughie was being treated as an honorary AIDS case, even though he'd had the anti-body test and not come out positive. There was so much contradictory advice that we forgot about sex – well didn't forget, just stopped having it. Now Hugh couldn't stay out all night when I was bad so he started bringing men home. Not that we'd ever been possessive. The nights didn't bother me, it was the mornings after.

Lights change **Hugh** *enters.*

Hugh You awake Gerry?

Gerry Yes.

Hugh Sleep well?

Gerry Off and on. Anyone I know?

Hugh Who'd you mean?

Gerry The Man Who Was Thursday. There's no need to hustle him out at the crack of dawn like I was your landlady. I could do with the company as much as you.

Hugh I'm sorry Gerry.

Gerry What's there to be sorry for?

Hugh For not being open about it.

Gerry Well next time I'll make breakfast for the two of you, OK?

Hugh Gerry, what are you saying? I mean they don't know about you, or us, or any of this . . .

Gerry 'They'. So there isn't *someone* in particular?

Hugh No, just Mr Thursday.

Gerry There should be.

Hugh What are you trying to do?

Gerry Be a saint. (*Pause.*)

Hugh You hungry?

Gerry A cup of tea'd be nice. Any left in

the pot?

Hugh I'll make a fresh one.

Lights change.

Gerry So maybe it was the best thing for both of us when I went into St Andrew's. Soon after that I got a letter from Hughie. A letter! From the man who so hated writing I had to sign all the Christmas cards from the two of us. He would always, but always, telephone. Would you pass that folder?

Peter This one?

Gerry Yes. Short and to the point.

Gerry *passes the letter to* **Peter**.

Hugh 'Dearest Gerry, I hope that you have settled into St Andrew's. Do let me know if there is anything else you need. I'm trying to get someone else to share the flat as I can't manage the mortgage alone – but no takers yet. I'd be sorry to leave a place with so many happy memories, but perhaps it's for the best. Love, Hughie.'

Peter So that was how it happened?

Gerry That was the sweet sorrow. (**Peter** *misses the reference.*) 'Good night! Good night! Parting is such sweet sorrow.' *Romeo and Juliet.* Lately I've become quite a literary bloke. You see when I resigned I had a lot of spare time, not being ill enough to be hospitalized, and got in the habit of going to libraries. Read everything I'd been promising I would and never got around to: Tolstoi and Proust and *Gone With The Wind*. That was when I started reading about AIDS. Kept copies of a few things. There was this one for instance, the ritual they used in the middle ages for casting out lepers. They'd take the person into the church and kneel them under a black cloth between two trestles, the ones they put coffins on. Then the priest would say: 'I forbid you ever to enter churches or go into a mill or bakehouse or into any assemblies of people.'

The company (*this speech to be recited by the rest of the cast*) 'I forbid you ever to wash your hands or even any of your belongings in spring or stream of water of any kind, and if you are thirsty you must drink water from your cup;
I forbid you ever to go out henceforth without your leper's dress that you may be recognized by others, and you must not go outside your house unshod;
I forbid you, wherever you may be, to touch anything you may wish to buy otherwise than with a rod or staff to show what you want;
I forbid you to have intercourse with any woman other than your own wife;
I forbid you to touch infants or young folk, whosoever they may be, or to give to them or to others any of your possessions;
I forbid you henceforth to eat or drink in any company except that of lepers. And know that when you die you will be buried in your own house, unless, by favour obtained beforehand, in the church.

Gerry Then the person was given a coat, shoes, clappers to warn of his coming, a cloak, knife, plate and other necessaries. Then, leaving, the priest would say 'Worship God and give thanks to God. Have patience and the Lord be with thee. Amen.'

Peter It's horrible.

Gerry But for me it does have ... resonances. Anyway I don't have to reconcile an all-loving God with Acquired Immune-Deficiency Syndrome and none of the priests who visit this place have had the impertinence to try. Sometimes I feel like that man kneeling in the church.

Peter But there are support groups for AIDS patients, there's counselling and meetings, even I've read about them.

You don't have to be on your own.

Gerry I'd just like to go somewhere without those four scarlet letters being the first thing that anyone ever knows about me. Only now there's nothing else for me *to* be.

Peter You still think life should be fair?

Gerry No, but not fucking vindictive!

Peter Tomorrow I'm going to take you out to meet some of the other patients. Mrs Richards, never smoked a cigarette in her life, got cancer of the throat so they hacked out her vocal chords. They didn't find the cancer and now she's on a chemo treatment as painful as anything you'll ever know.

Gerry And you? You've seen it all and suffered none of it!

Peter Sometimes the effects are similar. (*Pause.*) Let's take a walk.

Gerry A walk? It's dark!

Peter We'll wrap you up snug in a wheelchair, you can see the river from the grounds. I sometimes go there after a night shift and watch the sun rise.

Gerry You sound very lonely.

Peter There's a difference between loneliness and solitude.

Scene Five

The Lecture Theatre

Peter We were out for about half an hour. After that Gerry was tired, which had been the whole point, so I put him to bed. I saw quite a lot of him over the following week. His condition was very erratic, one day we'd practically have to lock him in and the next we'd be waking him for meals. He didn't seem to have any visitors, but if he had and he'd treated them the way he treated us they'd not have come back for more.

Scene Six

The Isolation Room, five days after Scene One.
Furnished as previously except it now contains a telephone.
Gerry *writes a letter.*

Gerry Dearest Hughie, I called you last week but am writing in case you did not get the message from Roy. I presume that he's now sharing the flat, he had the air of a man answering his own telephone. I never answered your note to me at St Andrew's. If there is anything of mine left in the flat then keep it. You were to – you will have it in any case. You may have heard I have now been moved to the East London Teaching Hospital where fate has been particularly unkind to me, I have a straight male nurse. He's actually quite amusing company, but in spite of rather than because of his attempts to be so. My white cell count is down to 2,700 and I am supposed to be in a 'stable condition', which means I'm no worse this morning than I was last night. I still think of you often and of the great times we had together even that rather fraught visit to your parents. I'm not going to ask you to visit me. There's no need for me to feel manipulative and you guilty. Perhaps you want your last memories of me to be happy ones. I like to think that's the reason. (**Gerry** *looks at the letter and tears it up.*) Hughie! Where are you?

Scene Seven

A bench beside the Thames, Evening.

Marie Come on Pete, let's go back to the car.

Peter I'm enjoying the fresh air. Why don't we sit out here for a while? You know in thirteen months of knowing you that's the first time I've ever spent a whole evening with your mates.

Marie Well, whenever they're not working you are! They enjoy seeing you.

Peter Well I hope I live up to their expectations. I mean I'm nothing special.

Marie That's what I said.

Peter Oh. You know them from school then?

Marie Most of them. Didn't you keep in touch with your schoolmates?

Peter No, remember I told you. I dropped right out of sight and then worked in a hostel for a year. After that they'd all gone their separate ways.

Marie It's odd the way people choose jobs isn't it?

Peter Most of us don't choose them.

Marie That's what I mean. I was offered the shop job and I'd been doing it for six months before I even thought about whether it was what I wanted.

Peter Is it?

Marie It'll do. My dad says I ought to pack it in and do a secretarial course.

Peter He's right. You'd earn more money than me.

Marie I do that already.

Peter No need to rub it in.

Marie You worried about your exam tomorrow?

Peter Nah, know I'm going to fail anyway.

Marie You always say that! But you never do. There's something on your mind though isn't there?

Peter Sort of.

Marie Tell me about it.

Peter One of the patients died last night. Mrs Richards. Cancer of the throat. Couldn't talk, had to use a pad and pen. When I came back on this morning she'd left a message for me, 'Hello Peter, I tried to hold on until you came back.' She left me a book of poems but I don't know when I'll have time to read them.

Marie I thought you'd be used to it by now.

Peter You always think you're immune until the next time. Take Gerry for instance.

Marie Who?

Peter He's been in the hospital a couple of weeks. Acquired Immune Deficiency Syndrome, AIDS.

Marie You never told me there was an AIDS patient in the hospital.

Peter It's quite normal these days, nothing to make a fuss about.

Marie You don't actually see him do you?

Peter Every day.

Marie They can't make you.

Peter No, but he's terminally ill like all the others. I can't pick and choose the illnesses I like you know. And we seem to be able to communicate. There's a sort of chemistry.

Marie It's the chemistry I'm worried about. I hope you're being tested or something.

Peter There's nothing to test, there's really no risk love. Anyway I was a bit fed up with him today. About lunchtime he gave me a letter for his mate Hugh. Suppose he thought it might evoke more guilt delivered personally. I hate being taken for granted.

Marie I know what you mean

Peter So I took the letter and drove down to this basement flat in Clapham.

Peter *stands in the doorway of flat.*

Compromised Immunity 65

Hugh (*offstage*) You going to answer that Roy?

Hugh *enters wiping his hands on a tea towel.* Hello.

Peter Hello, are you Hugh? I think he lives here.

Hugh I am. He does. You're not selling anything?

Peter No, it's personal.

Hugh You'd better come in. Sorry about the mess. It's not mine.

Peter I've come from the hospital, East London Teaching Hospital.

Hugh Is it bad news?

Peter I'm not sure.

Hugh You're not sure?

Peter No, Gerry asked me to deliver this letter. I don't know what it's about.

Hugh Oh, that's a relief, I thought something had happened to him.

Peter Well it has, hasn't it?

Hugh I meant something else. So he asked you to bring it round?

Peter Yes, I'm one of the nurses, Peter Dennett.

Hugh I'm Hugh, but you know that.

Peter Yes, Gerry told me all about you.

Hugh What makes you think Gerry knows all about me? . . . How is he?

Peter He's in pain and he's lonely and he's dying. I think he'd appreciate a visit.

Hugh That's not exactly what it says here.

Peter Well, if you read between the lines . . .

Hugh That is where he writes. Look, I'm sorry. Is there anything else you have to tell me.

Peter There's not much to tell. I've got to go. I've arranged to meet my girlfriend.

Hugh Of course.

Peter He's got a room of his own, you can come any time.

Hugh It would be difficult. It's been so long.

Peter Well it won't be much longer.

Hugh How bad is he?

Peter I've told you. He is dying.

Hugh But how long has he got?

Peter Why does everybody want a timetable? They've given up on the chemotherapy.

Hugh Is that all a modern hospital can do. Wait for someone to die?

Peter Sometimes, and it's not easy for us either. But I do try to be there. Why is it so difficult?

Hugh This is the way that Gerry wanted it. Did he ever tell you that? Everything's black and white to you isn't it? One person in the right, the other in the wrong, and you in the middle refereeing with so much professional commitment that you can even play the amateur social worker in your spare time. After all, if it becomes too much you can just scuttle off to your girlfriend and forget about it. Would you have been so self-righteous if Gerry had been a woman?

Peter I – I suppose so, yes.

Hugh So you interrogate the ex-lovers of all your patients do you?

Peter They don't all need it.

Hugh But you know who does huh? He really is better off without me.

Peter I'll see myself out. Of course I could drive him down here if that'd be more convenient.

Hugh You wouldn't dare!

Peter But only if he asked me to. I hope to see you again.

Peter *returns to* **Marie**.

Marie No wonder you look drained. You shouldn't take it personally....

Peter You have to take people personally. And anyway haven't I done exactly what Hugh said I would?

Marie What else could you do?

Peter I'm worried about Gerry.

Marie You're not going to tell him what his boyfriend said?

Peter No, not that. But tomorrow's my last day, then I move to the Operating Theatre.

Marie You've been looking forward to that.

Peter Yes, only Gerry doesn't know yet.

Marie You could get him a present.

Peter Good idea. I'll just have time after the exam.

Marie It's getting cold. Let's go back to the car.

Peter You coming to the hostel?

Marie I thought you had an exam tomorrow. All right.

They kiss.

Scene Eight

The Isolation Room the following afternoon. **Gerry** *is sitting on the floor surrounded by photographs.* **Peter** *enters with a wrapped present.*

Peter What are you doing down there? Praying to Mecca?

Gerry I'm well past prayer now. Sorting through my photographs.

Peter You've certainly got plenty.

Gerry Not enough. This is supposed to be a record of 36 years.

Peter Let me see. Is that a school one. Which one is you?

Gerry Guess.

Peter The cocky one in the back row.

Gerry Nah, that's Paul Wheatley, used to run the school protection racket, now he's a Detective Inspector. That's me, fourth from the end.

Peter Nothing like you.

Gerry Twenty years do not leave one unscarred, look what's happened to me in one. The boy next to me was sent down for aggravated assault six years later, that one's a rabbi, he lives in Ilford and drives a taxi. I've lost touch with the others.

Peter Any of your family?

Gerry I didn't keep them.

Peter What about this one, it must be your sister, she's so like you!

Gerry She is me. Dragged up to the eyeballs.

Peter Did you do that often?

Gerry No, it was some fancy dress do. Before I met Hughie... Good God, that's Gary Campbell, the man who put the camp in Campbell. So sweet to me he was, when I first came down to the smoke. Last I heard, he'd retired to Dulwich.

Peter Isn't that?

Gerry Yes?

Peter Nothing.

Gerry Yes Peter, that's Hughie, in Edinburgh. (**Gerry** *weeps*.) I'm sorry, I'm sorry.

Peter Can I get you anything?

Compromised Immunity

Gerry No, I'll be fine. I'm sorry about that.

Peter Drink this.

Gerry It's the first time it's happened in ages. I just remembered. (**Gerry** *cries.* **Peter** *holds him until he is calm. There is a moment of embarrassment.* **Peter** *releases* **Gerry**.)

Peter How are you feeling now?

Gerry Steady, as a Rock. So much for avoiding physical contact.

Peter I did it without thinking.

Gerry Maybe it's time you did some thinking Peter. You did see Hughie?

Hugh He was in when I took your letter round, yes.

Gerry Did he give you an answer?

Peter He hadn't read it properly when I left. I dare say you had a lot to tell him.

Gerry Only one thing actually. So when d'you think he'll be round?

Peter I don't.

Gerry But he didn't actually say that?

Peter No. Yes. I don't think he knows how to start again. He said something about it being the way you wanted it.

Gerry Perhaps it was. But I can't stop thinking about him.

Peter Well don't, he's fine.

Gerry It would just have been nice to see him again. I shut my family out of my life once – though the feeling was mutual. And as for my friends...

Peter I'm with you.

Gerry And I appreciate that, I don't think you can guess how much. But at the end of the day it is what you're paid for.

Peter And that means I have no real feelings?

Gerry It means I never know when you're being professionally nice and when you're doing it in your spare time.

Peter Does it matter?

Gerry It does to me. When you've moved from healthy relationships to being ill and having to depend on people like I relied on Hughie and I'm coming to rely on you then there's an imbalance. Things are never the same again.

Peter So I make things worse?

Gerry No, but only so much better. Peter, there are limits.

Lights change as in Scene Four. **Hugh** *and* **Gerry** *together.*

Hugh It's ten o'clock Gerry, do you want another chapter? (**Gerry** *nods.*) 'The Landlady Bares her Soul'.
  'OK' said Mona, downing her Verdicchi, 'what was the cryptic comment all about?'
  Mrs Madrigal smiled, 'What did I say?'
  'You said Barbary Lane chose me. You meant that literally didn't you?'
  The landlady nodded. 'Don't you remember how we met?'
  'At the –'

Telephone rings.

Gerry You'd better answer it.

Hugh 278 8745, hello?... Hi there Roy... Yes, it has been a long time... it was... Sure, me too... Right now isn't a good time. I'm looking after Gerry and there's trouble at work... no, not like that, just lots of compulsory overtime... it'd be nice to see you again, but it's not really possible... Why don't I ring you some time?... Yeah, yeah, Bye.

Gerry Who was that?

Hugh No one special.

Gerry Who was he?

Hugh Roy Haines.

Gerry I remember. The little guy from over the Common. You seeing him?

Hugh Not any more.

Gerry You shouldn't stay cooped up in here you know Hughie. When they take me into hospital permanently you're going to need people like Roy.

Hugh And you'll need me.

Gerry I'll need a nurse. Someone to check the drip in my arm, clear up the diarrhoea.

Hugh I want to be with you.

Gerry Liar. (**Hugh** *leaves.*) After that he took to the spare room Awaiting my departure and his honourable discharge, if you'll pardon the expression.

Peter It's got dark all of a sudden.

Peter *turns the light on.*

Gerry So you could say I'd brought this splendid isolation on myself. Did I do the right thing Peter?

Peter I don't know. Did it seem the right thing at the time?

Gerry I couldn't stand the thought of Hughie resenting me.

Peter Well, he doesn't.

Gerry Does he think about me at all?

Peter He did yesterday. (**Peter** *yawns.*)

Gerry Tired?

Peter Yeah, had an exam this morning.

Gerry You should have told me. I'd not have given you that letter if I'd known.

Peter You had more important things on your mind. Actually I didn't tell anyone. My mum and dad can't follow the technicalities of my medical career and my friends are in the profession so they know anyway.

Gerry And Marie?

Peter I told her, she's looking forward to me getting fully qualified almost as much as I am. Then I can specialize, paediatrics maybe.

Gerry Settle down?

Peter Yeah, buy a house, get married.

Gerry And pay the alimony from the overtime?

Peter What?

Gerry That might not be what she wants.

Peter She's never said so.

Gerry Have you asked?

Peter I don't have to.

Gerry ESP must make life so much easier.

Peter That reminds me, I've got something for you, a present. Here.

Gerry Peter. You shouldn't.

Peter It's just a –

Gerry Let me open it. Isn't this exciting? A scarf! Thank you Peter, it's a lovely pattern. Did you make it yourself?

Peter Autumn's coming on. It's for when you go out.

Gerry I'll not be going out.

Peter I've taken you out. You've got to learn to be more independent. It's a sort of a leaving present.

Gerry They're not moving me again are they! Where to this time?

Peter No, they're moving me. Janice, one of the other nurses will be looking after you from now on.

Gerry So that's it? You're going?

Peter Yes?

Gerry And did you really not know

about it until this morning?

Peter I didn't want to worry you.

Gerry You hoped I'd croak before the time came, huh? Well maybe it would've been better if I had. Well, what are you waiting for?

Peter Er, nothing.

Gerry Well you'd better get on with things then. Bid your tactful farewells to the other patients.

Peter Do you really have to make it –

Gerry Goodbye Peter! (**Peter** *exits.*) And good riddance! I'm quite able to die on my own. Just let you encourage me to put it off. (**Gerry** *takes a razor blade and tests it on his thumb.*) A drop of blood, looks just like anyone else's. If only I could squeeze it all out, like water from a sponge and start again. (**Gerry** *bares his wrist.*)

As the lights change **Gerry** *moans.*

Scene Nine

The corridor a few minutes later.

Coates Oh there you are Peter, I wanted a word with you about your transfer.

Peter Yes, I'm really looking forward to it Miss Coates, do you know which theatre it'll be?

Coates Well, it might not be that simple. What ever is?

Peter Oh?

Coates The AIDS case, Grimond.

Peter What about him?

Coates You know how difficult the other nurses find him.

Peter The others! I've just had a bloody great row with him myself. Told him I'd be leaving.

Coates That's the point. He's been fine with you. You just seem to have a way with him. Now I can't force anyone to look after him. I'm sure you realize that there's a lot of anxiety about AIDS and the Unions are keeping a very close watch on things –

Peter As they should Miss Coates.

Coates It would be a pity to make a scene out of a situation that isn't going to be with us for very much longer.

Peter So you're going to reassure the other nurses that there's no risk involved?

Coates I have done, repeatedly. But when every tabloid undoes what you're trying to do it isn't easy. There isn't any risk if you observe the right precautions. I was going to mention that too. I know Dr Hillman's instructions are something over and above the official guidelines at the moment but please be careful. One AIDS case in a hospital is a distinction Peter, two would be cause for concern.

Peter I know what I'm doing Miss Coates.

Coates I'd be convinced of that if you were willing to see it through.

Peter It's not fair! I had a go at Gerry for saying that not long ago.

Coates Dr Hillman reckons it'll only be for a couple more weeks.

Peter Oh, has he told Gerry? I just think you're taking the easy way out.

Coates I think you want to do that Peter. We're a team here.

Peter I know. I just sometimes feel like a one man band-aid. All right, I'll do it – so long as . . .

Coates Yes?

Peter So long as Gerry accepts it.

Coates Good, you're thinking of his feelings.

Peter You didn't hear the two of us just now.

Coates Well let's sort it out now then.

Peter All right. I've just about got time.

They enter the Isolation Room. **Gerry** *is wholly covered by bed linen.*

Coates I think he must be asleep.

Peter Hello Gerry! I expect you're surprised I'm back, but this time it's for good, if that's what . . . oh God!

Coates I'll get doctor.

Coates *exits.* **Peter** *takes tissues to staunch bleeding and holds* **Gerry***'s arm up.*

Gerry Am I dead?

Peter It's not going to be that easy. (*A pause.*) Come on!

Act Two

Scene One

Gerry *is in the Isolation Room writing his diary. Three days have passed.*

Gerry 1 October. There's nothing quite as embarrassing as failing to kill yourself. The first thing that people ask is 'Why did you do it?' Today it was a psychiatrist, in gloves and a mask of course, there can be few more frightening sights. 'It seemed a good idea at the time' I replied. Frivolous perhaps, but quite true. If they hadn't taken away my razor blades and started watching me more avidly than 'Eastenders' I'd do it again. Still no word from Hughie. So I fill my days keeping a diary, on the grounds that writing about doing nothing is marginally less boring than doing it. Perhaps I should ask the BBC if they could serialize it. 'Plagueround – an everyday story of terminal folk'. And that is about as much scintillating prose as I can manage in one day. (**Gerry** *reaches for the telephone.*)

Scene Two

The flat.

Hugh Roy? Roy!

Hugh *puts on answering machine and starts to unpack shopping.*

Roy (*on tape*) Hughie? I'm just calling to say there's a staff meeting at the school tonight, so I won't be in till late . . . Oh, and I think I forgot to feed the cat this morning. Sorry.

George (*on tape*) Hi Roy, hi Hugh. It's George. Look, sorry but I can't make the Garden Friday. Let me know if you can't get rid of my ticket. See you on the fifteenth.

Gerry (*on tape*) Hello Hughie. Yes, it's Gerry. I rang last week and spoke to Roy. He sounded kind of flustered, and you hadn't rung back so I just wondered if you got the message. Hughie, I – the number is 272 3965.

Sally (*on tape*) Mr Emmerson. Sally here, from the office. Just to say I've got the returns from the Quantity Surveyor –

Hugh *turns off the machine.*

Scene Three

The Isolation Room the following evening. **Gerry** *is asleep in the dark.*

Peter (*has been drinking*) Hey? What was that? Can't even find the bloody light switch. I know you're on the wall somewhere. There you are. (**Peter** *turns on the light.*) Oh, flowers, isn't that nice. What a lovely smell. I trod on them you know Gerry, did you hear me? I trod on your flowers. You should have asked for a vase. Gerry? GERRY!

Compromised Immunity 71

Gerry I can hear you. What do you want?

Peter I said you shouldn't've left those flowers there, I trod on them.

Gerry What are you doing here? You're off this evening.

Peter They're from Hughie aren't they? I told you he'd come.

Gerry He didn't come. He had them sent.

Peter Well, like I said, he was worried about you.

Gerry About himself you mean!

Peter I think it was a very nice thing to do.

Gerry If he'd waited a little bit longer he could've sent a wreath instead. What do I want with flowers anyway? I can't even smell them! Did you realize that?

Peter Probably just a temporary occlusion.

Gerry One by one my organs are coming out on indefinite stoppage and all you can throw me is medical jargon. Soon I'll be on a drip and my sight'll start to go. I'm an invalid Peter, that means in*va*lid, I don't count. Please take those flowers away. And turn the light off when you go. I had actually got to sleep you know.

Peter I'm not going. You're getting up.

Gerry It is half past nine in the evening.

Peter You got a razor anywhere?

Gerry You know they took it away last week. Now what are you –

Peter Thought so. (**Peter** *produces a razor from his pocket.*)

Gerry What are you doing? I'm not going anywhere.

Peter Sit still.

Gerry The water's too hot.

Peter Good. It'll clean out your pores.

Gerry I don't want a shave.

Peter Patients don't want a lot of things, but they get them anyway. Doctor's orders, well nurse's orders, which are the next best thing. Makes a change to shave someone at this end. Don't move your head. I'm not qualified to make incisions. There. That's much better. You do look pale though. Got any make-up?

Gerry You're drunk! What are you doing Peter?

Peter Getting you ready.

Gerry Ready for what?

Peter Ready to go out. How are you feeling?

Gerry I am cold and tired and in pain. And you are talking complete nonsense about going out.

Peter Actually I thought you might want to go out to Night Rites. (**Peter** *throws tickets on the bed.*)

Gerry It's a joke isn't it? Just leave me alone.

Peter It's not a joke.

Gerry It would kill me.

Peter Is that such a bad way to go? If it comes to that I'd rather face a disciplinary hearing without you around as a witness.

Gerry You've got the tickets and everything.

Peter Borrowed one of your magazines, didn't I? Hadn't the nerve to walk in Smiths and buy it.

Gerry They don't sell them in Smiths.

Peter Night Rites is all right isn't it, I mean as these places go?

Gerry Fine, I used to go there quite often.

Peter So, will you come?

Gerry I hate to turn down the offer of an evening at Night Rights with a handsome young man, but Peter, surely you can see. I can't even walk the length of this room and I'm not going to leave it upright. I'd be a spectre at the feast. I've said goodbye to all that. It literally doesn't matter a fuck.

Peter I do understand Gerry.

Gerry Understand what?

Peter What you're going through. You fancy men, I fancy women, we're not that different.

Gerry Do you think that's all it's about – screwing? You'll never understand.

Peter *exits.*

Scene Four

The Lecture Theatre.

Peter I almost hit an ambulance on the way out of the hospital. Went to Hugh's flat but there was no answer. Then I noticed the Night Rites tickets on the dashboard. Well, I thought he might be there, anyway . . . Anyway, I went. Huge place it was, music, lasers, all men of course, having a good time. Better than the gutted pubs that pass for night clubs down this way. Still I felt odd being the only straight bloke in the place and I couldn't see Hugh. With so many people I couldn't be sure. But, I didn't want to hang around in case anyone got the wrong idea, so I went for a walk by the river to clear my head.

Scene Five

A bench beside the Thames, same set as for Act One, Scene Seven.

Peter *is looking over the river.* **Ian** *enters unseen by* **Peter.**

Peter Gerry!

Ian So, who's Gerry?

Peter Who are you?

Ian Iain Edwards. Am I disturbing you?

Peter You must think I'm crazy, talking to myself.

Ian No, you could be drunk or not have anyone to tell what's on your mind. So who's Gerry?

Peter Gerry Grimond. He's in EL – the East London Teaching Hospital.

Ian What with?

Peter AIDS.

Ian That's why you were so distracted – in Night Rites I mean.

Peter You were there?

Ian Don't pretend you never noticed me.

Peter I didn't notice anything.

Ian Not even your own name?

Peter I was too full of Gerry and what he said when I tried to make him come out this evening. 'I'd be the spectre at the feast.' And he would. Too near the bloody bone. Gerry thought it'd never happen to him. So did three hundred other poor sods. So do we.

Ian Don't try and make me feel guilty. I've just run away from four years of that!

Peter I didn't ask you to talk.

Ian I'm sorry. I can see you're upset Peter, I would be if it'd hit me that close. What are you going to do about Gerry?

Peter There's nothing I can do, except be there with him. I don't suppose you've got a free evening this week?

Ian Yes, why?

Compromised Immunity

Peter No, it doesn't matter.

Ian No, go on.

Peter I wondered if you might be interested in maybe coming up to the hospital.

Ian The hospital?

Peter It'd be really great if you could. I was looking for a friend of his, Hugh, tonight. All he sees is me and nurses, medical people. He needs a breath of fresh air. He needs some new faces.

Ian OK.

Peter You sure?

Ian Yes.

Peter Thanks.

Ian I suppose you're quite genned up what with Gerry's illness. I was thinking of getting that test done.

Peter HTLV? Why?

Ian I've been worried, you know, about not sleeping, swollen glands and that. (**Peter** *feels* **Ian**'s *lymph glands.*) Oh! Your hands are cold!

Peter I don't think there's anything wrong there. But there's a clap clinic up at the hospital if you want to be sure. I can show you where it is.

Ian Would you?

Peter When can you come, tomorrow?

Ian Sure, damn! I've just realized. Sorry, not tomorrow, I'm working. The day after OK?

Peter Yes, it's just past Limehouse Crossroads. I should be around about seven-thirty. Not quite sure what my shifts are. If I'm not there go right in. Room 501. You'll not be interrupting anyone.

Ian I'll see you there Peter.

Ian *exits.*

Peter (*calls after him*) How did you know my name (**Peter** *realizes that he is wearing an identity badge.*)

Scene Six

Peter *enters the Isolation Room and affixes a drip to the unconscious* **Gerry**, *checks that it is in place and exits.*

Scene Seven

The Isolation Room two days later, **Gerry** *is in bed, his condition evidently worse.* **Ian** *enters with flowers.*

Ian Excuse me, is this room 501?

Gerry Yes, 101 was already engaged.

Ian (*not registering the reference*) And you're Gerry Grimond?

Gerry Yes, word's evidently got out. Might I be permitted to ask who you are?

Ian My name's Ian, Ian Edwards.

Gerry Hello Ian. Now what is this total stranger doing in my bedroom?

Ian It seems rather an intrusion when you put it like that.

Gerry It is.

Ian I saw Peter Dennett at Night Rites on Saturday night.

Gerry Ah, so he went on his own then?

Ian Very much so.

Gerry And did he ask you to come?

Ian Sort of. He seemed very low about it all.

Gerry I do wish he wouldn't see my condition as a sign of his own inadequacies. (**Ian** *expresses incomprehension.*) As a nurse I mean.

Ian He works here?

Gerry Didn't he tell you? He's my nurse.

Ian So there's nothing . . . between you?

Gerry Good God! You do know he's straight? (**Gerry** *laughs*.)

Ian He was acting strange last night – that would explain it. I thought he was cruising me. I did a dedication to him. 'Stranger in Paradise'.

Gerry Very appropriate!

Ian I was thinking of myself.

Gerry Make yourself comfortable Ian. It's about time a couple of Mr Dennett's complications got together.

Ian I brought you these.

Gerry You shouldn't, we're not even dating. Mind you neither were Gabriel and the BVM.

Ian What?

Gerry The Archangel Gabriel brought lilies to the Virgin Mary. You know, when God wanted her to be a surrogate mother. They're lovely. When Hugh sent flowers I was less gracious.

Ian Peter was looking for someone called Hugh last night. Were you lovers? (**Gerry** *nods*.)

Gerry Imagine the scene if Peter had found him! What would've we said? I'm better off alone.

Ian You're not alone.

Gerry I'm not am I? (*Pause*.) You know it's nice having someone whose not a doctor or a nurse around again. Where are you from Ian?

Ian You wouldn't know it. Ammanford, in South Wales.

Gerry And have you been in London long?

Ian Arrived at Paddington two months ago.

Gerry With a luggage label round your neck saying 'Please look after this homosexual'?

Ian Almost! I'm in a hostel at the moment. Still looking for somewhere to live.

Gerry Tried Gay Switchboard?

Ian I've tried everywhere. But it's the worst time – start of the academic year, see.

Gerry Hm, I might be able to do something. Open that case over there. Go on, it's not locked. There's a blue address book in the top.

Ian Here you are.

Gerry There's a guy, Gary Campbell, might be worth a call. He helped me out many years ago when I first came to London. He's retired now but he might have a room. Anyway he's the sort of guy who knows people. Here's the number.

Ian You're sure he won't mind?

Gerry Not Gary. Give him my regards. I don't think we've met in three years. I got out of touch with so many people. Hughie and I decided it was important to spend as much time as we could together.

Ian So that's why you're here on your own? Thanks. I wish I could do something in return.

Gerry Maybe you have.

Ian I'll come and tell you how I got on. Unless you'd rather . . .

Gerry Please do.

Ian See you tomorrow. Goodbye.
(**Ian** *exits*.)

Scene Eight

The corridor.

Peter Ian! So you came to see Gerry.

Ian Yes. He's tough, isn't he?

Peter That's one way of putting it. Thank you for coming. Whatever I try and say we don't really have much in common.

Ian That must give you plenty to discuss.

Peter I suppose it does.

Ian He's not got long has he?

Peter They reckon about a week.

Ian You know Peter, I followed you the other night. I wanted to speak to you.

Peter Really?

Ian Yes, I rather fancied you actually.

Peter I'm not gay.

Ian Well isn't that a shame? You will let me know if you change your mind?

Peter You lot are worse than Jehovah's Witnesses.

Ian I think we have more fun. Well?

Peter You're bloody persistent.

Ian That's how I'm still gay after eighteen years in Ammanford.

Peter You should be grateful to Gerry you know. A month ago I'd've smashed your face in for saying that.

Ian So what will you do?

Peter Thank you for the compliment. (**Marie** *enters.*) Marie, what are you doing here?

Marie Come to see you.

Ian I'd best be off then.

Peter See you tomorrow Ian. (**Ian** *exits.*) Well, what's the matter?

Marie You said you'd be moving to the Operating Theatre. Did you really think I'd never find out?

Peter I will be. There's just been a slight delay. I was going to explain.

Marie Explain what?

Peter Come with me. Come on.

Marie Where are you taking me?

They enter the Isolation Room.

Gerry Hello Peter, now who's this?

Peter This is Marie, I think I mentioned her. (**Gerry** *extends a hand,* **Marie** *hesitates and then shakes it.*)

Gerry Hello, I'm Gerry Grimond.

Marie At last. I'm not sure what I expected.

Gerry Not a pretty sight.

Peter I told you about Gerry didn't I? About how he's dying of AIDS, about how he's gay? What I didn't tell you is that he tried to top himself when I told him I was going to be moved. He didn't know I'd been asked to stay on. But I didn't want you worrying.

Marie You lied to me Peter. OK so I was worried. Who wouldn't be? I'm not stupid. Do you think it helps, you never telling me anything?

Gerry She's got a point.

Peter Gerry!

Marie Peter!

Coates (*from doorway*) Mr Dennett! Could I have a word please?

Peter Coming! (**Peter** *exits.*)

Gerry Well, aren't you going too?

Marie I can't. Not with her outside. She almost stopped me coming in when I asked her the way.

Gerry You know I really forced him into it with all my (**Gerry** *mimes his suicide bid*).

Marie Oh, if he'd asked what I'd thought I'd've told him to do it. Only he didn't.

Gerry You mean a lot to him you know.

Marie Yes, only I'm not sure how much he means to me. Guess I'm not cut out to be a hospital widow. Maybe it's me. Looking for this knight in shining armour.

Gerry Oh, so was I. Long as I had a can opener.

Marie Only I didn't really want that at all. If Peter's going to protect me by lying –

Gerry He was protecting himself. When I came here I was a right bastard. Rude, aggressive, hurtful. Peter was the only one to realise that under it all I was afraid. But to tackle that he had to get involved. Not here (**Gerry** *touches his temple.*) but here. (**Gerry** *touches his heart.*)

Marie He said that once. About thinking you're immune, until next time.

Gerry That's right. And it's a real slap in the face when one of your terminal patients tries to kill himself. I've not made things easy for him, or for you.

Marie I suppose I've been jealous of you.

Gerry Me?

Marie Yes. Never get involved with anyone in the medical profession Gerry.

Gerry I've not had much choice lately. Oh, thanks for the scarf.

Marie It was from Peter.

Gerry Yes, but it was your idea wasn't it? Did you get a staff discount?

Marie (*laughs*) It wasn't one of ours. (*A pause.*)

Gerry Well, you'd better say goodbye to Peter. And thanks for coming to see me.

Marie That wasn't why I came.

Gerry Wasn't it?

Marie But I'm glad I did.

Scene Nine

The Isolation Room six days later. It is full of cards and flowers. **Gerry** *is in bed. The telephone rings and he picks it up.*

Gerry This is Gerry Grimond coughing . . . sick bed humour . . . Oh hi Carlos. How'd' you get my number? . . . Oh, Gary? . . . (**Peter** *enters with a kidney bowl containing equipment for the scene.*) How are you . . . And Rupert? . . . He didn't! . . . Uh-huh . . . Awful to tell the truth. (**Peter** *takes* **Gerry**'s *pulse.*) Right now I'm being poked about by a nurse . . . Sorry about that . . . Sure, if you think it won't put you off your dinner . . . Room 501, Avard Wing, East London Teaching Hospital . . . They'll be putting up signs soon . . . OK Carlos, tomorrow . . . Goodbye (**Peter** *takes the phone from* **Gerry**.) Was that really necessary?

Peter Yes. You've been talking too much. (**Peter** *puts a thermometer in* **Gerry**'s *mouth.*)

Ian (*carrying a bag of shopping*) Can I come in?

Peter Well, he'll be sleeping soon. (**Gerry** *beckons to* **Ian**.) Right come on in Ian.

Ian Any visitors today? (**Gerry** *nods.*)

Peter Four. Five now.

Ian Let me guess. Angela Grey? . . . Yes. Mike and Alex? Do they count as two? Uh-huh. Can't think who the fourth might be. (**Gerry** *silenced by his thermometer, begins a charade.*)

Peter One word, two syllables, first syllable. Foot? . . .

Ian Mr Foot?

Peter Toes?

Ian One. One toe? (**Gerry** *nods.*) Leg?

Peter Knee? Tony. (**Gerry** *nods.*)

Ian Who's Tony?

Compromised Immunity

Peter I don't know. Tony who? (**Gerry** *begins another charade.*) One word, two syllables. First syllable. Dead? Reading a book? Finished?

Ian Done with? (**Gerry** *indicates 'shorter'.*)

Peter Shorter.

Ian Done. (**Gerry** *nods and mimes walking his fingers.*)

Peter Walking up a hill? Uphill? Hill?

Ian Tony Dunhill! (**Peter** *and* **Ian** *laugh.*)

Peter (*removing the thermometer from* **Gerry***'s mouth*) It's probably less tiring if you talk.

Ian I'm not disturbing you am I Peter?

Peter No, I can work round you. With all these flowers there's a lot to do. Did you have anything to do with this?

Ian Sort of. I've just got in touch with some of his old mates. They didn't even know you were here.

Peter There's some more post.

Ian D'you want to read it? Let me see. There's a card, from Philip and Tim. I don't know them.

Peter They were here the other day.

Gerry We used to work together.

Ian More cards. Alain, Amyn . . . You've been quite a cosmopolitan on the quiet haven't you? No wonder this one came in a plain envelope. We'll have to hide that from Sister.

Peter I think Sister's seen more male anatomy than that, professionally speaking.

Ian And a letter from Hugh Emmerson.

Peter Do you want it read out?

Gerry No.

Ian No?

Gerry No!

Peter Isn't this what you've been waiting for.

Gerry I don't want to read it. Hugh and I thought the answer to someone's problems was someone else. It isn't. It's everybody else.

Peter You mean Mike and Alex and Angela and Carlos . . . and Ian?

Gerry And Peter. (*Telephone rings, as* **Peter** *answers it* **Ian** *kisses* **Gerry** *goodbye and exits.*)

Peter Hello? Hello Gary. No, he's resting at the moment. He's got your number hasn't he. Yeah, I'll get him to call you back. Yes. Yes. Goodbye Gary! Switchboard! No more calls for Mr Grimond right now please, he's sleeping.

Gerry I'm not sleeping.

Peter Well you should be Gerry. I don't think you should have as many visitors. You know . . . your days are numbered.

Gerry So?

Peter So Dr Hillman prescribed complete rest. Look what happens. Each visit leads to someone else the next day. It'll happen sooner or later and I'd rather it was later.

Gerry Do you know why I'm still here? Because they are coming, because some of the doors I shut have started opening again. I'm gay and I'm dying. I know I said being gay doesn't matter any more. But it does. Ian helped me realize that.

Peter Yes, Ian.

Gerry I do have a soft spot for him.

Peter He said the same about me.

Gerry I won't judge his taste. What will you do?

Peter That's what he asked.

Gerry You can borrow 'The Joy of Gay Sex' if you –

Peter Thanks, I said no.

Gerry Pity, it'd've made a lovely ending.

Peter It was confusing, being on the receiving end of a proposition.

Gerry What are you and Marie –

Peter Open! I'm going to clean your teeth. (**Peter** *does so with a swab, thoroughly and tenderly.*) What a mess! And with all those visitors coming to see you. Suppose we should be thankful they're not taking photographs. Though no doubt that'll be next. I'd really think with being on a drip you'd keep your mouth in a better state. It's not as if it's ever used for anything except telling other people how to run their lives.

Gerry I get the message – you still have the technology. (**Peter** *puts vaseline on* **Gerry**'s *lips.*) Could I have some water please?

Peter Here.

Gerry Thanks. (**Gerry** *drinks. As* **Gerry** *dozes* **Peter** *combs his hair and sits beside him, reading his poetry book. A long pause.*) Could you read to me Peter?

Peter Sure. What? A magazine?

Gerry No, something soothing. What's that book you've got?

Peter Oh, one of the patients, Mrs Richards, gave it to me. Modern poetry, too depressing for you.

Gerry Please.

Peter All right. Here we are then.
I have a friend
At the end
Of the world.
His name is a breath

Of fresh air,
He is dressed in
Gray chiffon. At least
I think it is chiffon.
It has a
Peculiar look, like smoke.
It wraps him round
It blows out of place
It conceals him
I have not seen his face.

But I have seen his eyes, they are
As pretty and bright
As raindrops on black twigs
In March, and heard him say:

I am a breath
Of fresh air for you, a change
By and by

Black March I call him
Because of his eyes
Being like March raindrops
On black twigs.

But this friend
Whatever new names I give him
Is an old friend. He says:

Whatever names you give me
I am
A breath of fresh air.
A change for you.

Gerry What was that?

Peter 'Black March', by Stevie Smith.

Coates (*at the door*) Is he resting?

Peter Sorry, didn't see you there.

Coates Don't get up. You must be tired yourself.

Peter A little.

Coates Thank you. For staying, I mean.

Peter Thank you. For making me stay.

Coates I came to ask you something Peter. Dr Morley's been on to me, she's a psychologist over at the Special Clinic. Some of Gerry's visitors have been her patients, they call them 'clients' that side of the building don't they? She was quite intrigued by Gerry.

Peter Aren't we all?

Coates And wondered if she might see him.

Peter Well, he seems to want to keep open house. Whatever the consequences.

Coates And maybe bring a video camera, without any fuss or anything. Just a few pictures of Gerry talking.

Peter You told her it's impossible?

Coates What do you think Gerry?

Peter He's asleep.

Coates I've been in this profession long enough to know when someone's asleep.

Gerry I'm listening.

Coates Well?

Gerry Why not?

Peter Because it's ridiculous!

Gerry
Coates } Is it?

Peter OK Gerry, you do it.

Gerry We do it.

Peter 'We', look, I can't, I mean I'm not –

Gerry Tomorrow.

Peter Tomorrow.

Gerry I can wear my new scarf.

Coates Thank you Gerry, I'll ring Dr Morley, I have her home number. (**Coates** *exits*.)

Peter You really know how to make an exit don't you? Go to sleep. You'll need your energy tomorrow. Maybe we can deal with some of those letters in the morning eh? (**Peter** *tucks* **Gerry** *in. As he does so* **Gerry** *squeezes* **Peter**'s *hand*. **Peter** *raises* **Gerry**'s *hand to his lips, kisses it and puts it under the sheet*. **Peter** *adjusts the pillow*.) Goodnight.

Gerry Goodnight, Black March. (**Peter** *looks at* **Gerry** *for a moment, turns out the light and leaves. Lights change*.)

Scene Ten

The Lecture Theatre. **Peter** *is holding* **Gerry**'s *scarf.*

Peter Two days later I started work in the Operating Theatre. I think the main difference was that there you open up other people. Gerry taught me a lot about nursing and being nursed, about being ill and about being more than an ill person. I think that the most important thing I learned is dying can isolate people. But it can also bring us together. I hope it does.

Peter *wraps scarf round him*

This Island's Mine

Philip Osment

This Island's Mine was first performed as a staged rehearsed reading as part of the Gay Sweatshop Times Twelve Festival at the Oval House on 13 March 1987 under the direction of Philip Osment with the following cast: Paul Cowling, Nancy Diuguid, Robert Ray, Margaret Robertson, Richard Sandells, Peter Shorey and Ella Wilder.

The play opened as a Gay Sweatshop production on 24 February 1988 at the Drill Hall Arts Centre with the following cast:

Martin/Stephen/Prospero	William Elliott
Selwyn/Dave	Trevor Ferguson
Jody/Mme Irina/Debbie/Wayne	Diane Hall
Marianne/Maggie/Miranda	Suzy King
Miss Rosenblum/Vladimir	Margaret Robertson
Mark/The Director/Frank	Richard Sandells
Luke	Dougray Scott
Music and lyrics by	Sharon Nassauer
Directed by	Philip Osment
Musical director	Sharon Nassauer
Designer	Kate Owen
Lighting designer	Matt Shadder
Assistant director	David Benedict
Stage Manager	Sue Tandy
Poster design	Angela Spark
Set Construction	Karen Wood
Wardrobe supervisor	Marion Duffin
Administration	Suad El Amin and RaeAnn Robertson

All other parts are played by members of the company.

A revival of **This Island's Mine** opened at the Crawfurd Centre, Glasgow on 14 June 1988 when Jody/Mme Irina/Debbie/Wayne were played by Irma Inniss and the musical director was David Benedict.

Author's Note

This play is written in a mixture of narrative and dialogue and any production has to be flexible enough to incorporate both these styles. On the whole the actors narrate in character and the lines are informed by the character's attitude and state of mind – sometimes the narration takes on the flavour of direct speech such that it becomes almost part of the dialogue. At other times the actors tell the story in a more neutral way or with just a hint of characterization which becomes stronger in the dialogue scenes. In the first production all the actors were onstage all the time which helped the flow of the play and which meant that they were able to become, for instance, part of the crowd at the airport or the bystanders on the pavement with ease. Actors not involved in a scene also played music, sang, or made tableaux when appropriate. The doubling of **Stephen/Prospero** and **Marianne/Miranda** is important. **Debbie** and **Dave** were played by Black actors even though this is not specified in the text.

Music

There is an original score and lyrics written by Sharon Nassauer to accompany the text. The music and songs are used to heighten certain moments or to make links between different parts of the play. Certain characters or situations are associated with certain pieces of music which in the first production was played and sung by the actors.

The lyrics of the funeral song which is included in the text were written by Sharon Nassauer.

Scene One

Luke The bell rings for the end of school.
Luke packs up his books,
Decides,
With nervous resolution that tonight will be the night:
'I'll tell me Mam first –
When I get home –
Tonight won't be like other nights;
Sitting at the table,
Reading out the headlines from the local paper;
Instead,
I'll make her a cup of tea
Talk to her before our Dad gets home –
Potatoes boiling on the stove,
Chops sizzling in the oven –
Say quite simply:
'I've got something to tell you Mam,
I owe it you to tell you,
I don't want to hide from you.'
Luke strolls across the playground,

Schoolboy Fourth former behind his back,
Limply flaps his wrist.

Luke Luke (usually so quick to notice)
Fails to register the insult,
Lost in his preoccupation
Of how that kitchen-table conversation might proceed:

Maggie 'What's that my dear?
Oh, just turn on the gas under those peas,
Or he'll walk in
And we won't be ready.
Now, what is it you don't want to hide from me?
You've not taken up smoking have you?'

Luke The cycle sheds –
Luke straps his briefcase on his bike,
Pedals down the drive,
Waves to Dave
(His best friend)
Staying late for rugby practice,
'Would he be my best friend if he knew?'
Through the gates and up the hill.
He pants his reassurances in the rhythm of the ride,
'You didn't do wrong, Mam,
It's nobody's fault,
I'm happy as I am.'
Pause at the top for a view of the city.
'I always stop here on my way back from school,
It makes me feel . . .
Oh, I don't know . . .
Hopeful
The whole city spread out
You can see our house down on the estate,
And further along at Nethercliffe,
The closed-down factories where our Dad used to work.'
Everyday he has a rest up here,
After the climb,
Breathing in the view,
Looking right across the city to the moors on the other side –
'Where our Dad used to take us for Sunday picnics
When we still had the car.'
And way beyond the moors where they disappear in a blue haze,
Like his whole life spread out before him.
Full of possibilities,
Exciting prospects,
Dimly discernible hopes
In the blue, hazy horizon.
'Things you've only got an inkling of,
But you know they're there,
Waiting for you.
Gives me a funny feeling in my stomach
That's almost like an ache.'
One last look,
Then it's on down the hill,
Freewheeling,
Spirits soaring,
Wind in his hair,
Eyes smarting,
Building up speed,
Then slowing down again
To stop outside the newsagents.
Some headlines,

Voice One DON'T TEACH OUR CHILDREN TO BE GAY!

Luke Some front page headlines,

Voice Two GOVERNORS TAKE ACTION TO PROTECT HEALTH AND MORALS

Luke And he's down to earth with a sickening thud.
It's a different boy who wearily rides the last few hundred yards
Between the two rows of terraced houses,
Twin walls of normality
To stem the tide.
How stupid of him to think that he could fight that,
Be accepted here.
As he parks his bike in the shed
He blushes with shame
At the idea
Of what
He had planned to say.

Scene Two

Friend 1 London,

Friend 2 A restaurant

Martin And Martin eating out with friends
Is holding forth,
Late into the night.
'Once upon a time I was lonely,
I thought I was the only one in the world,
I was filled with self-disgust.
Then I discovered hope.
Pride.
I came to see that my body was mine,
To do with as I saw fit,
And guilt belonged to the past.'

Voice One The waiters look on glumly,

Voice Two Cough,

Voice One And tap their feet,

Voice Two And ask each other,
'Aren't these people ever going to leave?'

Martin 'Then, from somewhere, comes this disease
And they use it to say,
"Didn't we tell you?
It's divine retribution.
Look where your behaviour has got you!"'

Friend 1 They sense the manager listening

Manager As he counts the evening's takings

Friend 2 'Let's just pay the bill and go.'

Martin But Martin has to finish;
'They tell us what we can and cannot do,
Don't suck –'

Two The waiters exchange a knowing smirk.

Martin 'Don't fuck – '

Manager The manager drops his pile of coins.

Martin 'And if we're not careful
We'll all be locked up in our bodies again,
Scared of touching each other.'

Manager 'Gentlemen, please,
We want to go home.'

Martin As he pays the bill
Martin hardly notices the manager's disdainful look.

Manager 'Goodnight, gentlemen.'

Martin Out on the street they kiss goodnight on the corner.
'Is it true you can't catch it from a kiss?'
Martin walks home alone,
And decides...
To give the Heath a miss.
'Early to bed, early to rise...'

Scene Three

Manager In the cafe,
The manager blows out the last candle,

Stands at the bar,
Rattles his keys,
Waits for his staff to leave.

Mark Mark Leigh, assistant chef,
Proud of his work, glad of the job,
Passes the man, says goodnight,
And goes.
'Am I imagining it?
Or are they really being funny with me?
Ever since I mentioned Selwyn,
Told them I'd got a boyfriend.'
As he crosses the street he glances back:
Dimly lit by the light over the bar
He sees his workmates gather round his boss –
Like in some mafioso film –

Chef The chef,

Waiter 1 The waiters,

Cashier The cashier ...

Manager The manager holding out a newspaper,
Pointing to headline;

Waiter 2 They read.

Waiter 1 Eyes turn

Manager Towards the door

Mark Through which Mark has just walked.

Scene Four

Martin Martin lives in a run-down house that has seen better days,
Sitting there on the corner of the street,
Out of keeping with its neighbours
Who have been converted according to the gospel of the new age –
Their once spacious rooms
Divided into flats
Cut down to size
In order that no tenants get more than their fair share of space.

Miss Rosenblum Not so the house on the corner,
It still retains its former grandeur
(In spite of damp patches on the walls
And cracks in the moulding on the ceiling)
Built to house a wealthy merchant and his family,
Now just two people live there:

Martin Martin

Miss Rosenblum And his landlady, Miss Rosenblum.
One morning,
Miss Rosenblum,
Seeing Martin in the hall,
Stops him between stair and door.

Martin (Martin just popping out to buy some milk for his tea.)

Miss Rosenblum There amongst the potted plants and yucca plants
She warns him:
'Beware!
It can happen again.
I see the signs, Mr Martin,
They want someone to blame.'

Martin Martin, smiling politely,
Tries to figure out a way
Of getting through the front door to the shop
As quickly as possible, without hurting her feelings.

Miss Rosenblum Miss Rosenblum –
A retired piano teacher,
Spends each morning –
Nine-thirty till twelve –
In an alcove at the library
Scanning every newspaper
Clicking her tongue and sighing,
Muttering to herself in Viennese German,
Reading between the lines
Looking for the signs ...
Her afternoons are spent
In a patisserie on Finchley Road,
Where she plays the piano
Every tea-time from three till five.
Afterwards she eats Strudel with her friends –
Ilse, Freddi and Hutch
And talks to them about what's

happening in the world,
Mindful of the time,
When driven out of house and homeland,
She fled the terror that swept away half her family.
'Last time, Mr Martin,
We were the pestilence,
Now you people are spreading a plague.
I see it.
You must watch.
You must be prepared.'

Martin Martin, imagining his tea going cold in the pot,
Tries to reassure her
And moves towards the door.

Miss Rosenblum But the old lady halts him,
Pinching his arm in a bony grip:
'Do not think it cannot happen here!'

Martin As he closes the door,
He hears her slowly climb the stairs
Talking to her ginger tom,

Miss Rosenblum 'Ja, Vladimir, so ist es, So wird es sein!'

Scene Five

Luke Saturday mornings,
Luke gets up late,
Has the house to himself.
His Mam and Dad catch the bus to town,
To get the week's groceries.
Luke lies in bed and hears the back door slam,
Remembers a time when his father wouldn't be seen dead on a bus
Let alone in a supermarket.
But now,
His male pride battered by lack of work,
He looks forward to these weekly outings with his wife,
The biggest event of his week.
Luke hears the bus stop at the bottom of the road
Creeps out of bed,
Pulls back the curtain,
Watches them board.
Then its out the door,
Along the passage,
Into their bedroom.
Stealing across to his Mother's dressing-table,
He catches sight of himself in the mirror,
Looking guilty as a thief.
Then continues.
Slowly opening the top right-hand drawer,
There where she keeps her jewellery
(Such as it is)
And face creams
Her lipstick and mascara,
Reminding him of other Saturdays,
When he'd crept in here, lured by the need
To open the box
And let the Pandora trapped in every man
Parade around his parent's bedroom
Decked out in his Mother's finery.
But not this morning.
He passes over the make-up and the necklaces
And reaches right to the back
Where his mother hides her brother's letters
Carefully wrapped up in tissue-paper,
Out of sight and out of mind of the rest of the family.
Letters from his uncle,
In London.
He opens one and reads the address,
Repeating it to himself several times,
Committing it to memory.
Then returns it to its envelope,
The envelope to the pile
Which he wraps in tissue as before
Placing the package, how he found it, in the drawer.

Scene Six

Martin While at Heathrow,

Martin waits to meet his wife –

Marianne Oh yes, he has a wife –
Returning from an extended trip
To visit friends and family in the States.
Marianne, a southern belle,
Escaped to England to become a dyke
Away from the persistent scrutiny of her
  North Carolina family.
From a mother whose little girl can do
  no right
And a father whose little girl can do no
  wrong –
Both impossible to live up to.
And so to England.
A marriage of convenience with Martin,
Arranged by a mutual friend,
Dual nationality was hers.
Although she sometimes feels she has no
  nation
That she's stuck somewhere in the
  mid-atlantic.
An exile in both countries.

Martin Martin, at the barrier, smiles at a
  man –
Attractive if a little tipsy –

Man Who smiles back.

Martin Is he?
Isn't he?
Martin's radar can't quite decide.

Man He asks Martin if he's meeting
  someone off the New York flight?

Martin 'Yes I am.'

Man 'So am I. I'm meeting my wife.'

Martin ('Ah well, you can't win them
  all.')
'Really? I'm meeting my wife too.'
And there she is –

Marianne 'Hi, hon, thanks for meeting
  me.'

Martin 'That's alright. You OK?'

Marianne 'Oh, Martin, Berta's dead.'
Mrs Berta Jones,
The Black woman who raised Marianne,
Nursed her through illness,
Consoled her when upset
Had been more of a Mother
Than the brittle doll-like figure who was
  her biological parent.
Marianne can still remember those
  happy hours
Spent in the kitchen with Berta.
Making bread under her all-seeing
  supervision
Or sitting in her lap
Face pressed to her bosom,
Listening to the words resonating in her
  chest
As Berta told stories,
The smell of dough mingling with her
  perfume and sweat.
Sometimes
In the arms of a lover,
The memory – so sweet –
Returns to choke her with emotion.

Jody Then there was Jody,

Marianne Berta's youngest,

Jody Jody Jones,

Marianne Marianne's childhood friend,

Jody Jody,
Light brown skin,
Hair plaited and beribboned,
Eyes,
One moment flashing with anger,
The next brimming with tears of
  tenderness.

Marianne Those long hot summer
  afternoons
Sitting out back on the porch

Both try to do headstands.

Marianne 'I hate you, Jody Jones,
You pushed me over.'

Jody 'Your legs were all bent,
I was trying to put them straight.'

Marianne 'I'm never gonna talk to you
  again.'

Jody The misery.

Marianne Then the making friends
  again:

Jody 'Marianne? . . .
Marianne? . . .
You can wear my new ribbon if you wanna . . .'

Marianne 'And you can play with my roller skates.'

Both The joy.

They hug.

Marianne Those years of their childhood –
At the time they seemed to last forever,

Jody But all the same they rushed by.

Marianne Marianne was sent off to a private school in Virginia
Where she excelled.

Jody While Jody went to the local state school.

Marianne And later,
Marianne's father paid for Jody to go up North to college

Jody Where *she* excelled.

Marianne And so Jody and Marianne

Jody Went their separate ways,

Marianne Lost contact –

Jody Until they came face to face over Berta's grave.

Marianne 'My Daddy and I went to the funeral,
He wanted to pay his last respects.
Of course Mom didn't go –
She said she had a migraine.
There were so many people there,
She had so many friends.'

All We too shall come to the Riverside
One by one, one by one,
And lay our garments all aside
One by one, one by one.
The Lord is with us on the tide
One by one, one by one
As one by one he carries us
To home, to home.
We shall be gathered, fording the river
One by one.

Marianne 'Then I saw Jody standing amidst the mourners –
I recognized her at once:'
'Hi, Jody.'

Jody The other woman turning away,
As if she had not heard.
Detaching herself from the group at the graveside
Heading off towards the waiting cars:

Marianne 'Jody, don't you recognize me?'

Jody 'Hello, Marianne.'

Marianne 'I'm sorry about your Mom, Jody.'

Jody 'Thanks.'

Marianne 'She was the kindest woman I ever met,
I loved her dearly.'

Jody 'You're looking well, Marianne.'

Marianne 'You, too.
Are you working?'

Jody 'Yes.'

Marianne 'What are you doing nowadays?'

Jody 'I work for Oxfam,
I spend a lot of my time in Africa.'

Marianne 'Oh, you've done well, I'm glad.
Did you see Daddy?'

Jody 'Yes I did.'

Marianne 'Come over and say hello.'

Jody 'I can't do that, Marianne.'

Marianne 'Why not?
He'd sure like you to.'

Jody 'Your Daddy and I don't get along anymore, Marianne.
I had a big fight with him the last time I was home to see Mom.
She was furious with me,
She never forgave me.'

Marianne 'What did you fight about?'

Jody 'Ask him, Marianne.
I have to go.'

Marianne 'Well, look, here's my address,
If you ever get to London,
Look me up.'

Jody 'OK.'

Marianne 'And she just left without explaining anything.
I mentioned it to my Dad
And he said it all came down to a misunderstanding.
My Mom clammed right up when I asked her about it.
It's a mystery.'

Martin *puts his arm around her.*

Martin Martin tries to comfort her,
Picks up her suitcase
And they leave.

Marianne 'He was always so good to her.
I can't believe she'd be so ungrateful without reason.
It's weird.'

Scene Seven

Prospero Awake, dear heart, awake!
Thou hast slept well.
Awake!

Miranda The strangeness of your story put
Heaviness in me.

Prospero Shake it off. Come on.
We'll visit Caliban, my slave, who never
Yields us kind answer.

Miranda 'Tis a villain, sir,
I do not love to look on.

Prospero But as 'tis,
We cannot miss him. He does make our fire,
Fetch in our wood, and serves in offices
That profit us. What, ho! Slave! Caliban!
Thou, earth, thou! Speak!

Caliban There's wood enough within.

Director 'No, no, no, no, no.'
In a draughty hall in Belsize Park
Rehearsals are not going well:
'Selwyn, darling,
Caliban is a primitive,
He tried to rape Miranda,
So don't try and give us the noble savage,
It just won't work,
It's an oversimplification
It will destroy the balance of the play.
Prospero is the hero,
Not Caliban.'

Selwyn Who is Selwyn to argue with England's greatest playwright?
Anyway,
He doesn't want to be labelled as a troublemaker.

Director 'He's raw physicality and sex.
We'll dress you up in something skimpy
Give the punters a treat.'
Under his breath:
'God why have I got the only black actor
Who doesn't know how to use his body?'

Selwyn Selwyn,
Proud of his work, glad of the job,
Finds it difficult to stand his ground with tinpot theatre gods.
But still explodes that night,

Mark When Mark tells him the latest news from the restaurant,
How the manager took him aside:

Manager 'Come into my office, Mr Leigh.
Now this is a rather delicate situation.
The rest of the staff have asked me to talk to you.
They have expressed some concern about working with you,
I'm sure you can understand their fears;
And so to avoid painful situations,
I've no alternative but to give you your cards,
And thank you for your hard work here at the restaurant.
There's a month's full pay.'

Mark Mark speechless,
Unable at first to reply,
Then a halting, 'Why?'

Manager Is assured that it's nothing personal.
The manager is not at leave to go into details,
Is unwilling to prolong
What must be an embarrassing interview for both of them.
Tells Mark he needn't work out his notice –
'Someone is filling in for you,
So that's taken care of.'
Brushes aside Mark's shocked protests
And ushers him out.

Mark Mark on the street,
With a bulging pay-packet,
But no job.

Selwyn *takes* **Mark** *in his arms.*

Selwyn 'They can't do that to you.
You should have told that bastard where he could stick his job!'

Scene Eight

Miss Rosenblum 'Mr Martin, Mr Martin,
There is a young man at the door for you.'

Martin Martin stumbling out of bed,
Bleary-eyed and overhung,
Kicks over a glass half-full of Marianne's duty-free
Left over from the night before.
Swears,
Puts on his dressing gown
And opens the door.

Miss Rosenblum 'I thought I should wake you up.'

Martin 'Thank you, Miss Rosenblum.'
Only then becoming aware of the fair-haired boy standing behind her.
An Adidas bag over his shoulder,
Looking incongrusous in the dusty hall,
There amongst the potted palms and yucca plants,
As if lost on his way to some squash court
Or swimming pool.

Luke 'Hello, Uncle Martin.'

Martin Martin's brain is not yet in gear.

Luke 'I'm your nephew, Luke.
I've run away from home.'

Martin Martin peering at him fuzzily,
Seeing the family likeness –
('Great,
This is all I need.')

Miss Rosenblum 'Well, Mr Martin,
I go to the shop now,
To buy my Vladimir his breakfast.'

Martin 'Right, thank you Miss Rosenblum.'

Miss Rosenblum 'Goodbye, Mr Martin.
Goodbye, junger Mann.'

Luke 'Goodbye.'

Martin 'Well, Luke, you'd better come in.'

End of part one

Scene Nine

Miss Rosenblum So once again the old house gives refuge to one in flight
As it has done many times before.
It serves a purpose
Though falling now into disrepair:
Slates on the roof are missing,
Window frames are beginning to rot,
The cold water tank has sprung a leak,
Electricity needs rewiring.
Miss Rosenblum often thinks of selling up
Buying herself a little box somewhere
But she can never quite bring herself to do it.

Vladimir Meanwhile Vladimir wanders freely through its decaying rooms
And up the carpeted stairway at its heart.
Pausing now to sit on the window-sill

halfway up the stairs
Where the dust rises in the shafts of light.
He looks out on the overgrown half acre of garden
And the alley which runs along the back
(Once his favourite nocturnal haunt)
He narrows his eyes in the autumn sun
Radar ears twitching and scanning every movement –
Each falling leaf might be prey –
Building up a picture of his surroundings with all his senses,
For sight and sound and touch are not separated out in his cat's brain
Just as the past and present are all one;
He is old now
But still feels like that kitten
Left on the doorstep in a cardboard box
By some well-meaning child
(In those days everyone knew
That the Russian lady who lived here then
Would always take in a stray).
Vladimir becomes bored with falling leaves,
'Too old now to be chasing pigeons.'
He arches his neck to give his ginger chest a desultory lick,
Then jumps down with a thud onto the landing
(Limps have lost their spring)
To continue his leisurely stroll up through the house.
At the top are the servants' quarters,
A depository now for bits of junk and discarded furniture;
Vladimir squeezes through the half-open door
And sidles up to an old velvet armchair
Rubs himself against the worn and faded fabric –
There where his claws were once
Dug in
And sharpened by his youthful self.
He clambers onto the seat,
Curls up,
And sleeps,
And dreams.
Who knows what pictures now flit across his mind?
Does the chair fill up with the figure
Whose pointed elbows made the worn patches on its arms?
Whose hair stained the headrest?

Mme Irina Does her perfume linger?

Vladimir So that Vladimir imagines he is sleeping in her lap?

Mme Irina Perhaps for him she is not dead and he can feel
A bejewelled and wrinkled hand stroking his fur.

Madame Irina was a White Russian princess
Brought to London by a far-seeing aunt in 1913.
The story goes that she brought with her
The family jewels
Disguised as a box of truffles
Each gem cunningly coated in chocolate.
She lived out the rest of her life here in this house
With a string of paid companions and cats,
Waiting for the day that never came,
When Erkaterinburg would be avenged
And she would return to Mother Russia.
So she ended her days
Sitting in this chair
With her cats around her
At her side a bell
To summon Miss Rosenblum,
Popping chocolates between her pampered lips.

Vladimir So Vladimir sleeps at the top of the house,
Till he hears below
The sound of Miss Rosenblum opening a tin.
The dream forgotten,
Wide awake,
He scampers almost skittishly down the stairs
To his food dish,
Leaving the ghost alone in her chair.

Scene Ten

Martin 'We've got a spare room upstairs
A sort of junk room.
I'm sure Miss Rosenblum won't mind
 you using it for a few days.'

Luke 'Thanks.'

Martin 'I think we should phone your
 Mum,
Let her know where you are.'

Pause.

Martin 'Do you want me to phone?'

Luke 'Yeah.'

Martin 'Do you want to talk about why
 you ran away?'

Luke 'I just had to get away for a
 while . . .
I need to think.'

Martin 'What about?'

Luke 'About myself . . . about . . .'

Martin 'Yes?'

Luke 'I think I might be . . .'
 And so Luke tells his uncle why he left,

Martin And Martin
Remembers other times
When he himself arrived in London
On the brink of self-acceptance,
With his law degree from a Northern
 University
And his long hair
To the still swinging London of 1969
With its happenings and its
 demonstrations
When everything seemed possible –
Or nearly everything –
For though men talked of brotherly love
It did not include the kind of love
That Martin felt for other men.
Then came the rumours from New York
Of riots in Greenwich Village,
And a new sort of Pride was born
Which quickly spread to Europe.
Remembers the first rallies in Hyde Park
The excitement of it all,
The joy.
The Isle of Wight and Shepton Mallet
Had never felt as good as this.
'Where's that photo –
I've got it somewhere –
Of me in drag with an ostrich feather in
 my hair,
My arms around David and David
My two lovers?'
(In those days you had to have at least
 two,
Now even one seems excessive to
 Martin.)
Remembers the bystanders on the
 pavements,

Voice One Some faces jeering,

Voice Two Some perplexed,

Voice Three The angry ones

Voice Four And ones which showed
 disgust.

Voice Five Faces where the envy turned
 to hate.

Voice Two But scattered in amongst
 them were faces
Which spoke of a battle going on inside.

Martin Remembers the day when in the
 crowd
He saw a little nuclear family –

Frank Husband,

Maggie Wife,

Luke And child,

Martin Looking lost and scared.

Maggie Suddenly the woman's eyes
 meet Martin's,
Her hand goes to her face.
When she takes it away,

Martin Martin recognizes his sister.

Frank Now the man has seen him too,
He shields the child's face from the sight
And pulls his wife away into the crowd.

Martin 'I've still got that letter she
 wrote –'

Maggie It was a surprise visit

We went to your house in Notting Hill
They told us you were at a rally in Hyde Park.
We didn't know what sort of rally it was
But we thought we might be able to fnd you.
So we stood at Speakers Corner –
For ages we couldn't make out what the banners said
And when we did we couldn't believe our eyes.
I thought you must be there as some observer.
Then we saw you,
You were with all those queers
I hardly recognized my own brother.
You were marching with them
With your arms around another man.
There was no doubt.
Frank says he doesn't want you in the house,
He's afraid of the effect you might have on Luke.

Martin (That had stung more than anything,
He'd lavished love and attention on his baby nephew
The last time he was home.
Now the child had to be protected from him.)

Maggie Frank says he always thought if anything were to happen to us
Then you would be the one to look after Luke.
He's taken it very badly.
It was such a shock
Seeing you there
Shouting it on the streets.
I think it's best we don't see each other for a while.

Martin Martin had never been able to forgive his brother-in-law
And felt that now there was some rough justice at work
That the boy was taking shelter with him.
And so he phones his sister,
Calming her,
Telling her that Luke is worried about his exams.

Maggie A few words with her son help to reassure her.

Martin 'He can stay with me for a few days, Maggie,
I'll look after him.'

Maggie 'Thank you, Martin,
I'm so relieved,
And Frank will be too,
He couldn't be in better hands.'

Scene Eleven

Marianne On the tube
Marianne takes the badge from her pocket
Looks at it
Then with nervous resolution pins it to her lapel.
Rushing wildly up the stairs at Green Park
Risking her life crossing Piccadilly in the rush hour
Colliding with the fur-clad lady at the entrance to Fortnum and Mason's,
Finding at last the restaurant –

Waitress 'A table for one, Madam?'
The waitress eyes her leather jacket with alarm.

Marianne 'Uh, no, I'm meeting someone.'
She narrows her eyes trying to bring the scene before her
Into focus.
Spies in the corner the man in his mid-sixties –

Stephen White hair in stylish cut
Tanned urbane face
Expensive grey suit
Looking half his age
Relaxed and powerful.

Marianne She falters,
Regrets her decision to dress down for the occasion,
Fingers go nervously to her lapel,

Remembering Debbie's words this morning:

Debbie 'What do you want a badge for?
You don't normally wear badges –
And that's an old one – vintage '86.'

Marianne Seeing him sitting there,
She wonders herself what she's trying to prove.
'Ah, damn, I said I'd wear it and I will!'
A deep breath
And she's edging between the tables.

Stephen As if he senses her presence the man looks up from the menu.

He rises to meet her and they hug.

Installs her in a chair as if she were in full evening dress.

Marianne 'Sorry I'm late, Dad,
I had to give Debbie's kid his tea
When he got home from school.
Trying to make this reference to her
English lover seem
Natural and spontaneous.

Both Chasms open.

Stephen He hands her the menu.
'I've only just gotten away myself.
It all took longer than expected.'

Marianne 'What exactly are you doing in London, Dad?'

Stephen 'There's a conference on health in the Third World –
I'm here to talk about what our company can offer in equipment and supplies.
In some countries there's a chronic shortage.

Marianne That look of concern and sadness
How well Marianne knows it.
When she did something bad as a child
She feared that look more than any scolding from her Mother.
'How's Mom?
Is she . . . well at the moment?'

Stephen 'She went through a rocky patch in the Spring.
She seems to have come through that.
She's given up booze – for the present anyway.
Shall we order?'
Every now and again his eyes come to rest on her badge,
Then they're off again
Uncertain of what they have seen.
'When I was in England during the war,
We used to come to London on leave.
Fortnum and Mason's restaurant became one of our regular haunts.'

Marianne 'Bit posh.'

Stephen 'Well, we were living it up.
We were based down in Wiltshire
On some godforsaken hill
So it was grand to be in the big city.
Mind you, it wasn't just Soho that brought us up here,
We were interested in art and theatre.
England had so much culture and history.
On one of our visits
My buddy took me to the British Museum
To see the Egyptian Mummies.'
But he doesn't mention to Marianne
The meeting with the young Jewish girl.

Miss Rosenblum Coming from the reading room
Where she had been studying the newspapers
For any scrap of information about the camps.

Buddy 'I dare you to speak to her.'

Stephen 'OK, I will . . .
Pardon me, ma'am,
Can you tell me where I can find the Egyptian section?'
Persuading her to accompany them,
'This seems a dull place to spend your afternoons.'

Miss Rosenblum And she told him that Karl Marx came here to write.
Later she took him to afternoon tea at Fortnum and Mason's.

Stephen 'You know, Marianne,
We carved a white horse on that hill
down there in Wiltshire.
There's chalk underneath the turf
You can cut it away and make a picture.
Some British regiments carved out their insignia,
But we yanks carved a horse.
It's still there.'
And he remembers that last afternoon with Luise.
The walk to the top
To see the newly finished landmark.
From up close it didn't look like a horse at all.
Remembers her saying.

Miss Rosenblum 'The English people do not know how dearly they buy their victory.
Today they give you a piece of hill,
Tomorrow they will sell you their souls.'

Stephen She was an oddball,
With oddball ideas.
And yet he'd nearly married her.
Back home,
Later,
When Senator McCarthy and J. Edgar Hoover were out hunting for witches,
He believed he'd had a lucky escape.
And yet as he grew older,
He thought of her more and more.
'Hell, Marianne,
What is that button you're wearing?'

Debbie 'You must really care about what your Dad thinks of you,
Going to all that effort to provoke him.'

Marianne She hands it to her father.

Stephen He holds it
A tiny badge
In his large paw
With its raw message:
US BASES OUT OF BRITAIN.
He looks at it for several moments
Then hands it back.
'Have you ever considered buying a place to live over here, Marianne?'

Scene Twelve

Luke Luke sits in the velvet armchair
In that room at the top of the house.
While putting his clothes in a drawer
He found a cardboard box
With old birthday cards and Christmas cards:

Irina 'To my dear Luise,
From one old maid to another,
Yours Irina.
Christmas 1960.'

Luke Letters
And photos –
One, faded and torn,

Stephen Of a soldier

Miss Rosenblum And a young girl

Stephen Standing under a statue.

Luke On the back:

Miss Rosenblum Piccadilly Circus, 1945.

Stephen *and* **Miss Rosenblum** *pose as in the photo.*

Luke A tap at the door –
Luke hides the box guilty behind a chair.

Miss Rosenblum 'Junger Mann,
My cat is up the tree,
He cannot get down.
I am worried for him.
Can you help please?'

Luke Luke follows her outside to the tree at the bottom of the garden.

Vladimir Where Vladimir sits in the topmost branches,
Blinking at them defiantly.

Luke Luke runs to get a ladder
And coaxes the stubborn cat down.

Scene Thirteen

Selwyn After rehearsals Selwyn pays a

visit to the library,
Mindful of last night's row with Mark.

Mark Mark,
Sitting at home all day
Depressed.
Watching the clock.
Playing records,
Going to the launderette.
Watching the clock.
Cleaning the flat,
Cooking Selwyn's meal . . .
Watching the clock –
Potatoes boiling on the stove,
Chops sizzling in the oven –
Listening for steps on the stairway
And watching the clock.

Selwyn Then the tetchiness when he does arrive
As if Selwyn is somehow at fault,
For working when Mark is unemployed.
'Look, I'm going to find out about your rights,
He can't just sack you like that.'
And so the trip to the library.
Finding the book he wants:
GAY WORKERS: TRADES UNIONS AND THE LAW.
Hesitating at the checkout
Trying to look unconcerned as the librarian reads the title.
He puts it in his bag
Under rehearsal clothes
And dog-eared script.
Then takes the short cut home
Along tree-lined streets,
So unlike the streets of his childhood
Lined with council blocks
With wafer-thin walls
And lifts that never worked.
Selwyn feels pleased with himself –
He's made it in a white man's world,
No need to feel victimized.
Now turning up the alley
That runs along the back of spacious gardens.
Half past six,
He starts to run,
Scared of Mark's reproachful look.
Racing out of the alley onto the busy main road

One Where a van screeches to a halt beside him

Two And three policemen jump out:

Three 'Where do you think you're going in such a hurry?'

One 'What are you doing in these parts?'

Two 'What have you got hidden in the bag, then?'

Selwyn Selwyn backing away
Remembering trips to the West End with his brother, Wayne.

Wayne 'If they stop us, just turn and run.'

Selwyn 'Why, we haven't done nothing?'

Wayne 'That won't stop them, just run.'

Selwyn So now he has to fight the impulse.

One 'Just don't try doing a runner.'

Two They hustle him into the seclusion of the alley.

Selwyn 'I haven't done anything, let me go.'

Three 'So, you won't mind us looking in your bag then, will you?

One 'Fucking Ada – a book,
That's an interesting title.'

Two 'He's a poof.
You a black pansy then?'

One 'I thought you only got pink ones.'

Selwyn 'Oh, very funny.'
Selwyn tries to sound defiant and strong.

One 'Watch your lip, poof,
Unless you want a truncheon up your arse.'

Two 'No, he'd enjoy that, too much.'

One 'Here's something to remember

us by, mate.'
Punch.

Two 'Try to be a bit more careful what you carry around with you.'
Kick.

Three 'Come on, you two, let's go.'

One They leave him in a heap.

Selwyn Selwyn falls through the gate
Lips bleeding, ribs bruised,
Into the back garden,

Luke and Miss Rosenblum *rush towards him.*

Miss Rosenblum Someone's back garden.

Luke A young boy with a ginger cat in his arms
States at him in amazement.
Luke remembers that night during the strike,
When his father returned from the police station
With swollen lips and bruises down his back.

Miss Rosenblum Miss Rosenblum remembers that night
When they took away her father
Professor at the University
For questioning.
And later,
When they returned to burn his books.

End of Part Two

Scene Fourteen

Mark That night, in bed, Mark comforts Selwyn:
'Selwyn?'

Selwyn 'Mmmmmm?'

Mark 'You OK?'

Selwyn 'Mmm.'

Mark 'You sure?'

Selwyn 'Mmmm.'

Mark 'Good of that bloke Martin to drive you home.'

Selwyn 'Yeah, he was nice guy.'

Mark 'Who was the other one, the young one.'

Selwyn 'Dunno.'

Mark 'Do you think they're lovers?'

Selwyn 'I dunno,
I didn't ask them.
Why are you so interested anyway?'

Mark 'No reason.'

Pause.

Mark 'He's a solicitor, you know.'

Selwyn 'Who?'

Mark 'Martin.'

Selwyn 'Oh.'

Mark 'Perhaps you could lodge a complaint through him.'

Selwyn 'Mmm. Ha.'

Mark 'What you laughing at.'

Selwyn 'Who'd believe me? There were no witnesses.'

Mark 'But you can't let them get away with it.'

Selwyn 'They do. All the time.'

Pause.

Selwyn 'Owww. Mind my ribs.'

Mark 'Sorry.'

Selwyn 'Just leave me alone, will you?'

Mark 'Don't take it out on me, it's not my fault.'

Selwyn 'Who says?'

Mark 'What?'

Selwyn 'Nothing.'

Pause.

Selwyn 'Saturday tomorrow, think I'll go over and see my Mum.'

Mark 'Oh.'

Selwyn 'Oh what?'

Mark 'I just thought we could spend the day together,
I quite fancy playing nurse.'

Selwyn 'I'm not hurt that bad.'

Mark 'You sure you're up to going out?'

Selwyn 'I wanna see my Mum.'

Mark Mark thinks back to the festival in Victoria Park
When they came face to face

Mother With Selwyn's Mum.

Selwyn Selwyn had already told his Mother about Mark.

Mother But neither side was prepared for this chance meeting –

Mark All through the embarrassed conversation
She avoided looking at Mark.

Mother 'Your sister was asking after you last week,
She says she hasn't seen you since Christmas.'

Selwyn 'Yeah, well, I've been busy.'

Mother 'It's like you're living in another country.'
Before they parted she told Selwyn to be sure to visit her –
'Don't listen to that brother of yours
His fists will be his downfall.'
Then off she went
Sighing about the ungratefulness of the young.

Mark 'What was that about your brother, Wayne?'

Selwyn 'He's threatened to beat me up if I go home.
He shouldn't worry,
I won't be going back.'

Mark Mark lies there and broods.

Selwyn 'Look, Mark we don't have to be together all the time you know.'

Mark 'I know.'

Selwyn 'Stop sulking then.'

Mark 'Why've you suddenly decided that you've got to go over to Hackney.'

Selwyn 'I just wanna.'

Mark 'Has it got anything to do with what happened today?'

Selwyn 'Of course it's fucking to do with what happened today!
I wanna talk to someone about it.'

Mark 'You can talk to me.'

Selwyn 'You understand, do you?'

Mark 'Course I do.'

Selwyn 'How can you?'

Mark 'What, because I'm white?'

Selwyn 'Maybe.'

Mark 'It's never bothered you before.'

Selwyn 'How do you know what's bothered me before?'

Mark 'What is this?
Suddenly everything's coming down to black and white.
It's you I love,
The colour of your skin's not important.'

Selwyn 'Are you sure?'

Mark Mark can see it now –
The first time they made love,
The shock he'd felt when their bodies first made contact;
Fair skin against dark skin,
Their legs intertwined
Looking down at their bellies touching,
The stark contrast.
Taking his head in his hands
Feeling his hair,
At one point,
Catching a glimpse of the two of them in the mirror –

Not just man with man
But black with white as well.
The rush of excitement at the breaking of taboos
Long-held by his race.
'No, Selwyn, I'm not sure.'

Scene Fifteen

Debbie 'Marianne,
I can't tell you whether you should let your Daddy buy you a house!'
Debbie is at the end of her tether!

Marianne 'Oh, God, it's such a big decision.
What do I do?
If I say yes,
Then I'll feel that they've gotten a hold over me again.
It'll be like I never left the States.'

Debbie 'Then say no.'

Marianne 'If I say no,
It just feels like a childish gesture.'

Debbie 'Then say yes.'

Marianne 'It's not that simple.'

Debbie 'Give me strength.'

Marianne 'You don't understand.
The first thing to happen will be that my Mom will want to come over and visit,
She'll start asking questions and criticizing:
"Why aren't you living with that nice husband of yours Marianne?"
"Because he's gay, Mom,
And I'm a lesbian."
"Oh, Marianne, don't use such words.
You know how it upsets your Daddy!"
I can't go through all that.'

Debbie 'Then don't.'

Marianne Marianne feels that Debbie isn't being very sympathetic.

Debbie 'She wants sympathy now!
She's got the luxury of being able to torment herself
About whether she accepts a handout of seventy thousand quid,
She spends hours bellyaching to me about it,
Till I'm ready to climb up the wall
And on top of that she wants sympathy!
My heart bleeds!'

Marianne 'I think you're jealous.'

Debbie 'Me jealous?
Never.
I've got this whole stack of people
Just waiting to buy me houses –
My only problem is whether to choose the mansion in St. John's Wood,
Or the modest maisonette in Hampstead.
Course I'm bloody jealous.'

Marianne 'You don't have to be,
You could always come and live with me.'

Debbie 'Don't even think it, Marianne.
I've made my choices.
My kid,
My home,
My independence.
It took me five years to get out of my marriage,
Now
I feel great,
I've got my freedom.
I'm never going to give it up again.'

Marianne 'But we could have our own spaces.'

Debbie 'I've got my own space,
It's this tatty council flat in dear old Peckham,
And I love it.'

Dave The doorbell interrupts their conversation –

Marianne Marianne opens the door to Debbie's ten year-old son.
'Hiya kid, howya doin?'

Dave 'Where's my dinner?'

Marianne 'Dave, I said Hi.'

Dave 'Hi, Marianne.
Where's my dinner, Mum?'

Debbie 'Oh god, the lord and master returns',
Debbie can see that her son is in one of his
"I'm the man of the house moods".
'Marianne's cooking tonight.'

Dave 'Uhhhh.'

Marianne 'Well, gee honey,
You know how to make someone feel appreciated.'

Dave 'I'm hungry now,
Can't I have sausage and chips?'

Debbie 'But Marianne's bought us some lovely fish.'

Dave 'Don't like fish.'

Debbie 'Dave, what's the matter with you?
What's wrong with you tonight?'

Dave 'Nothing's wrong with me.'

Debbie But Debbie knows her son,
Underneath the macho nonchalance she senses something else.
'Look at you your coat's all torn.
Have you been in a fight?'

Dave 'No.'

Debbie 'Dave . . .'

Dave 'I haven't.'

Debbie 'Well, what's this scratch on your face?
Who did that?'

Dave 'It was . . .'

Debbie 'What?'

Dave 'It was just something that happened on the way home.'

Debbie 'What?'

Dave 'Ian Parker and Derek and that lot,
They were saying things.'

Marianne 'What did they do to you kid?
Shall I go and beat them up?'

Dave 'No!'

Debbie 'What sort of things?'

Dave 'Things about you and Marianne.'

Debbie 'Like what?'

Dave 'They said you were Lesbians,
They kept on shouting it.
And then . . .'

Debbie 'Then?'

Dave 'They said I was a nancy boy,
And started grabbing me.'

Marianne 'Are they still out there?'
Marianne rushes out the door and down the stairs
To find the bullies.

Dave 'Where's she going?
It's none of her business.'

Debbie 'She's angry for you, Dave.
And so am I.
Come on let me give you a cuddle.'

Dave 'No, leave me alone.'

Debbie 'Dave . . .'

Dave 'Leave me alone,
I hate you
I want to go and live with my Dad.
I don't want to live with you and Marianne.'

He cries in her arms.

Debbie 'Dave, Dave.'

Marianne *returns.*

Marianne 'They've disappeared,
But I'll get them,
Don't worry, Dave.'

Debbie That night Debbie tucks him up in bed,
It's the time of day when they have their heart to hearts,
When David becomes a small boy again
And lets the hardman's image slip

Just a little.
'Dave?'

Dave 'Yeah?'

Debbie 'If you really want to live with your Dad,
We could ask him.'

Dave 'I know.'

Debbie 'Do you want me to ask him?'

Dave 'No.'

Debbie 'You sure?'

Dave 'Yes,
I didn't mean it really.'

Debbie 'That's good,
Because I like having you live with me.
And Dave?'

Dave 'Yeah?'

Debbie 'Do you want me to pick you up from school tomorrow
And walk home with you?'

Dave 'No, I'll be all right.'

Debbie 'Night, then, love.'

Dave 'Night.
Mum?'

Debbie 'Yes?'

Dave 'Tell Marianne,
I liked the fish.'

Debbie 'OK, I will.'

She joins **Marianne.**

Marianne 'You have to admit, hon,
That living in a council flat in dear old Peckham
Does have its disadvantages.'

Debbie 'OK, I'll think about it.'

Scene Sixteen

Martin ('Hate discos,
Never come to them')
Thinks Martin
As he hands over seven quid to the man on the desk.
('Music too loud,
Air too smoky,
People too busy posing to even look at you
Let alone smile at you
Or even talk.')
Looks at Luke –

Luke Eyes-a-sparkle –

Martin And recalls how desperately hopeful he felt at that age.
Going to the bar for drinks
He catches sight of himself in the mirror,
Noting the wrinkles around his eyes,
The grey hair at his temples.
'A rum and coke and a pint of lager, please.'
Looks around for Luke,

Luke Already deep in conversation
With an attractive young man

Mark In a pair of torn jeans.

Martin Martin recognizes Mark from the previous evening,
When they drove Selwyn home.
('Wonder if they're lovers?')
Now edging his way back through the crowd,
'Excuse me.
Excuse me.'
('God, if that bloke doesn't move,
I'll pour this pint down his back.')
'Thank you so much.'

Luke But Mark and Luke are off to dance.

Martin 'Oh, fine,
I'll hold your drinks.'
('Don't mind me,
I like standing around on my own at discos
Trying to look casual and self-possessed
When all the time I'm feeling totally inadequate
Because these bright young things with their careless elegance

Are making me think that life has passed me by
And I'm on the junk heap at thirty-eight.')
Martin chances a smile at a flat-topped youth –

Youth Who looks right through him.

Martin ('Is that what we fought for all those years?
Where did all that coming together go?')
When Mark and Luke return
He's well into his second pint.

Luke 'Do you want to dance, Uncle Martin?'

Martin ('Does he have to call me that?')
'No thanks, I don't like dancing.'
('Not here anyway,
We used to dance in the streets.')
And so the evening wears on
Martin becoming more and more morose
With each drink.

Luke 'Have you got a pen and paper, Uncle Martin?'

Mark Mark wants to take down Luke's telephone number,

Luke 'We're going to see a film on Monday night.'

Martin ('So they're not going home together tonight,
A good old-fashioned courtship, eh?
Very romantic,
That's a sign of the times.')

Mark *and* **Luke** *kiss.*

He watches them say a fond farewell
Fighting back a sentimental sigh:
('Ah, young love –
Let's hope we can go home now.')

Luke 'That was a really great evening, Uncle,
Thanks ever so much.'

Martin 'That's OK, Luke.
Do you like him – Mark?'

Luke 'Yes I do.
You know he thought at first you were my boyfriend.'

Martin ('What a preposterous idea!')

Luke 'But I told him who you were.'

Martin ('I should think so too.')

Luke He said he wished he had a sexy uncle like you.'

Martin ('Pah, humbug,') thinks Martin
As they run to catch the last tube home.

Scene Seventeen

Mother When she saw his bruises
Her anger knew no bounds.
But she was pleased to see him,

They embrace.

Welcomed him with open arms,
Took him out to the High Street to buy him a new pair of shoes,
Cooked him a special meal
And invited all the family round –

Selwyn His aunt and her new bloke,
His sister and her new baby,
Even Wayne turned up –

Wayne Very quiet, cool, not giving much away,

Selwyn But Selwyn saw his presence as a sign
That a truce had been called!

Mother Then at bedtime their Mother said,
'Selwyn, your sister's using the spare room,
You'll have to share with Wayne tonight.'

Selwyn This was unexpected.

Wayne Wayne said nothing
Went straight to his room.

Selwyn Later,
When Selwyn climbed into bed,

Wayne Pretended to be asleep.

Selwyn Both of them lying there,

Wayne Wide awake,

Selwyn For over an hour.

Pause.

Selwyn 'Don't worry, Wayne, I'm not gonna touch you.'

Wayne 'I never said I was worried.'

Selwyn 'It's not your fault I'm gay, you know.'

Wayne 'What you say that for?'

Selwyn 'Do you think I don't remember what we used to do?'

Wayne Both of them could remember other nights
When they had shared this bed,

Selwyn When hands reached out

Wayne Under the bedclothes,

Selwyn Under the cover of night,

Wayne And they had caressed each other's bodies –

Selwyn Something secret that happened after lights were out

Wayne Never acknowledged or spoken about in the cold light of day.

Selwyn Then,
Years later,
Selwyn came out;
The unmentionable was mentioned!

Wayne 'That was just fooling around, guy.'

Selwyn 'So why do you feel so guilty?'

Wayne 'Who says I feel guilty?'

Selwyn 'Why else would you wanna mash me up
When I said I was gay?'

Wayne 'Look, man, I'm not a battyman, if that's what you're saying.'

Selwyn 'That's not what I'm saying,
But you're scared, man, scared
That I'll blow your cover,
That someone might find out
That Wayne isn't the he-man he's cracked up to be.'

Wayne 'Fuck off, will you?
I'm trying to get to sleep.'

Pause.

'You should never've gone to that drama school
Letting all them white poufs have your arse.'

Selwyn 'Yeah, the first man I slept with was at that college,
He was the dance teacher,
He was Black.'

Wayne 'Tttt.'

Selwyn 'That surprise you?
Did me.
Till then I thought I was the only one
Who'd been letting the side down.
He was a really good teacher
In more ways than one –
I had a hard time of it at that college to start with,
Trying to fit in with all those white kids,
Trying to make myself into a proper actor.
Then he said to me,
"If you don't fit the mould,
Don't start cutting off bits of yourself,
Break the mould."
That's something that applies to all of us, Wayne.'

Pause.

Wayne 'How's your bruises?'

Selwyn 'All right.'

Wayne 'Hey, man, I didn't mean it, you know,
I wouldn't really've hurt me own brother though?'

Selwyn 'No.
We should leave that to the filth,
They're good at that sort of thing.'

Wayne 'Yeah,

Night mate.'

Selwyn 'Night Wayne.'

Wayne Sleep comes quite easily

Selwyn To both of them.

Interval

Scene Eighteen

Luke Suddenly he's wide awake –
Something has disturbed him.
Lying there frozen
His heart pounding.

Miss Rosenblum A low moan.

Luke He looks towards the chair
Moving his head on the pillow as noiselessly as possible,
And sees her,
Sitting in the velvet chair
Silhouetted against the window
Where the dawn light is creeping in.
At first Luke thinks he has seen a ghost.
Then he realizes it is Miss Rosenblum.

Miss Rosenblum Her hair unpinned and loose around her neck,
Giving her an unfamiliar outline.
She has been walking in her sleep
And is dreaming of the past –
Those early years
When she had just arrived in England,
With her letter of introduction
To a Mrs Goldsack of West End Lane
Who employed her to scrub floors –
This girl from a rich Viennese family.
With the outbreak of war the Goldsacks decided to emigrate,
And so the young Fraülein Rosenblum
Was forced to look for other work.
One day, passing a newsagent's on Finchley Road,
She saw a card in the window.

Irina FOREIGN LADY REQUIRES GENTEEL COMPANION.

Miss Rosenblum So it was that the skinny eighteen year old orphan
(Though she didn't yet know she was an orphan)
Approached the house for the first time.
It loomed up out of the smog
Like a haunted castle,
Laurels almost blocking the path,
A dingy porch with wrought-iron bell-pull
That sent a tinkling sound throughout the house.
A long wait,
Then footsteps,
And a light,

Irina A figure behind the frosted glass
Who opens the door.
'Yes?'

Miss Rosenblum In her mind's eye she can see her still,

Irina Irina Petrova,
Standing in the doorway
In her long black dress,
Ivory brooch at the neck,
Hair piled up on top of her head,
With three cats rubbing themselves against her skirts.

Miss Rosenblum 'I've come about the advertisement.'

Irina 'Ah, come in.'

Miss Rosenblum At first she had been scared of her new employer,
But the work was easier than cleaning –

Irina 'Oh, you play the piano?
Good, I like to listen to music.'

Miss Rosenblum And the room at the top of the house was cosy,
Felt like home.
So she stayed.
They only ever disagreed when Fraülein Rosenblum wanted time off.

Irina 'So, you are going out again this afternoon, Luise?'

Miss Rosenblum 'Yes, I'm going to the British Museum as usual.'

Irina 'Ah, yes, to read the newspapers.'
But one day Irina followed her
Keeping well out of sight,
She boarded the bus which took them –
Not to Russell Square,
But to Piccadilly Circus

Stephen Where a tall GI awaited his girlfriend under the statue of Eros.

Stephen *and* **Miss Rosenblum** *pose as in the photo again.*

Irina She followed them down Piccadilly and into Fortnum and Mason's
Sitting in the corner of the restaurant
Spying on them.
Then slipped out as discreetly as she could
And hailed a taxi home.

Stephen 'What's wrong, Luise?'

Miss Rosenblum 'I'm sure that was Irina Petrova who just left.'

Stephen 'Your Russian Princess?
What would she be doing here?'
And they let the subject drop

Miss Rosenblum And talked instead of Stephen's imminent return to the States.

Stephen 'I can't wait to get back home, Luise,
It's a great country,
With a great future.
You wait,
We're gonna build a better world,
Where there's no more war,
No more hunger,
No more disease.
Everyday new discoveries are being made
To make our life on earth a better one –
We're on the edge of a new age
My country will lead the way forward
And I'm gonna be part of that.'

Miss Rosenblum 'Oh, brave new world that has such people in't!'

Stephen 'Huh?'

Miss Rosenblum 'That's Shakespeare,
The greatest writer in the English language,
Your language.'

Stephen 'I speak American.
Now,
You're gonna come down to Wiltshire before I leave?'

Miss Rosenblum 'Ja, next week,
I shall take the whole day off, I shall tell Irina
That I am meeting with Ilse.'
That evening as she sat with Irina in her room
As if by chance,
Their conversation settled on the topic of marriage:

Irina 'Of course I was very popular as a girl,
There were several young officers after my hand.
I remember at a ball in Petersburg
Two young men had a violent argument
Over me.
I believe they fought a duel,
Although I can't remember what the outcome was.
Pass me those chocolates my dear.
But, of course, I cannot think of marriage at the moment
With my country suffering under the Soviet yoke.
Help yourself, Luise, –
Oh, please, don't take that one,
The truffles are my favourites.
I suppose, soon, you will find some young man to marry,
And you will be coming to me and saying,
"I am handing in my notice, Irina Petrova."
And I shall be left on my own again.
But please don't throw yourself away on just anyone, my dear,
You have so many talents
And there are so many charlatans in the world nowadays.'

Miss Rosenblum And the young girl shuddered inwardly

At the thought that she might end her
  days
Sitting in that velvet chair
Regretting the past,
Alone.
Instead she turned her thoughts to her
  rendezvous
With her shining knight
On that windy hillside
Where a white horse is carved in the
  chalk.

Luke 'Miss Rosenblum, are you all
right?'

Luke *gets out of bed and wakes* **Miss
Rosenblum.**

Miss Rosenblum 'Oh, I'm sorry, junger
  Mann,
I must have walked in my sleep.
This happens sometimes.'

Luke Luke guides her down the stairs.

Miss Rosenblum On the landing she
  grips his hand:
How old are you, junger Mann?'

Luke 'Nearly eighteen.'

Miss Rosenblum Standing there in the
  early morning light
She peers into his face
Long
And hard

Luke Until Luke begins to feel quite
  unnerved.

Miss Rosenblum 'Ja, junger Mann,
We must make of our lives what we can,
That is most important.'
And she releases him
And moves on down the stairs.

Luke Luke can see her through the
  bannister
Looking frail and childlike
In her long pink nightgown.

End of Part Three

Scene Nineteen

Martin 'Luke?
Luke?
Are you going to be much longer?'
It's half past seven,
Martin has been waiting to use the
  bathroom since half past six.
'I want to have a bath and wash my hair.'

Luke 'OK, I won't be long.'

Martin ('Kids, who'd have 'em?')
Martin stomps back into the kitchen,
Picks up a file,
Reads through the barrister's notes on
  tomorrow morning's case.
And waits.
And waits.

Luke 'Sorry about that –
I was getting ready to go out.'

Martin 'So I gathered.
I did want to go out myself tonight, you
  know.
You're looking smart.'

Luke 'Thanks.'

Martin 'What coat are you wearing?'

Luke 'I dunno.'

Martin 'Well, you can't wear that blue
  kagool.'

Luke 'Actually . . . I wondered –'

Martin 'Yes?'

Luke 'If I could wear your denim
  jacket.'

Martin 'OK.
It's hanging on the stand by the front
  door.'

Luke 'Thanks ever so much, Uncle –
I mean, Martin.'

Martin 'What time does the film start?'

Luke 'Quarter to nine,
But I'm meeting Mark at half past eight.'

Martin 'Well you'd better go or you'll be
  late.'

Luke 'Yeah.'

Martin 'Nervous?'

Luke 'A bit.'

Martin 'Well there's no need.'

Luke 'No . . .'

Martin 'Come on, what's wrong?'

Luke 'Nothing really, just . . .
Do you worry a lot about AIDS?'

Martin Suddenly the penny drops
And Martin understands his nephew's worried look.
God, it makes me so angry
He shouldn't have this to fret about
As if it isn't difficult enough already!
So he sits him down
And explains all the ins and outs –
As it were.
('I feel like an anxious father explaining the birds and bees!')
'So just make sure you're safe, that's all.'

Luke 'Right.'

Martin 'OK?'

Luke 'Yeah.
I really appreciate it, Martin
What you've done for me.'

Martin 'It's a pleasure, Luke.'
('Except when you spend two hours in the bathroom.')
'Right, now, off you go.'

Luke 'Yeah,
Bye then.'

Martin 'Bye.'
Martin hears the front door slam.
(*Sings.*) 'Everybody's going out and having fun.'
('Now, eight 'o' clock,
Let's have that bath,
Then – well, perhaps I'll go out for a drink.')
Martin finds the bathroom swimming in water,
By the time he's cleaned up the mess it's twenty to nine.
('And he's used up all my shampoo.
What do I wash my hair with –
Fairy Liquid?')
Martin lies in the bath listening to the noise from upstairs.

Miss Rosenblum Monday nights are Miss Rosenblum's musical evenings.

Ilse And Ilse –

Freddi And Freddi –

Hutch And Hutch –

Miss Rosenblum Have all come round.

They gather around her.

Martin Now Martin's dried and dressed and ready for action –
He looks at his watch –
It's nine forty-five!
Martin decides it's too late to go out for the evening,
So feeling sorry for himself he settles down to work.
Falling asleep over a client's affidavit –

Miss Rosenblum There's a knock on the door at quarter past ten.
'Mr Martin,
I hope we don't bother you with our music,
I am teaching Ilse a new song.'

Martin 'No, I can hardly hear you.'

Miss Rosenblum 'Are you on your own tonight?'

Martin 'Yes, Luke's gone out on his first date.'

Miss Rosenblum 'Ohho.'
So the old lady insists
That Martin must come up and join them.

Martin Martin at first reluctant follows her upstairs.

Ilse/Freddi/Hutch Ahhhhhhhh!

They welcome him.

Miss Rosenblum And Luise plays the

piano till way past midnight

Ilse With Ilse singing –

Hutch And Hutch on violin.

Martin 'This has turned out to be a lovely evening,'
Thinks Martin.

Freddi As Freddi fills his glass with tonic and gin.

Scene Twenty

Debbie 'Look, Marianne, she was an old schoolfriend.'

Marianne 'So I gathered.'
Marianne and Debbie are having a row in bed.

Debbie About a woman called Helen, Who Debbie went to school with.

Marianne Who rushed up and hugged her,
When they were going to catch their tube.

Debbie 'She always was boisterous.'

Marianne 'Boisterous, is that what you call it?'

Debbie 'Shhh! You'll wake Dave.'

Marianne 'A loudmouth, I think, would be more accurate.'

Debbie 'I was really pleased to see her again after all these years.
We didn't know about each other at school.'

Marianne 'Yes but did she really have to announce it to everyone on King's Cross station?
"Debbie, I thought it was you.
You're a lesbian.
How fantastic!"
That ticket collector's eyes were nearly popping out of her head.'

Debbie 'OK, you didn't like her.'

Marianne 'But you obviously did.'

Debbie 'What I like is to keep up with people from my past.'

Marianne 'Yes I've noticed that.
Melissa, and Sian, and Kate,
And Sian's lover Caroline,
Who you later had a relationship with
And Caroline's ex-lover and flatmate –
The other Caroline –
Who Melissa went off with after you and Melissa split up.
It's so incestuous,
Half of them have got the same names.
I get so confused.'

Debbie 'You get so jealous.'

Marianne 'It's not that,
I just get fed up of worrying,
Whether you're going to be able to fit me in to your busy schedule.
And now, it's not just ex-lovers,
But ex-schoolfriends as well!
When you arranged to meet her Thursday night,
I couldn't believe it.
That's the night you said you'd come out with me and my Dad
It's his last night in London.'

Debbie 'Your Dad?
What's he got to do with all this?
You want me to plan my week around your Dad?
I thought I got away from in-laws when I left my marriage!
You're obsessed with your bloody Dad.
And then you accuse me of having incestuous relationships!
To hell with your Dad!'

Marianne 'And to hell with you!'

They turn away from each other.

Debbie 'Marianne?
Marianne?
Those women are like my family.
They know things about me that no one else can know.

People from the past are important to me.
Like Jody's important to you.'
Debbie reaches across to the bedside table,
Picks up the postcard that arrived three days ago
From a village somewhere in the Sudan.
'I was glad for you when you got this,
Glad that she got in contact,
That she wants to meet up with you whilst she's in London.
Because she's someone that you care about.'

Marianne 'It's just that sometimes I seem to come real low-down on your list.'

Debbie 'Marianne, I love you.'

Marianne 'I know.'

Debbie 'Trust me.'

Marianne 'It's hard.'

Debbie 'Look, if you really want me to come out with you and your Dad,
I could cancel,
I could always see Helen on another night.'

Martin 'No, don't do that.'

Debbie 'You sure?'

Marianne 'Yeah.'

Debbie 'Come on, let's get some sleep.
It's Tuesday tomorrow,
You've got to look your best for Jody Jones.'

They kiss.

Scene Twenty-One

Selwyn On Tuesday morning,
Selwyn sits having coffee with Miss Rosenblum,
And Martin.
'I just wanted to thank you all
For looking after me last week
When I was beaten up.
I was going to come round sooner,
But I've been staying over in Hackney the last few days with
my Mum.'

Miss Rosenblum 'I am pleased you have recovered, junger Mann,
He gave us quite a shock, didn't he, Vladimir?'
The cat answers her with a feeble and throaty miaow.
'Ohhhh, he's not feeling well.
Willst du dein Frühstück nicht fressen, mein Liebling?
He has not eaten for two whole days.'

Selwyn 'Well, I must be off.
I haven't been home since Saturday morning,
Mark must be wondering where I am.
I've got to call in there before rehearsals.'

Martin Martin almost mentions seeing Mark at the disco,
Then decides not to.

Miss Rosenblum 'Oh, ja, the play.
When does it start?'

Selwyn 'Thursday.'

Miss Rosenblum 'And can we come and see it?'

Selwyn 'Of course you can,
Come on the first night.'

Miss Rosenblum 'Mr Martin, will you come with me?
The Tempest is my favourite Shakespeare play,
I would love to see it again.'

Martin Martin sees Selwyn to the door,
'When Luke gets up,
I'll tell him that you called.'

Selwyn 'Thanks.
Bring him along on Thursday too.'
As he leaves,
Selwyn bends down to pick up something from the mat,
'The postman's been,

112 Gay Sweatshop

There's a letter for you.'

Scene Twenty-Two

Martin On Tuesday morning,
Martin reads the letter from his sister:

Maggie 'Dear Martin,
Thanks for looking after our Luke.
I wish he'd told us he was so worried about his exams,
We could have helped.
But I meant it when I said he couldn't be in better hands,
I'm sure you'll say all the right things.
Perhaps it will bring us all closer,
And we'll be able to let bygones be bygones –
This rift has gone on far too long.
I know Frank said some hurtful things
But he didn't know any better
Neither of us did.
And you know,
Sometimes I feel you could have helped us more, Martin.
That pride of yours makes you so unforgiving,
I remember that from when you were a kid.'

Martin The treachery of a sister
Who promised to take him to the fair
Then went with her boyfriend instead!
No peace offerings,
No nougat,
Or coconut
Would ever make him speak to her again!
He kept it up for two whole weeks.
But then came the fall,
Head over heels off his bike.

Maggie 'Come on, our kid,
Let's get you indoors and clean you up.'

Martin He had to speak to her then, didn't he?

Maggie Frank always feels that you think he isn't good enough for me –
But I'm not complaining,
He's been a good husband.
He gets his moods of course –
Especially since the strike,
He's very bitter about being out of work
Having to accept redundancy –
But he's changed a lot you know, over the years,
The strike was a big eye-opener for us all.
When we had the big demonstration
There were several banners
From the lesbians and the gays.
There was this group of lads being right daft
Whistling at them
And being limp-wristed –
You know how they can be –

Frank 'All right lads, that'll do,
Their support group have given us £300 for the strike fund.
How many of you have ever been on one of their marches?
People have got to stick together
Help each other out,
Not bash each other over the head.
You should have learnt that by now.'

Maggie I was right proud of him.
I suppose what I'm saying, Martin,
Is that I hope you'll come and visit us
Next time you're up this way –
It'd be good to see you after all this time.
I'll phone you up in the week,
Take care of our lad,
Tell him we love him,
We always will,
No matter what.
Your sister,
Margaret.

Martin And scrawled at the bottom in a different hand,

Frank Hope you're well, Martin,
Come up and see us,
Frank.

Martin Martin reads the letter,
Feels suddenly ashamed,
Takes it upstairs to show it to Luke,
Thinks somehow it will help the lad.
But Luke's bed hasn't been slept in . . .

Scene Twenty-Three

Selwyn On Tuesday morning Selwyn returns to the flat,
Anticipating recriminations,
Surprised to notice the bedroom door is still closed.
('Mark can't be up yet.
Funny,
He's usually such an early riser,
Unemployment must be really getting to him.')
Mark's notebook lies beside the 'phone –
So easy to pick it up,
Flick through,
Find clues,
See how he's spent his weekend.
('Thus coupledom doth make detectives of us all!')

Mark Saturday pm: Sainsbury's for food,
Cut jeans for club tonight –

Selwyn ('Ohhhh!')

Mark Read booklet Selwyn got from library.

Selwyn ('Well, that's good.
At least he hasn't been sitting around moping.')

Mark Notes from booklet:
No good,
Haven't been working there two years
Can't go to tribunal.
Should have been member of union.

Selwyn ('Over the page . . .')

Mark Sunday am: Phone L.

Selwyn ('Who the hell is L?')

Mark Check times for film for tomorrow night –
Monday cheap night at Cannon . . .

Selwyn ('He's certainly been living it up.')

Mark Ask L if Martin knows anything about unfair dismissal.

Selwyn ('Martin? . . . Martin! L!
Luke!')

Mark Meet L outside Cannon 8.30 tomorrow.
Monday am.
Buy *Advertiser* to look for a job . . .

Selwyn ('Yeah . . . yeah . . .')

Mark Look in Newsagent's window on Finchley Road.

Selwyn ('Mmmmmm . . . Oh!')

Mark Buy Selwyn card for opening night.

Selwyn ('Well, thanks for remembering my existence.')

Mark Monday pm:
Wash jeans,
Haircut,
Have bath,
Put clean sheets on bed.

Selwyn ('Uh uhh.')
Selwyn catching sight for first time of a blue denim jacket
Over a kitchen chair,
('Well, that's not Mark's.')
Looking at the closed bedroom door with new eyes.
('Shit. And I'm supposed to be the fickle one.')
Selwyn leaves the flat
Closing the door as silently as possible.

Scene Twenty-Four

Luke It's Tuesday morning
But no Tuesday morning was ever this bright!
Heart in his mouth,
Luke lies there
With Mark curled up at his side,
Both of them drifting in and out of sleep.
Savouring again the images of the night.
'This morning,
Early,

I heard the dawn chorus,
And I knew my life had changed.
Then,
People waking in the flats below,
Somewhere the smell of bacon.
Even that seemed strange and new.
Later,
Car doors slamming
Outside
As people went off to work.
Later still,
Children calling to each other
Running off to school.
School.'
Luke remembers that other life
When Tuesday mornings meant double Maths.
'Is that life still going on out there, somewhere?'
A moment's fear
And guilt.
He can hardly believe the enormity of his crime.
'I've done it now,
No going back.'
He looks again at the man sleeping beside him –
'Oh, it felt so good.
But this painful peace
Is even more intense.
I'm in love. I've got a lover,
I'm in love.'
He whispers it to himself
Over
And over
Again.

End of Part Four

Scene Twenty-Five

Marianne 'Oh, Debbie,
I feel so naive,
I really thought my Dad could do no wrong.'

Debbie Debbie sits Marianne in a chair
Tries to calm her,

Marianne While Marianne tells of her meeting with Jody Jones.
Sitting in a coffee bar in Leicester Square
Listening to stories
Of war,
Hunger
And disease.
And then this latest story,
A story about blood,
Unscreened,
Cheap blood.
(The tests are so expensive.)
Shipped off to the Third World –
A cargo of potential disease and death.
'As if this virus needed any help!
There was a lot of noise about it in the newspapers back home –
Jody showed me cuttings.
There was this letter from my Dad,
Where he admits that a consignment of blood
Had not been properly tested
And then goes on to say
That the risks involved were minimal.
How could anyone be so irresponsible?
Of course I knew that sort of thing went on,
That there were people without scruples
On the lookout for a fast buck.
But my Dad?
All these years he's been making out
He cares about the world's poor.'

Scene Twenty-Six

Caliban You taught me language, and my profit on't
Is, I know how to curse. The red plague rid you
For learning me your language.

Prospero Hagseed, hence!
Fetch us in fuel, and be quick, thou'rt best
To answer other business. Shrug'st thou, malice?
If thou neglect'st or dost unwillingly

What I command, I'll rack thee with old cramps,
Fill all thy bones with aches, make thee roar
That the beasts shall tremble at thy din.

Caliban No, pray thee.
(*Aside.*) I must obey. His art is of such pow'r
It would control my dam's god, Setebos,
And make a vassal of him.

Prospero So, slave; hence!

Director 'OK,
Let's have a tea-break now.
Back in fifteen minutes everyone.
Selwyn, darling,
Where's the West Indian accent?
I thought we agreed you were going to do it with a strong accent!'

Scene Twenty-Seven

Marianne 'But that's not the whole story –
Later I took Jody through to St James Park
And we sat there watching the ducks.'

Jody 'I'm sorry, Marianne,
I thought you'd know,
I thought you'd have read about it.'

Marianne 'Well, I guess the story wasn't taken up by the British press.'

Jody 'When I saw you at the funeral
I felt myself getting real angry.
"She sits in England publishing books of poetry
While our father commits murder."
That's how it struck me then.'

Marianne 'What did you say?'

Jody 'Oh, I know that's not fair.
I've often come across books you've published,
They're good.'

Marianne 'No, I didn't mean that.
Did you say "our father"?'

Jody 'Yeah, sure.'

Marianne '*Our* father?'

Jody 'You mean you didn't know?
Oh Marianne, Marianne,
I thought everyone knew about that.'

Marianne 'You mean father and Berta . . .'

Jody 'Yeah.
From what I understand he pursued her,
When she was in the house
Cleaning or cooking,
And your Mom was out,
Suddenly he'd be there
Watching her,
Touching her.
What was she to do?
He was white,
A man
Her boss.
She was black
A woman
His maid.
And it was 1949.
Of course it was all hushed up
And no one was supposed to know –
It was my aunty May told me all about it.
She said he told Berta he loved her.
Hmmm.'

Marianne The past replays itself in Marianne's head –
Suddenly everything fell into place,
The missing clue had been found.

Jody 'You know, Marianne,
As a kid,
I always felt like a freak.
I'd brought shame both on my Mom and Dad.
I just felt I was bad.
And then there was you –
You were everything that I was not –
It was like I was the negative
And you were the positive
The perfect picture.
God, I so wanted to be you.
Then, one day, while I was still at college,
Berta told me about you;
How you'd gone off to England to live

with another woman
How you had unnatural tastes as she called it.
I felt this immense relief;
It was the best gift you could ever have ever given me,
Not because I'm gay,
I'm not –
At least,
Well,
I don't think I am,
At the moment anyway –
But because
You were not normal either.
It was like a weight had been lifted off my shoulders.
So when I saw you at the funeral,
With your beloved Daddy,
I felt you'd let me down.
That's why I got mad at you.'

Marianne 'Oh, Jody.'
In St James Park,
Amidst the office workers eating their lunch
And the au pairs out with their infant charges
Two sisters sit crying in each other's arms.

Jody 'Welcome home, Marianne.'

Scene Twenty-Eight

Martin (*on the phone*) 'Maggie,
It's Martin.
Luke's coming home.
Yes, he's fine, but he's got a lot to talk to you about.
Well, wait, he'll tell you.
He's getting the early train tomorrow,
He should be up there by lunchtime.
Look, I don't know if he's coming home for good –
Well, talk to him.
Actually I thought I might come up one weekend.
Yes,
Well, I'd like it too.
OK, I'll let you know when – give you lots of warning.
Yes.
All right then, bye.
Yeah, bye – oh, Maggie –
Give my regards to Frank.'

Scene Twenty-Nine

Selwyn (*on the phone*) 'Mark?
It's me.
Hi.
I'm OK.
At rehearsals.
Look, I came to the flat this morning.
Yeah.
I don't mind.
You don't need to apologize.
You weren't to know I was coming back.
Anyway that's not why I'm phoning you –
I've been thinking,
I wanna move back to Hackney.
No, I've been thinking about it all weekend,
I'd already made up my mind before this morning.
And I wanted to warn you, see,
So's you'd know,
And you'd have time to think about it.
Of course I still love you
That's why I wanna move,
'Cos if we carry on living together I think we'll split up.
That's one reason anyway –
The other one is –
I don't feel at home over this side of town,
There's a flat near me Mum's,
She thinks she can get it for me.
Look, we'll be able to talk about it later,
I gotta go now.
Yeah, I'll be there about seven.'

Director 'Selwyn, love, hurry up,
We're all waiting for you.
Positions for Act Two.'

Scene Thirty

Marianne They sit there in the hotel lobby,
Marianne pale,
Nervous,
Her lip trembling at the audacity of her accusations.

Stephen Her father quiet,
Thoughtful,
Listening to her,
Allowing her to finish.
Then –
'But honey,
You're talking as if some crime has been committed,
Those governments knew what they were getting,
They knew that blood hadn't been screened.
If they're so careless about what they do with it,
Then we can't be blamed, now, can we?'

Marianne 'But you must have known they can't afford to screen it,
That they don't have the facilities.'

Stephen 'It's their responsibility, Marianne.'

Marianne 'Did you really need the money that much, Daddy?'

Stephen 'Oh, come on now,
We were providing them with blood they needed badly,
And a helluva lot cheaper than they could get it anywhere else.
Was that a bad thing to do?
As for Berta and Jody –
Hell, I'm no saint, Marianne,
But I'm no devil either.
I paid for what happened between me and Berta,
And I think she forgave me.
It was all so long ago;
I was desperate,
You've no idea what it's like
To be sharing your life with someone
And to find that there's no love –
Love was something I only ever found once,
And that was when I was very young.
I should have grasped it, kept it,
But I let it go.
Losing that love soured my life for many years.
Do you know who brought the sweetness back?
You did, Marianne.
When you came along I couldn't believe my good fortune.
You're not going to turn against your old Dad now, are you?'

Marianne 'I . . .'

Stephen 'And you'll come out with me on Thursday night?
It's my last night in London.'

Marianne 'I don't know if I can now.'

Stephen 'But you promised,
You told me you were gonna take me to the theatre.'

Marianne 'I know.'

Stephen 'So, can we still go?'

Marianne 'Well . . . I guess so.'

Stephen 'What's the play? Is it one I know?'

Marianne 'I dunno, it's a Shakespeare.
You remember Martin?
You met him last time you were over.'

Stephen 'Uhhuh.'

Marianne 'Well, he's taking his landlady
And he thought we could make it a foursome.'

Stephen 'Who's this landlady?
Are you trying to get me hitched?'

Marianne 'No.'

Stephen 'Well, that will be grand,
I'll look forward to that.'

Marianne 'Good.'

Stephen 'Do you love your old Dad, Marianne?'

Scene Thirty-One

Miss Rosenblum And so the stage is set
For wartime lovers to be reunited.
Actors are preparing
Audience is gathering
But one of the principal characters is about to miss her entrance.
Fate intervenes
In the shape of a ginger cat
A negative *deus ex machina*
And a pattern of co-incidence is casually thrown awry.
Vladimir is dying;
He has not moved from his place in front of the gas fire for days,
Except to stagger to his food dish,
Sniff at the contents disconsolately
And return,
As if exhausted by all this effort,
Without touching a single morsel.
Miss Rosenblum stands looking at him,
In hat and coat,
Gloves in hand
Waiting for Martin to come and collect her
And take her to the play.
Outside there is a distant rumble of thunder
Miss Rosenblum looks out of the window at the angry dark clouds
Heightening her sense of foreboding.
'Na, mein Liebchen,
Ich lasse dich nicht allein.'
And she takes off her hat and her coat,
Kneels down beside him.

Martin This is where Martin finds her later,
When he comes to take her to the play.

Miss Rosenblum 'No, Mr Martin,
I cannot leave my Vladimir.
I shall stay with him.
You must go without me.'

Martin Martin tries to reassure her
But leaves eventually –
Rather late –
For the theatre.
The play has already started as he arrives in his seat
Soaking wet from the downpour which caught him
As he ran from the tube.

Miranda If by your art, my dearest father, you have
Put the wild waters in this roar, allay them
The sky it seems, would pour down stinking pitch.

Marianne Marianne shoots Martin a questioning look,
'You're late.
Where's your landlady?'

Martin 'Couldn't come.'

Director 'SHHHHHHHH!'

Martin 'I'll explain later.'

Marianne And they settle down

Martin To watch the play.

Scene Thirty-Two

Miss Rosenblum Miss Rosenblum is out in the garden in a thunderstorm,
Digging,
Down on her knees,
Her thin hair plastered to her head.
The rain,
Mingling with her tears,
Drips off her nose,
As she scrabbles at the earth with an old garden trowel.
Beside her on the ground is a small bundle of fur,
Brownish and sodden –
Miss Rosenblum is burying her cat.
Feeling a pain in her chest from all the effort,
She decides the grave is deep enough.

She mimes picking up the dead **Vladimir** *and burying him.*

'Ja, Irina,
He was all that was left of you,
And now he has gone too.'

She stands with some difficulty.

'I don't know why I'm crying,
He had a good life.
Perhaps I cry for you, Irina,
For your wasted one;
Sitting there in your chair
Eating your chocolates
Complaining right until the end
About this country,
About the riff-raff they were letting in.
You never seemed to realize that we were
   part of the riff-raff.
Waiting for the day when you would
   return to your land of dreams,
Where men in uniform whisked you off
   to the ball.
Poor Irina,
You were so bitter.
And you never understood
That I did not feel like you.
You called yourself an old maid
Who no one wanted
But that was not how I saw myself!'

Stephen 'Well, there it is, Luise,
What do you think?'

Miss Rosenblum She had taken the
   train from Paddington station,
Excited at the prospect of seeing him,
Knowing that today was to be an
   important day in her life.
Her spirits had soared when she saw the
   white horse from the train,
Trotting proudly across the hill.
Now,
From up close,
It was rather disappointing,
It didn't look like a horse at all
Just an expanse of dirty chalk –
Huge
And drab,
And uninspiring.

Stephen 'This country's dead, Luise,
Like the ground we're standing on,
Chalk,
Calcium,
Compressed bones.
Come with me,
Come to the States.

I love you,
I want to take care of you.'

Miss Rosenblum He was saying all she
   had hoped he would say,
And more,
And yet it wasn't right.
'I love you, Stephen,
I love you dearly,
But I cannot marry you.'
And she stood on this hill
Looking over the rolling countryside,
And it was like her whole life spread out
   before her
Full of possibilities,
Exciting prospects,
Dimly discernible hopes
On hazy blue horizons.

'This is my home now,
Here's where I must make my life.'

She did not look back that night
As the train pulled out of the station.
She closed her eyes
And only opened them again
When the hill
And its white horse
Were way behind and out of sight.

'Ja!'

Miss Rosenblum picks up the trowel
And goes indoors.
Her shoes squelch on every step
As she climbs the stairs to her room.
There,
She sits in front of the gas-fire,
Drying her hair with a towel
And toasts herself a teacake.

Scene Thirty-Three

Caliban I must eat my dinner!
This island's mine by Sycorax my mother
Which thou takst from me. When thou
   camst first,
Thou strokst me and made much of me;
   wouldst give me
Water with berries in't; and teach me
   how

To name the bigger light, and how the less,
That burn by day and night. And then I loved thee
And showed thee all the qualities of the isle,
The fresh springs, brine pits, barren place and fertile.
Cursed be I that did so! All the charms
Of Sycorax – toads, beetles, bats, light on you!
For I am all the subjects that you have,
Which first was mine own king; and here you sty me
In this hard rock, while you do keep from me
The rest of the island.

Scene Thirty-Four

Luke The first snowflakes of winter are falling
As Luke pedals up the hill,
Wrapped up in scarf,
And hat,
And gloves.
Pause at the top for a view of the city –
Lungs burning from the effort.
Standing there looking at the unfamiliar view
And yet not seeing it,
Eyes smarting,
Heart aching,
From the pangs of first love,
Unrequited.
Unable to imagine that this pain will ever end.
Taking the letter from his pocket once again –
He knows it now almost off by heart,
But reads it all the same.

Mark 'I hope we can still be friends.'

Luke 'How can he say that?
It's not fair!
I love him,
I want to be with him.'
And so a new journey starts
As he stands there wiping his eyes,
'Just two more terms
Then I'll be leaving this dump.'
Snow now falling fast around him.
Those distant hills
Already thickly coated in white
Beckon him, even more distinctly,
Into that unknown future.

Twice Over

Jackie Kay

Twice Over was first presented by Gay Sweatshop at the Drill Hall Arts Centre, London on 27 September 1988 with the following cast:

Evaki 17, *black*	Adjoa Andoh
Cora 59, *white*	Pamela Lane
Tash 17, *black*	Thelma Lawson
Sharon 17, *white*	Amanda Martin
Maeve 58, *white, Irish*	Mary Ellen Ray
Jean 48, *black*	Cleo Sylvestre

Directed by Nona Shepphard
Designed by Kate Owen
Lighting by Sue Tandy
Soundtrack composed and recorded by Helen Glavin

Acknowledgement

I would like to thank Sallie Aprahamian, Philip Osment, Nona Shepphard and Louise Roscoe for their invaluable help and support in developing the play.

The play is set in the autumn of 1988.

The stage is broken up into different areas: **Maeve**'s *kitchen,* **Cora**'s *coffin, the street,* **Jean**'s *shop,* **Tash**'s *room. The set should not be totally naturalistic, so one or two objects indicating the above areas should be enough.*

Act One

Cora *is in her coffin, the others are grouped around her singing 'The Lord's My Shepherd'. On the second verse* **Cora** *rises.*

Cora It is so ironic to be lying next to my husband after all these years. (*She gazes around at the mourners, then sits.*) Being dead gives me a new perspective on things. If I could have lived all my life twice over, I would have never pretended.

They disperse. **Maeve** *is left alone.*

Cora But look at Maeve.

Maeve *goes to her room.*

Cora It's her I feel sorry for.

Maeve I have to talk to somebody. I'll go out of my mind if I don't talk to somebody. You're never allowed a second chance at life are you? That's it – over. Cora? I know you're here. I can feel you listening. You always were a good listener weren't you Cora? I could always trust you with my secrets and know you wouldn't go blabbing your mouth off to every Jessie, Janet and Edna. Cora? I can't remember how to laugh. We had some good belly blasts didn't we?

Evaki *is rumaging through* **Cora**'s *belongings sorting them into piles. All of her belongings are inside the coffin.* **Evaki** *puts them into black bin bags.*

Evaki Nan would probably have hated this you know. She was always kind of private. Never poked her nose into anybody's business and expected the same treatment for herself. Mind you, when she got mad at something there was no stopping her. (*Laughs.*) Like that time that lot was on my case calling me Darkie and beating me up. When Nan saw the mess my face was in, she was ready to go and get them herself. Personally. Do you think Auntie Jenny will want this? Jumble pile, family pile. OK into the jumble with you.

Cora My god! How on earth did I manage to accumulate all that junk? Chuck the lot out Evaki, give it away.

Evaki *picks out a hat, tries it on.*

Evaki I think I'll keep this. Well, you never know it might come round again. (*She finds some photos in a box.*) This is me with my Dad. What a state! I must have been about eight then. That was a year before he died. It makes me sick. Why my dad? My Nan? You know my little brother Tunde can't even remember him now. Funny that, how I got memories and he ain't.

Cora You know that funeral really put me through the paces! They were all there, quite a good turn out, wasn't it?, everyone in my life who mattered, commemorating me. Only one small problem – it isn't me they're remembering. I refuse to go through my death the same way I went through my life. That's expecting too much of a person.

Cora *moves decisively to the coffin, reaches for a photo of her and* **Maeve** *and places it before* **Evaki**.

Maeve I can't find any photos of her you know. Not one. I know we didn't have that many. But we had a few. I mean what about . . . ?

Cora *approaches* **Maeve** *smiling.*

Cora May I have the pleasure?

Maeve The pleasure's mine.

Cora *and* **Maeve** *waltz and freeze, looking into each other's eyes.*

Evaki Nan never showed me this one. I never knew they went dancing. How embarrassing. I'm just glad I was never there. I hate seeing old people dance.

Cora Come, come, Evaki. I bet I've got more rhythm in my left foot than you've got in your whole body. Have you seen her dance?

Cora *gets out a letter and places it in front of* **Evaki**

Evaki Wonder what this is about? I feel a bit like a spy prying into her business. The dead have no privacy, do they?

Cora I'm up to here with privacy. Go ahead read it!

Evaki Nah. I'll leave it out. I reckon it's none of my business.

Jean I know it's none of my business, but I do think it's a bit off, Maeve not coming back to work. You hardly need a whole day off for a funeral. Apparently she called Timothy and told him she won't be in all week! I'm upset too, but I'm here working. Honestly, next she'll be asking for compassionate leave! I was surprised this morning at the funeral. There was me crying the first tears in I don't know how long, and there was Maeve dry eyed. I said to her, 'I'm awful sorry Maeve, it's a shock, must be hard on you.' And she just nodded. Not a word about it's hard on all of us Jean, no. And to cap it all she had this expression on her face as if she was the only one who was going through it. Never mind Cora's family. I just thought to myself, what would Cora have thought of that?

Tash *is drawing in her room.*

Tash I was about to tell her too.

Cora What Tash? Tell me now love.

Tash I'd almost got it together to tell her.

Tash *concentrates on her drawing.*

Sharon I won't never tell anybody about this. I know what they'll say already – slag. I told him right, I told him, use a condom. I'm not catching AIDS from you mate. He says he won't go in just play around outside. So, his thing is outside me one minute and the next it's in. And he spurts inside me. I never told him I was a virgin cos he wouldn't have believed me anyhow. Sorry, he says. Couldn't help myself. I went home with his stuff dripping down my legs. I hope he keeps his mouth shut. I'll say he's bragging; I'll say his prick's so tiny he couldn't fuck a flea. Anyhow, I reckon I'm safe. I can't be that unlucky. It's just a warning.

Whilst **Maeve** *sings* **Cora** *listens.*

Maeve (*sings*) Her eyes they shone like diamonds
They called her the queen of the land
Her hair hung over her shoulder
Tied up with a black velvet band

She stops singing abruptly.

Nobody understands. Nobody.

Cora (*upset*) Can't you see why Maeve? Nobody knows.

Cora, *determined, walks to* **Evaki.**

Evaki? Where's that letter. Read it will you? get it over with

Evaki *gets out the letter again.*

Evaki She's not to know is she? Anyhows I'm curious.

Maeve My dearest ever Cora,
Well here I am back in the old country missing you so much. Mam isn't as ill as expected. I think she just called the alarm because she wanted to see me. Though it is good to be home again. You forget how much you miss it.
How's Evaki doing? Settled down at school? She's a right wee charmer, she'll learn fast.
I've had lots of time to think since I've been here Cora, about that conversation we were having just before I left. And I agree with you, sometimes it feels a bit like lying. But I still think it's best that nobody knows but us. They wouldn't understand what we have Cora. How could they? I don't like feeling like a criminal, but I love loving you. And I won't give that up for anybody.
I'll be back sooner than you'll know it.
All my love as always, Maeve xxx

Evaki *re-reads the letter, horrified and disbelieving whilst* **Tash** *talks.*

Tash This is too much this is. Last night he just stood and stared like he does. His eyes are always angry. Thing is, part of me feels sorry for him. Evaki says, how come you're so quiet Tash? I wonder what she'd say if she knew how come. Half the time I think, nah, it's not really happening. When I'm sitting in school doing my maths, I think, nah, it's not real. And then I go home. The only thing that's real is this. (*She points to her drawing.*)

Cora Tash. Tash. Tash.

Evaki This is doing my head in. Mum? I'm going out for a bit.

Maeve I should really get out, get some fresh air. Not that the air's very fresh in this bloody country. Do you know what I'd really like to do? Go back home.

Sharon *and* **Tash** *are in the street.* **Evaki** *approaches them.*

Evaki So how come you two aren't at school. Your granny hasn't died has she?

Tash Evaki!

Evaki What?

Tash Show some respect.

Evaki Yeah well, I would if she had, know what I mean.

Tash Nope.

Evaki Forget it.

Tash I don't understand you sometimes, Vak.

Evaki Don't bother trying.

Sharon Hey you two, is this a private conversation, or can anybody join in?

Evaki What?

Sharon I'm bored. Bunking off school isn't exactly dangerous is it? I mean why don't we do something exciting.

Tash Like what?

Sharon I don't know about you two wimps, but I could do with some booze.

Tash Yeah, but it's the money isn't it?

Sharon Who says anything about paying for it?

Evaki You're on, and I know exactly where we can get it from.

Jean For the love of God! They've landed me right in the soup, oh but they wouldn't have considered that, would they? Honestly. I said to Timothy, 'I knew nothing about this.' I don't know whether he believed me or not. Probably thinks all black people are thiefs underneath it all. Well, he looked at me kind of funny, as if I was implicated. Those three upstarts could cost me my job! Why did they have to pick my shop? That's what I'd like to know. Cora, hardly cold in her grave yet. Such blatant disrespect for the dead. It makes me think something awful might happen. The dead don't like being made a fool of.

Cora Oh for goodness sake Jean, it was only a couple of bottles of champagne. That lot ripped me off all my bloody life.

Jean If Maeve had been there it would have been her they'd have landed in it. I should pop round and see Maeve, tell her to pull herself together. You'd think Cora was family the way she's behaving.
I better get back down to my till. It's so embarrassing. I wish I worked somewhere else.

Maeve I can't face going back to work. Cora and I were there for . . . my god, twenty six years. For the last while Cora sat at till no 8 in the food department, I was in the women's clothes section, but I could always see Cora from where I sat. Oh, it'll be strange going back, but I'm not going to get another job at my age. Cora was due to retire in a couple of months. Ah, what's the use going over and over the same things?

Sharon You're just too much you are Tash. It was all your fault, you stupid cow.

Tash What was that?

Sharon I said some fucking lookout you were.

Tash I told you we should have never done it. They must have a camera or something.

Sharon They don't have no cameras fool. I should have known better than to pull anything off with you. You should stay at home doing those fucking doodles, that's all you're good for.

Evaki Lay off her Sharon. It just didn't work out. It's no big deal.

Sharon Maybe not for you. What's the matter with you anyway. You look like you couldn't give a toss?

Tash No big deal? How can you say that Evaki? When that store manager rang the pigs to see if we had any previous convictions, I suppose that was no big deal either? Jean will probably broadcast the whole story to your mum and she'll tell my dad.

Sharon So what? My dad's fed up with people ringing telling him things about me. He just tells them all to piss off. As for Jean, well what a laugh it was seeing her face. Serves the bitch right.

Evaki What's she ever done to you?

Sharon (*laughs*) She looked like she was shitting herself. Probably thought her boss would think she was trying to help us. She'd have trouble ripping off a hair pin.

Tash You know something Sharon, there's something wrong with you. You actually enjoy other people's . . .

Sharon Shut your face. You've got about as much nerve as a fucking hamster. I told you, you should stay at home. Outside's too dangerous for you.

Evaki I said leave it out Sharon.

Sharon If it weren't for her, we'd be drinking champers.

Evaki Who cares?

Tash Why's everyone blaming me?

Evaki So we didn't pull it off. So. There's always the next time.

Tash Not for me there's not.

Sharon And who'd ask you? Oh I'm fed up with this. I'm off home.

Sharon *goes to her corner.*

Tash I told you we should never have done it. That Sharon put us up to it.

Evaki I said forget it Tash.

Tash It's all very well for you. Whose going to give you any trouble?

Evaki My mum. She'd blow a fuse OK? Let's change the subject shall we?

Tash *is silent.*

Evaki Come on. What are you doing tonight? Fancy going down the club? We could have a game of pool.

Tash Nah. I'm going home to draw.

Evaki You're always drawing Tash, don't you do nothing else?

Tash What else is there?

Evaki Boyfriends.

Tash I'd rather draw.

Evaki You've never really had one have you?

Tash Not one that lasted. Hey Evaki, do you reckon you'll get married?

Evaki Suppose so. Eventually.

Tash I've been thinking, lots of people get married just because that's the done thing, then they end up pulling each other's hair out.

Evaki Not all of them. My mum and dad never fought.

Tash Well that's exceptional isn't it?

Evaki Nah.

Tash My parents hate each other for true.

Evaki Hate's a bit strong isn't it?

Tash No. I can't work out why they ever got married in the first place.

Evaki Well, there must have been something there.

Tash Can't see it.

Maeve Sean and me didn't have a bad marriage. Course, being a Catholic I don't consider myself divorced. I thought about it a lot at the time, and decided there was no point in living together anymore. That's what my conscience told me me. Sean took it all right in the end. I suppose it was lucky we weren't able to have any kids.

Cora When I think of how long I was married for before George died, it's staggering. Twenty one years. It's a long time. Well, we were happy enough. It was only through being with Maeve that I realized how much my marriage didn't give me. Twenty one years of my life.

Evaki So what would you do if you didn't get married then?

Tash Dunno. I reckon I could be happy living on me own, not having to answer to anybody, with a room I could draw in that's got lots of light.

Evaki You're not serious Tash, you'd get lonely.

Tash I'm lonely at home already.

Evaki Tash don't talk like that man, it's depressing.

Tash I wish we hadn't done that now. I feel dead guilty. When he asked about records I nearly fell through the floor.

Evaki Don't worry about it. In a few years time, we'll look back and laugh.

Tash Not if my dad finds out we won't.

Evaki You're scared of your dad aren't you?

Maeve I'm terrified of losing her you know. Her face is fading. I'd like to catch a memory and still it.

Cora *gives* **Maeve** *a small glass.*

Cora A little present for you.

Maeve Oh! What did I do to deserve this?

Cora Just being yourself darling.

Maeve Cora! You shouldn't have.

Cora Do you remember it then?

Maeve Of course I do. It was in that little shop in Cork. I've been kicking myself for not buying it ever since we got back from Ireland. But, I wasn't hinting that day.

Cora Course you were. Just as well I picked it up eh?

Maeve The cheek of you sometimes. Oh I'll treasure this Cora.

Cora Have a drink on me when I'm gone.

Maeve Don't talk like that Cora, you frighten me. Anyway, it'll be more than one drink I'll be having when you go.

Evaki I still can't believe it you know. I can't stop remembering things now. Come to think of it, I can't understand why I didn't see it before. Now that I know, it's all over the shop! Like that time I went round to Nan's early in the morning and she and Maeve were still in their nighties. And Nan said –

Cora Evaki! I didn't expect you this morning.

Evaki I thought I'd surprise you, see what you were up to!

Evaki And they both started getting dressed in front of me. And I said, you don't need to do that for me.

Cora Pardon?

Evaki I'm not royalty. And then Nan said –

Cora Would you like an egg now that you're here?

Evaki And she knew that I hated eggs. There were lots of times like that now that I come to think of it. It's just that I would have never dreamt they were both . . . Fucking hell. I just don't believe it.

She starts rummaging through **Cora**'s *things again. She discovers the diaries.*

Evaki Shit. Look at these. I suppose there's more about it in here. In for a penny in for a pound. God. It's fascinating as well as disgusting.

Cora Thank you for the compliment.

Evaki *opens one diary and closes it.*

Evaki Weird really. If I was her I wouldn't have gone writing nothing down. Somebody was bound to find this. I wish I could just shut them up, forget I ever found that letter.

Tash *is in her room trying to draw.*

Tash Listen to them! If they'd get me a Walkman, I could drown them out. (*She concentrates on the drawing.*) Miss Michael says I'm improving. Says, 'You've got talent Tash.' Talent! Funny drawing and painting's the only thing I like these days. I did this one of my mum and dad. It's more real than all the smiling photos they've got in the albums. They've got no photos of my white grandparents you know. They disowned my dad after he married mum, so he burnt all the photos to pretend they never existed I suppose. But he can't burn his memories can he?

Maeve She wouldn't have remembered giving me that glass. It's years back now. We always lived for the moment didn't we Cora? I wonder Cora, do you remember the same things?

Cora Some of them Maeve.

Maeve Probably not.

Cora I wish you would listen to me Maeve. It is so frustrating being dead. Nobody listens to you anymore.

Maeve My mam used to tell me she talked to her dead. I wish I could see my mam now. But she wouldn't know how to comfort me. What do you think Cora?

Jean Well I wonder what Cora would have thought of that!

Cora Why's everyone so suddenly interested in what I'm thinking? It's only because I'm dead. I mean I don't remember everybody asking me 'What do you think of this or that Cora?' every couple of seconds when I was alive.

Jean Evaki was her favourite. She spoiled that girl rotten.

Cora I did not!

Jean Oh, she'd deny it, I'm sure. If you ask me the girl's gone funny with Cora's death. She obviously just can't handle it. Death drives us all a bit different. I remember when my sister died I thought the world had a bloody nerve carrying on with the traffic jams, the hanging out of washing. Evaki's a far cry from the sweet little nine-year-old that Cora first introduced me to. Was I shocked! Cora hadn't mentioned anything about having black in her family. Well, her grandchildren are mixed, but you still can't call them white. And Evaki is really quite dark! I always thought Cora was different from other white women her age. I said to my Eddy when he said 'what do you want hanging around with an old white woman –'

Cora Is that what he said? Cheeky sod!

Jean I said, Cora's OK. I knew that from the beginning. I was adding up this white woman's groceries, you know the usual, ready made meals. This woman had bought enough to keep up with every Mrs Jones in the entire street. And you know when it's quality, it certainly doesn't come cheap. I said that'll be £34 something please. And she said –

Cora I remember that – It's not that I don't trust you people to add up, but are you quite sure?

Jean So Cora who I hardly knew at the time says –

Cora 'She's sure. The machine adds up.'

Jean Nice one eh? And she left without so much as a by your leave and Cora said –

Cora 'She should be an undertaker, then nobody would have to listen to her!'

Maeve *goes to* **Cora***'s.* **Evaki** *answers the door.*

Evaki Maeve! I didn't expect to see you round this way.

Maeve Well, I know it's hard work clearing up after . . . I just came to see if I could lend a hand.

Evaki Aw, come off it Maeve, you came to see if we were giving away any of Nan's best clothes.

Maeve I did not!

Evaki Actually Mum and me are managing just fine. So thanks but no thanks.

Maeve Well, I'll just come in and have a cup and a chat with your mum anyway.

Maeve *steps in.*

Also Evaki, I was wondering if you'd come across a little glass on your travels.

Evaki Plenty of glasses here.

Maeve No, this one was special. Cora gave it to me.

Evaki And you left it here?

Maeve Yes. I kept meaning to take it down the road. But you know how it is.

(*Pause.*) It's strange being back in this house. You know I keep expecting Cora to come through the door.

Evaki Well unless her ghost is prowling around you're out of luck!

Cora Evaki!

Maeve How's school?

Evaki Fine.

Maeve Are you still going out with that boy?

Evaki Which boy?

Maeve I can't remember his name.

Evaki It don't matter to you anyway.

Cora Evaki.

Maeve Sorry?

Evaki Nothing.

Maeve Oh Evaki, please help me look for that little glass.

Cora Go on Evaki!

Evaki Oh all right then.

Cora *leads* **Evaki** *to the coffin and puts the glass in front of her.* **Evaki** *picks it up.*

Evaki Is this what all the fuss is about then?

Maeve (*rushes towards her and takes the glass*) Oh yes! You're a darling an absolute darling!

Maeve *goes to embrace* **Evaki** *who backs away.* **Evaki** *goes and gets a diary out of the coffin.*

Evaki Well I better be getting back.

Maeve I'll get you down the road, I'm going too.

Evaki Sorry. I'm in a hurry.

Evaki *goes to the street.* **Maeve** *is upset. She wraps the glass in some newspaper carefully, ties a scarf under her neck and returns to her kitchen.*

Cora Well. Well. Where's she going with my diary? 1968! That was the year that George died. I think that's why I took to writing the diary in the first place. I was only 39, felt like I had the rest of my life stretched out ahead of me. Thought I might as well record my thoughts. I was lonely not having anyone to tell them to. And then once I started, I got hooked. I never told anyone. Funny, Evaki being interested in that far back. She wasn't even born then.

Sharon, **Evaki** and **Tash** *are in the street.*

Sharon How you doing Tash, all right?

Tash Piss off. I don't want nothing to do with you Sharon. You're nothing but trouble.

Sharon Trouble am I? That's rich coming from you.

Evaki Don't start Sharon.

Sharon You two always stick up for each other don't you? Well, I'm pissed off with both of you.

Evaki Oh come off it. Why don't we try again some place else?

Sharon Yeah?

Evaki Yeah.

Tash Well you can count me out.

Sharon Don't worry wimp, we wouldn't even consider you.

Tash Well I'm off. See you later Evaki.

Evaki (*ignoring her*) So where do you reckon we should try?

Sharon The off licence on the corner. That old geezer in there sleeps half the time. I reckon he's permanently sozzled.

Evaki All right. Now let's plan this one properly cos I could do with a stiff drink.

Tash *goes to her room.*

Sharon Me too. Hey, Evaki, why do you hang out with Tash, man. She's wet. She's a waste of space.

Evaki I like her.

Sharon Suit yourself.

Evaki We've been mates since we was twelve.

Sharon Stop it, you're breaking my heart. Some things you just have to grow out of, know what I mean?

Evaki Nah. I reckon Tash and me will be mates for the rest of our lives.

Sharon You're having me on. What are you both – lezzies?

Evaki Fuck off.

Sharon Just you seem so dedicated.

Evaki Drop it. Are we going to get this booze or not?

Sharon Course!

Evaki I'll meet you on the corner in half an hour then.

Tash I can't stop thinking about this dream I had last night. It was weird. My mum came into my room and told me she was going to die. Then she went out. I ran after her but I couldn't find her anywhere in the house. Then I was by the sea and I knew I was going to have a baby. I was swimming and it was swimming inside me. Then my dad came into the water and said we'd need to go home for mum's funeral. He was looking at me funny. I said, 'You bastard', 'What was that? Tash? Tash?' I woke up and he was standing at the bottom of the bed. He said, 'What's the matter?'

Maeve I don't know what's the matter with me. Too full of memories. We both worked in the same shop, Cora and I. After a year or so, Cora invited me round for dinner. George was still alive then. After . . . you'd think we'd have got fed up of the sight of each other. Working in the same place all that time. To tell you the truth I never tired of looking at Cora.

Always saw something different in her face.

Cora You never told me that!

Maeve Do you know that in all that time we never ran out of things to talk about? Mind you Cora was always joking that if me and a stranger landed on a desert island after a couple of days the stranger would be hiding from me! Well I'm not saying I don't like to talk. Now and again. When I'm in the mood. I remember us joking that time and Cora telling me I was romantic, no *a* romantic she said.

Cora Did I?

Maeve Have a drink on me she said. Well, I don't mind if I do. (**Maeve** *pours herself a drink in her little glass.*) The truth is I get scared of what they might be finding round at Cora's. Prying with her business. I wish I could just go and check. Take away anything that might offend. It's all they need right now, to find out something like that.

Cora It'll be good for them.

Maeve I'm trying to remember what she said to me before she died.

Cora I said tell the truth about me.

Maeve And I can't for the life of me think what it was. I remember it was odd. Not a Cora thing to say.

Cora And what on earth is that?

Maeve Mind you Cora, you were always full of surprises. I'd just be thinking I know you better than I know myself and then you'd do something or say something.

Tash Sometimes you think you know somebody and then they go and spoil it.

Maeve Oh Cora, why did I leave you that awful night. Why in the Lord's name did I not trust my own instinct. You told me you weren't feeling yourself and I knew it. You didn't look well Cora. I suggested to Jan that I stay and look after you. She said 'You get off home Maeve, I'm sure Mum probably just needs some rest.' I wasn't happy leaving Cora. I just didn't want Jan to think . . . Oh! For goodness sake, it's ridiculous! If only I hadn't bothered about what Jan thought you might have been alive right now. The doctors said you had a heart attack and died between 2 and 4 am.

Cora So I did. Massive bloody great thing. Took me by storm I can tell you.

Maeve Was it lonely dying, Cora? If I'd just been with you. If I'd just told you again how much I love you. Cora. Cora.

Cora Maeve! Don't do this to yourself my love. All that guilt. It doesn't matter from here, I promise you. Actually it's harder for you than it was for me. OK. So there were things I would have still liked to do. And dying wasn't fun exactly, but it's not the end of the world. I'm doing fine now love. Absolutely fine.

Evaki *goes to* **Maeve***'s.* **Maeve** *jumps at the bell, answers it.*

Evaki Hello Maeve. Just thought I'd pop by on my way home from school.

Maeve Well, isn't this a treat? You'll stay for a cup?

Evaki Nope. Haven't got the time. Maeve, I was wondering . . .

Maeve What were you wondering darlin'?

Evaki I never knew Nan kept diaries, did you?

Maeve No I did not.

Evaki Hmmn. I thought if anyone would know, it would be you Maeve. Interesting isn't it. See this, (*She pulls a diary out of her bag.*) this is the first one, 1968. They go all the way up to now you know. Fact she changed to five year diaries and the last one's supposed to go up to 1990, but she didn't make it did she?

Maeve They should have buried them with her.

Evaki Oh no, that would have been a crime. It's good stuff this is. I'm thinking I might even try and find a publisher.

Maeve You haven't been reading them, have you? What would you want prying into her business? It's bad luck you know, sneaking up on the dead.

Evaki I'm not superstitious. Well, I have to be going. (*She notices* **Maeve***'s glass.*) Is that you drinking in the afternoon Maeve? It's not good for you. You should get back to work, keep yourself busy. I'll give your love to Mum shall I?

Maeve Yes . . . yes do.

Evaki *and* **Sharon** *meet at the corner, then go to* **Cora***'s with a bottle of gin.*

Cora Don't upset yourself Maeve.

Maeve I think I need a drink. (*She knocks back a drink, pours another.*) That's done it Cora! That's the last bloody straw. First you die on me and now these bloody diaries. I'm finished. You can find some other poor fool to grieve for you. What on earth were you doing keeping diaries Cora? Answer me, damn you! You had no business writing about me without telling me. Now my life's an open book as well as yours. Did I not love you enough? Was it not good enough? What did I do to deserve this Cora? I thought we had no secrets from each other. Damn you Cora! (**Maeve** *knocks over the glass and it breaks.*)

Cora Maeve. Maeve. You've got me all wrong.

Maeve Cora are you there? I've smashed my little present. I've broken the glass.

Evaki *and* **Sharon** *are drunk on the gin.*

Evaki What's up? I thought this was what you wanted.

Sharon Nothing.

Evaki *puts her arm around* **Sharon** *drunkenly.*

Sharon Geroff. Lezzie cow.

Evaki What did you call me?

Sharon I said you're a lezzie cow.

Evaki Piss off. Go on, get out.

Sharon Aw come off it. I was pulling your leg. Mind you, it must be true for you to act like that. Evaki! Darling, why didn't you tell me?

Evaki Shut your fucking face I'm warning you.

Sharon You don't think I'd hang around with you if I really thought that, do you?

Evaki Yeah, well slags aren't usually that choosy.

Sharon What was that?

Evaki You heard. Everyone knows you're a slag, Sharon. Steven's been talking. I don't mind. What was it like then, go on tell me?

Sharon I didn't do anything. He's a lying bastard.

Evaki So what if you did, we all need a bit of . . .

Sharon Speak for yourself. Where are you getting yours?

Evaki Actually I'm celibate at the moment.

Sharon Oh, celibate are we? Little Nun are we becoming. Well. Well. You know what they say about nuns.

Evaki Shut it.

Sharon (*shouts*) They're all lezzies!

Evaki I think you've had too much to drink. You better fuck off home.

Sharon Don't worry I'm going. (*She gets up angry, then stops.*) Vak?

Evaki Yeah.

Sharon There was something I was going to tell you.

Evaki Oh yeah?

Sharon Nah, it's nothing. I'm just pissed. See you tomorrow?

Evaki Yeah. Yeah.

Sharon *goes back to the street.* **Evaki** *gets out all the diaries.*

Evaki Well. Nothing can shock me now anyway.

Maeve Did you write about us? From the beginning? I remember the first time as if it was yesterday.

Evaki *reads while* **Cora** *talks.*

Evaki September 12th 1973.

Cora Maeve stayed the night last night.

Maeve We'd just been to a concert. Mozart I think. Cora was a one for the classical music.

Cora She came back for a nightcap and ended up staying over.

Maeve I remember saying that music's made me tingle all over.

Cora It was wonderful. I feel so high today. I can't believe it. Me a grandmother. I'm 44 years old and I feel like I've got a brand new lease on life.

Maeve She said, 'listen to you, tingling all over. You're so dramatic. You should sing arias yourself.'

Cora I said something that hurt her. I can't remember what it was but I said 'I'm only teasing.' (I didn't realize she could be so touchy.)

Maeve I was put out. Oh I'm a one for sulking now and again. And Cora said I'm only teasing. (**Maeve** *grabs* **Cora**'s *hand and kisses it.*) I don't know what came over me.

Cora She kissed my hand. I don't know what came over me. I said, now it's me that's tingling all over.

Cora *kisses* **Maeve** *on the lips.*

Maeve I'll never forget that kiss. I said to her bold as brass 'I've wanted you to do that for the past two years!'

Cora Everything fell into place last night. All these feelings I've been having for Maeve and hiding from myself. All those times I've been anxious to see her and just put it down to other things. I've been in love with Maeve all these years and I only really found out last night. All those times I'd pretend to forget something just so that I could kiss her cheeks goodbye again. Her fine, fine cheeks.

Maeve She sat down on the sofa and said –

Cora Come here.

Maeve I remember thinking absurdly to myself that my skirt was sliding over my knees as I walked towards her. I suddenly felt absolutely terrified. What would? And my man? And me 43 years old.

Cora Last night I thought 'Cora you're 44. You can do exactly as you please'.

Maeve And then we were through with the talking.

Cora And then we were through with the talking.

Maeve And do you know, the shame of it. (*She giggles.*) We never even made it up to bed. Our first passion on Cora's living room sofa. Even now when I'm round there, with Cora gone, I think to myself as Jan sits on that same sofa drinking tea, little do you know. And then I say, 'Oh Maeve, you're terrible, terrible.'

Evaki It's written down here in my Nan's own hand, and I still don't believe it. I can't keep all this to myself much longer man, it's doing my head in.

Cora Well then. What's stopping you?

Act Two

The stage is the same as before, except some of **Cora**'s *things are packed away in plastic bags.* **Evaki** *is still reading the diaries.*

Evaki I can't put them down. Well, I'll say one thing for Nan – she knew how to write.

Cora Thank you Evaki.

Evaki There's so much about me in these you know. Weird, reading about myself as a kid. It's like looking at old photos. January 12th 1980.

Cora Evaki and Tunde are staying with me to give Jan a break. What a new year for all of us! Not a word's warning. Mpenga died two nights ago of a brain tumour. We'll all miss him terribly, especially Jan. Poor dear. I know it sounds awful but I'm missing my Maeve. She and I can't behave the same way with my grandchildren here. Evaki is a nosey little thing, full of questions.

Evaki Fancy that! My dad just dead and they were at it even then. It's been going on since 1973 you know. I was only two when they got started.

Cora I've been thinking a lot about how silly this is. Hiding my real life from my grandchildren so that they won't tell my daughter.

Evaki Mum would have a heart attack if she knew, she would.

Cora I often wonder what Jan would do if she knew, whether she'd still let them stay with me or not. It'd break my heart if she didn't. I love those kids to pieces. One day maybe Jan will know and accept. I can't see me carrying on this secrecy for the rest of my life. It'd be intolerable.

Evaki Well. Too bloody late now.

Cora It makes me jumpy too. I mean it's unnatural.

Evaki She's right there.

Cora Unnatural jumping when a six-year-old or a nine-year-old comes into the kitchen, just because Maeve is kissing my cheek. Actually, it's undignified. I have to tell Maeve this, see what she thinks we should do.

Maeve When did you find the time to write them Cora? All those words. I'm scared stiff of anyone finding out Cora, but now I know why you wanted to tell. It's lonely not. Dead lonely. I should get some sleep Cora, it's late. But my bed is so empty without you. Last night I reached out for you Cora. Why on earth did you have to go?

Tash I wish I could get out of this house. I hate it. It's been going on for years you know. I was thinking that today when I was drawing a picture of a kid. Fact, as I remember, it was my eighth birthday. I couldn't believe how nice everyone was being to me. Mum gave me a game she used to play with in Trinidad. That night I was in my room looking over my presents when my dad came in. He had his fingers to his lips to tell me to be quiet. But I didn't make a sound anyway. Maybe I should have. Maybe it's my fault.

Sharon It's all my own stupid fault. This is no joke now. That bastard Steven, he's got nothing to worry about has he? Well they say if you worry they don't come. So I better stop worrying. But, what if I've got AIDS? I hear you catch it from sleeping around. I betcha that Steven's had more girls than I've had hot dinners. How do you know if you've got it? I've not been feeling too bright recently. Shit. If they don't come tomorrow, I'll have to do something drastic.

Evaki's *still reading the diaries.*

Cora Look at her! I've been dead eight days now and she still hasn't told anybody. It's getting so frustrating, I can't tell you. I wish I was the kind of ghost who made an impact, like Cathy in *Wuthering Heights*.

What is the matter with that girl? I was counting on her big mouth. She always used to tell me all her secrets.

Evaki You know I used to tell Nan everything. More than I tell Mum. I felt I could trust her. She always gave good advice. But I reckon I didn't know her at all.

Cora Course you did. You just didn't know everything that's all.

Evaki I can't get over how long they did it for. It's all over the shop. (*She flicks through the diary maniacally.*) May 12th 1979.

Cora Maeve said to me yesterday, 'Are you aware it's been six years now Cora?' 'What has, love?' I asked.

Maeve Do you know the funny thing? I can remember Cora years ago more clearly than I can days ago. This morning I woke up thinking about that gold chain she gave me for our anniversary. I think it was the seventh.

Cora I'll never forget the look on her face. I love her so much it scares me sometimes. I told her that Jean and I had chosen it together, and that I'd told Jean it was for her 50th birthday. Late that night we made love as if it was the first time all over again.

Evaki I wonder what they did. I mean I wonder how they did it.

Cora Our passion still amazes me. It was never like this with George.

Evaki Poor Grandad.

Cora Just as I was nodding to sleep, Maeve said to me –

Maeve Cora? If you told Jean it was for my birthday, what will happen when my real birthday comes?

Cora Honestly!

Evaki I wonder if anyone else knows about it. Maybe Jean does, I reckon I'll go and see her, find out for myself.

Cora Great idea! About bloody time too.

Tash Haven't seen Evaki for yonks. She's probably dumped me to hang out with Sharon. I thought we was good mates too. It's better not to trust anybody, then you don't get let down, do you?

Sharon Evaki must have gone back to Queen of the Wimps. What a waste. We had a good time drinking the other night. I nearly told her too. Shit. I wish I had somebody that would be that fucking loyal to me. What am I going to do?

Evaki *goes to* **Jean***'s shop.*

Jean Evaki! I didn't expect you here. I'm surprised you can show your face.

Evaki I've come to apologize.

Jean And so I should think. Your grandmother would . . .

Evaki Would you say you knew my Nan well, Jean?

Jean Yes, very well.

Evaki So you knew!

Jean Knew what?

Evaki Knew that she kept diaries.

Cora Chicken.

Jean No, I didn't, but that's not all that unusual you know. Are you surprised because you don't expect grandmothers to keep diaries?

Evaki There's a lot you don't expect grandmothers to do.

Jean Sorry?

Evaki Anyhow these diaries are very unusual as it happens. Fact, they're like a grand collection of everybody's secrets.

Jean What are you on about? I thought you came here to apologize.

Evaki So I did. Sorry.

Jean Yes well, you'd better be off with you. The shop's about to close.

Evaki OK. I'm going. Jean? There was one more thing . . .

Jean What now?

Evaki It's about Maeve . . . I'd rather she didn't get to hear about the other day, it would only upset her.

Jean Well I won't say anything, but I can't vouch for the rest of the shop. You know how people love to gossip. Mind you, by the time Maeve's back, it'll probably have blown over.

Evaki Is Maeve sick?

Jean Well, I think it's your Nan's death that's taken the wind out of her sails. They did practically everything together.

Evaki Not practically, everything.

Jean Well, you'd better be off.

Evaki OK. See you Jean.

Jean I don't remember telling Cora anything too private. Well, I told her about my Eddy always finding ways of reminding me he's seven years younger. Oh, and I'd have a moan about him and how he'd expect me to be thankful he's not getting it from someone younger and skinnier. Cora and Maeve, now they must have talked more intimately. Cora always seemed hellbent on pleasing Maeve. If you ask me, it was ridiculous.

Cora *and* **Jean** *mime looking in shop windows with umbrellas up.*

Cora No, that won't do. It has to be finer.

Jean For God's sake Cora, it's pounding down.

Cora Maeve's most particular.

Jean Well, so am I about getting my clothes soaked.

Cora Just one more shop. It's for her 50th birthday after all.

Jean We found the fine gold chain as the rain stopped. I hadn't known the two of them for more than a year then. I remember thinking I wish I had a friend that would go to all that trouble for me.

Jean *goes to* **Maeve** .

Jean Hello Maeve. I thought I'd pop by and check you're OK. We were a bit worried about you in the shop.

Maeve Come on in. Doing away. You know, I could do with a holiday someplace nice. Cora and I were planning on going to Dublin you know?

Jean Were you? You and Cora did a lot together, didn't you Maeve? Why don't you still go on your own?

Maeve I couldn't. Anyway, I'll need to get back to work soon.

Jean Oh there's no hurry.

Maeve I bet that's not what Timothy is saying.

Jean To hell with Timothy.

Pause.

Jean You must be missing Cora.

Maeve Oh yes I miss her.

Jean I do too, she was a fantastic person, Cora.

Maeve That she was. Not many like her.

Jean Have you seen Evaki recently?

Maeve Yes, yesterday.

Jean I think she's behaving a little strangely.

Maeve What do you mean?

Jean Well, she came round to the shop and was asking me if I knew that Cora kept diaries and said that they were like a grand collection of everyone's secrets.

Maeve She did not!

Jean I was surprised. Yes, you could have knocked me down with a feather. I can't imagine Cora writing diaries. I always think of solitary people doing that sort of thing. Did you know?

Maeve No, no I didn't. That girl's got a nerve on her.

Jean And the other strange thing. Well, I don't really know how to say this, but I thought it better you hear it from me rather than someone else.

Maeve (*panicked*) Hear what?

Jean Well, a couple of days after Cora's funeral, Evaki came round to the shop with a couple of her friends. I was glad you were spared the agony of being there Maeve. I'm sure you'd have been so embarrassed. Evaki's changed – I wouldn't have thought her capable . . .

Maeve Of what? I don't understand what you're saying.

Jean Well the long and the short of it is that the store detective caught them with a couple of bottles of champagne in their bag and I had to take them to see Timothy. They were bloody lucky they got off. I mean that would be all Jan needs, eh?

Maeve They tried to steal them?

Jean Yes two bottles of champagne of all things.

Maeve (*laughing*) Why the little devils!

Jean I thought it was disrespectful actually with Cora just fresh in the ground.

Maeve Terrible. Terrible.

Jean And you know how people gossip.

Maeve Yes.

Jean Well, I thought you were bound to hear.

Maeve Thanks for telling me Jean. I'm sure Jan would be upset, so we mustn't let her get to hear of it.

Jean Young people surprise me all the time. Even my own. They do things I'd never expect them to do. Yesterday I found a packet of condoms in Steven's underwear drawer. He's the same age as Evaki! In fact I'm sure one of the girls with Evaki is the same one Steven's been hanging around with.

Maeve Is that so? Well anyway it's better than getting her pregnant.

Jean I suppose so. Well, I'd better be off. Ring me if you need anything, and you know where I am if you want to chat with anybody.

Maeve Thanks Jean. I'll be back to work on Wednesday.

Jean That's right, life must go on.

Jean *goes back to the shop.* **Maeve** *sits laughing to herself.*

Maeve What a laugh Cora. You know this is the first time I've laughed since you died. You'd have thought that funny too Cora. I know what I'll do . . .

She puts on Fats Waller's 'The Jitterbug Waltz'. **Cora** *and* **Maeve** *dance together.*

Maeve I like the way you dance.

Cora We should go dancing together. Get all dressed up.

Maeve I used to hate dancing with Sean. He had two left feet. He'd step on my toes every third step.

Cora George was a good dancer. He liked the foxtrot.

Maeve Did he now? Did you prefer him to me then?

Cora Oh no. His waist wasn't nearly so nice to hold.

Maeve That's because he didn't have a girdle on!

They laugh.

Cora Lets go dancing. Get all dressed up. People will think we're widows or divorcees having to take each other as second best.

Maeve You are a widow and I'm almost a divorcee. Had you forgotten?

Cora (*laughing.*) Oh so I am! Well you know what I mean – little do they know.

Maeve You look lovely.

Cora You don't look too bad yourself.

Maeve Kiss me.

They kiss. **Cora** *goes to her place.* **Maeve** *is left dancing on her own. She is disconcerted.*

Maeve What year was it that we went to that dance Cora? 76? 77? You looked fantastic that night. Dancing like there was no tomorrow.

Sharon *and* **Tash** *meet up in the street.*

Sharon Hello Tash. Seen Evaki?

Tash Nope. I thought you'd know where she is.

Sharon Nope. Haven't seen her for a couple of days.

Tash Did you pull if off then?

Sharon Yeah man, a whole bottle of gin.

Tash Worth it was it?

Sharon Nah, not really. (*Pause.*) Tash, I think something's up with Evaki. She's gone a bit loopy. I reckon she might even try and top herself.

Tash Evaki? Never! What are you talking about?

Sharon Maybe it's my imagination.

Tash Yeah.

Tash *gets ready to go.*

Sharon Tash?

Tash Yeah?

Sharon I'm sorry I was such a bitch to you. It was nothing to do with you. I've got problems.

Tash What problems?

Sharon I think I'm pregnant.

Tash Oh no, Shar. I'm sorry.

Sharon It was that bastard Steven.

Tash They piss me off they do. Boys. They're all the same. Out for what they can get. And then they piss off and leave you in the shit.

Sharon Aw come on. Some of them are OK.

Tash Like who for instance?

Sharon Dunno. What am I going to do Tash?

Tash We could go to a clinic.

Sharon You mean you'd come with me?

Tash Course.

Sharon I'll wait a couple of more days.

Tash Yeah, well, don't wait too long.

Sharon Tash? Don't tell nobody, not even Evaki. I don't want no gossip.

Tash I won't. I promise.

Evaki *is still reading the diaries.*

Cora Give it a break! I'm getting bored. Honestly, it's really getting me down. I've got no control over it all. It reminds me of when I was alive. I thought being dead would be totally different. I want it out in the open once and for all. Not just for me, for Maeve. Funny, I thought it'd be enough Evaki knowing. But it's not.

Evaki This is a good bit. February 13th, 1973. Evaki is talking away these days. I'm still amazed at how children learn to copy sounds. It's a wonder we have any individuals. Evaki even pretends to smoke and she's not yet three. She rolls up a piece of paper and lights it by pressing her thumb down on her clenched fist. Then puffs out and chuckles. She is such a character. If Jan didn't smoke then she wouldn't be imitating, but who am I to judge?

Maeve I can't stop thinking what if Jan finds out? The thought of my own family knowing still makes my stomach turn. It's ridiculous still being scared at 58 of my mam finding out who I am.

Evaki I can't remember things without remembering other things. They took us all in, they did. Must have had a good laugh at our expense.

Cora It wasn't funny.

Evaki And I liked Maeve too. And I loved my Nan.

Maeve I told this friend once. I trusted her. And what did she do. She said she couldn't trust me anymore.

Cora Enough, Maeve! Give yourself a break. Are you going to spend the rest of your life going over and over these petty details till you drive yourself to the grave? It really isn't worth it. Take it from me – I'm dead.

Evaki I just hope it isn't hereditary, that's all. Cos people say it's in the hormones and it's catching. Nah. I would know, wouldn't I? I've got boyfriends, not right now, but still. Mind you Nan was married to Grandad. I would have never guessed. They both wore skirts.

Cora What me and your grandad in skirts?

Evaki And they don't look like men or walk like men. They just don't look like lezzies, do you know what I mean? Shit. It never rains but it pours. Nan used to say that all the time. I'm pissed off with her. I wish she was around so's I could tell her how pissed off I am. Mum? I'm finished here.

Evaki *puts the bags inside the coffin and closes it.*

Sharon Tash is all right. I don't reckon she'll tell anyone. I reckon she knows how to keep her mouth shut. I feel a bit bad about being so rotten to her, but there you go. I was trying to work out what I'll do if I am pregnant. The old man and old dear would die. I couldn't bring myself to tell them. I'd have to go away. Tash said she could lend me some money. I wonder where she gets money from. I reckon Evaki's still mad at me for calling her a lezzie. Silly cow.

Jean Maeve didn't even seem to mind about those three stealing from our shop. I think it's Cora, affecting her. I tell you those two were so close, I sometimes wondered about them! But that's monstrous. They're too old. Mind you I had an aunt like that. It wasn't her fault. Well you know some of them are born that way. But no, Maeve and Cora were married. I was quite fond of my aunt actually. But my mum never forgave her for not being normal, which I always thought a bit unfair. I mean, she couldn't choose her hormones could she? For myself, I can't see the attraction in it. I like men to be men and women to be women, then everybody knows where they are. Maeve and Cora couldn't have been actually. I can't imagine either of them playing the man. Mind you, Cora had quite a dominant personality.

Evaki You know Miss Michael, do you reckon it's true what everyone says?

Sharon That she's a lezzie? Dunno. I don't think so. We'd know about it.

Evaki How?

Sharon Aw come off it. You can smell a lezzie a mile off.

Evaki Oh yeah?

Sharon Yeah man. What's the matter with you. She'd have been eyeing us up for starters. Then there's the way they walk, the jobs they do.

Evaki What are you talking about?

Sharon Most of them walk like men and do men's jobs, you know building sites, shit like that.

Evaki That's crap Sharon.

Sharon Even the clothes they wear. I'm telling you, they're all fucked up. They all think they're men so they wear men's stuff, do their jobs, it's sick man.

Evaki That's crap too.

Sharon I'm not talking crap. I'm talking common knowledge. Where've you been? I've even seen some. Yuck, it's horrible. Can you imagine doing it with another woman? It's so dirty it's not true. You have to watch lezzies though, it's catching.

Evaki What are you talking about?

Sharon You know you might get caught under their influence.

Evaki That's rubbish too. You ought to hear yourself Sharon, you're talking absolute garbage.

Sharon All right then. How come you know so much about it then?

Evaki My Nan was one.

Sharon (*explodes laughing*) That's a good one Vak. Oh you haven't lost your sense of humour. Queer grannies. What a laugh. Can you imagine two wrinkled up old ladies doing it together? What a joke.

Evaki I'm not joking.

Evaki *walks off to* **Cora**'s. **Sharon** *stares open mouthed.* **Tash** *goes to* **Cora**'s.

Evaki Tash! I was just thinking about you.

Tash Yeah?

Evaki Yeah.

Tash Are you alright Vak?

Evaki Yeah, why shouldn't I be?

Tash No reason.

Evaki Actually Tash, I've got something to tell you.

Tash Spit it out girl.

Evaki You know I was helping my mum clear out my Nan's things?

Tash Yeah that must have been depressing Vak.

Evaki Yeah well. I came across lots of stuff.

Tash Yeah.

Evaki First of all, right, I found this photo.

Tash Oh what a picture. They look great, don't they?

Evaki Then I found this letter. Here, read it.

Evaki *hands* **Tash** *the letter.*

Evaki You see it'd been going on for ages.

Still reading.

Tash What has?

Tash *finishes the letter.*

Tash My god, that's amazing!

Evaki Is that all you can say.

Tash I mean that's incredible.

Evaki After I read this letter and reread it about a million times. Shit Tash, I just couldn't believe it. I found her diaries. There was no going back then. I was obsessed. The diaries go right back to 1968.

Tash You shouldn't have read her diaries Evaki.

Cora I don't mind Tash. Nice of you though.

Evaki Is that all you can think of? I'm telling you I've got a queer Nan and you're bothering about me reading her fucking diaries!

Tash Don't say queer like that. Show some respect Evaki. She's dead.

Evaki You don't even see them on the box, queer grannies. If they was to make a soap, it'd get taken right off.

Tash So what did you find in the diaries?

Evaki Lots. I read bits about me and stuff about my mum and dad. Lots about Maeve and her being really close. Fact, Tash, I couldn't put the bloody things down. I found out so much about Nan that I never knew. How she would have liked to write stories rather than sit at a till all day. How she liked music. How much she loved Maeve. How Maeve filled a spot she never knew was empty till it was filled.

Cora Did I write that? That's eloquent isn't it?

Evaki And about how I am her favourite grandchild, even though she said she shouldn't have favourites and . . . and . . . (**Evaki** *breaks down.*) I reckoned she must have meant me to find them because there is so much about me . . . At first I thought. I can't tell this to nobody, no matter how bad I feel cos it wouldn't be fair on her. Till I realized that she didn't want it secret anyhow. She says in her diaries over and over again how she hates her life being a shame. Hates covering up and lying and pretending all the fucking time. That's what decided me to tell you Tash. And she liked you too.

Cora At last!

Evaki You know every so often I think this has to be a dream and I'm going to wake up . . . Just like I think that Nan dying is a bad dream and I'm going to wake up and she'll be there talking with me and stuff, except now that I know all this, I don't know what I'd say to her.

Tash I don't think there is anything wrong with it, you know. I mean they weren't doing nobody any harm. Just getting on with their lives. They were happy, weren't they? And happiness don't grow on trees.

Evaki But don't you think it's disgusting Tash?

Tash Not really. What's disgusting about it?

Evaki Come on Tash. Two women. Two old women. It's unnatural you've gotta think that.

Tash I reckon natural's what you make of it.

Evaki Aw leave it out Tash.

Tash I'm serious. My mum and dad staying together when they hate each other's guts, now *that* ain't natural, but people would say that it is. Anyhow they were good to you, weren't they?

Evaki Yeah. Suppose so.

Tash So why think differently about them just because of this? Don't you love Nan no more?

Evaki Don't talk crap Tash. She's dead.

Tash You can still love someone even if they is dead.

Evaki I was going to tell Maeve that I knew.

Cora Tell her then. Tell her!

Evaki I almost did. But I was angry then. Anyhow I don't know what she'd say.

Tash Well we could find out, couldn't we? Come on, let's pay Maeve a visit.

Jean I can't stop thinking the whole business is odd. Ever since I had that peculiar thought about Maeve and Cora being that way inclined, I haven't been able to stop remembering things. And they all add up, I can tell you. At Cora's 55th, there was something going on. I walked into the kitchen and there they both were, cuddling like sweethearts. Oh, I put it down to the wine at the time. But Maeve had that same expression on her face that she had yesterday, as if she'd been caught. What a shame really. I mean they weren't doing anybody any harm. It must be terrible for Maeve now. Not a soul to talk to about it. I don't suppose she's ever told anybody, she's so secretive. Maybe I should broach the subject with her. No she's so private, she'd resent it, I'm sure. I better just mind my own.

Maeve Do you know what the awful thing is? I keep seeing her. Every time I go out, I catch a glimpse of her or somebody who looks like her. I try and catch up and when I do the face changes and I feel like an old fool. There were so many things we still had to talk about. So many promises we'd made ourselves. Do you remember us talking about going on a cruise Cora?

Cora Hell, I wish we'd just gone last year instead of worrying about the money.

Maeve I'll really need to stop this. Stop thinking I'll just pop round to Cora's and then the thud of remembering. Stop waking with this long list of if onlys. Cora? I know I'm being pathetic, you'd hardly recognize me. I can't help myself.

Sharon *is reading the instructions of a pregnancy test.*

Sharon Right. The results are in the window. If there's a definite blue line you're pregnant, if there's not you're not. (*She peers at it.*) Jesus. Well what bloody colour is that? (*She stares again.*) Wait a minute. There's no blue line. (*She squeals with joy.*) Well thank fuck for that. You can't be too careful. This bloke Simon's asked me out tonight. I wonder what I should wear. Well, I've got my new lipstick. He's really good looking. I don't know why people say looks don't matter, they do. Everybody's after him. But there'll be no hanky panky tonight. No way.

Tash *and* **Evaki** *go to* **Maeve's.**

Maeve Evaki! Tash! Come away in. This is a surprise. To what do I owe the pleasure?

Evaki We were passing by and . . .

Maeve Oh, I'm all right. Bored today, mind you. Still, I've got company now. Usually on a day like this, if Cora and I had the same day off, we'd go someplace, Brighton or somewhere for the day. But I don't feel like going on my own. It's not the same is it? I miss your Nan Evaki.

Cora I know Maeve.

Evaki I know Maeve.

Maeve No doubt you do too.

Evaki I've been thinking about her a lot.

Maeve Yes I know love, it's hard. But there's no bringing her back.

Tash I was really fond of Cora too, she was like a gran to me.

Cora What is this an admiration society?

Maeve Ah well, so what have you two been up to then?

Evaki Nothing much. School and stuff. Oh, Maeve I brought some things I thought you might be interested in. (*She hands* **Maeve** *the photo.*)

Maeve Oh! I've been looking everywhere for this. Cora loved the dancing you know?

Evaki No I didn't. Maeve? I know you and my Nan were close.

Maeve (*still laughing at the photo*) Oh yes we were close all right. Best of friends your Nan and I.

Evaki No that's not what I mean. I know about you and Nan Maeve.

Maeve What on earth are you getting at?

Evaki Well I read this letter that you sent Nan from Ireland.

She gives **Maeve** *the letter.* **Maeve** *reads it and is embarrassed.*

Maeve Oh this isn't the way it sounds Evaki. You're surely not implying that your Nan and me –

Evaki were lesbians. Yes. You don't have to deny it to me.

Maeve Oh this is absolutely preposterous! I can't believe you're sitting in my house talking such rubbish. This bit here about I hate feeling like a criminal, that was just because I felt guilty that I wasn't going home to stay in Ireland for good. You see if you'd read the letter properly, you would realize that my mam was sick. Well she wanted me to move back lock, stock and barrel. And as for the love. Well, yes, I won't deny I loved Cora.

Cora Thank goodness for that.

Maeve But not in the dirty way that you imply. What on earth do you take me for? Evaki you've got a nerve on you coming here upsetting me like this. Goodness knows what your Nan would have said if she'd heard these accusations! Mind you she'd have probably laughed them off, they're so bloody ridiculous.

Evaki Nan would have been honest about it, I'm sure of that. She was fed up with lying.

Maeve Listen to you lying. What age are you? 17 years old and you don't understand a damn thing. Get out of my house. I don't have to sit and listen to this nonsense in my own home. No, there are some things I don't have to do.

Evaki What about this then?

Evaki *gets out the diaries.*

Listen. October 28th, 1975.

Cora Maeve and I are still having a good time.

Maeve Shut up, I don't want to hear her bloody diaries. You had no right reading them.

Cora I'm convinced we'll be together for the rest of our lives. We love to joke about how we'll perm each others hair and make ginger wine when we're old ladies.

Maeve Ginger wine! Nonsense. I can't stand ginger wine. Cora was a one for fabricating. I don't suppose you knew that Evaki, but she liked to tell a story.

Cora And go on cruises. We've always wanted to go on a cruise.

Maeve *starts crying.*

I'd love to see so many places with Maeve – China especially, for some unknown reason. Still no word to the family. I'm fed up with this hiding. This double life. I can't put up with it for much longer. Why should we be ashamed of our love?

Evaki At first when I read all that, I'll be honest, I wasn't exactly jumping for joy. Fact, quite the opposite. Then I started thinking what it must have been like for my Nan going all these years without telling a soul. I mean secrets are terrible things, in't they Tash?

Tash Yeah.

Evaki And I thought I was lucky cos I haven't really got any secrets from anybody. I'd tell my Nan. And now I tell Tash all my business. And then I started remembering all these things that I hadn't even thought I'd noticed. Like all those times you stayed at Nan's and would act odd if I came by surprise.

Maeve All right! All right! For Christ's sake just be quiet. Oh, you've been a right little detective, haven't you. I suppose you're proud of your handy work. Think you're clever, do you?

Evaki It's nothing to do with being clever.

Maeve Reading letters, reading diaries, working out this and that. You'd think you were the bloody police coming to get me with your substantive evidence. Well I hope you're satisfied now that you've proved your case. You can go home. Leave me alone.

Evaki Maeve, don't take it like that.

Maeve How am I supposed to take it? How would you like it if I snooped around in your private business reading your love letters, your diaries. I tell you Cora, will be turning in her grave.

Evaki No she won't. She wanted me to know. Her diaries say so. I reckon she'll be peaceful now.

Maeve After all those years, being so bloody careful, hiding this, faking that. All those years and my own hand gives it away in the end. If you hadn't found that letter, you would have never known. Would you?

Evaki I suppose not. But that ain't the point is it?

Maeve It was our business. Our private business. That's the point. We knew most people wouldn't approve, so we kept it to ourselves. I suppose you've already told your mother?

Evaki No, but I am going to. I reckon she's got a right to know.

Maeve Oh she has, has she? Well then she's got a right to know about her daughter stealing bottles of champagne. Or trying to steal I should say. You didn't make it did you?

Tash How do you know about that.

Maeve Oh I hire my own private detective too.

Tash Don't worry Maeve, Evaki won't tell her mother.

Evaki Yes I will. And you can tell her what you want. I don't care anymore about all that.

Tash But I do. Your mum would ring up my dad or something.

Maeve That's right, so she would. How you could think of it, when Cora had only been buried two days. It's a disgrace.

Evaki I was angry. All right. I was angry at you and her and everything. I can explain all that. Look, Maeve, you ain't making things easy for me.

Maeve And why should I make things easy for you? Listen to who is talking!

Cora Girls! Girls! This is all getting out of hand.

Maeve I mean it's all very well for you to come here and wreck my life and Cora's out of it isn't she? She's safe in her grave? Have you thought of what it would mean for me if everyone knew. Look at someone like Jean. She would ostracize me. And your mother, Evaki. It's lonely enough as it is with Cora gone. I can't cope with everyone turning odd on me.

Evaki But I don't think they would. I reckon mum would be all right. Given half the chance.

Tash Yeah. Not everybody thinks it's wrong Maeve. I don't.

Maeve Would you listen to them! What do you know? I've lived my life. Do you want to know how long your Nan and I were lovers, do you?

Evaki I know – fifteen years.

Maeve That's right, fifteen years. It's a long time. And during that time we told a few trusted people and they always, and I'm not exaggerating, they always let us down. I know what I'm talking about. I tell you, I would have never imagined sitting here talking about all this to you two.

Evaki Well then.

Maeve I suppose it hasn't killed me.

Cora That's the spirit.

Evaki I've missed you too Maeve as well as my Nan.

Tash Are you all right Maeve. You look miles away?

Maeve sees Cora for the first time.

Maeve and Cora sit down together. Evaki and Tash watch them.

Cora That's done it! Evaki this morning. I almost swallowed my egg when she said, you don't need to worry about me. I thought she knew. This is silly Maeve. Pretending all the time. It's driving me mad. I'm fed up with being deceitful to my own granddaughter. Me, being scared of her!

Maeve I'm telling you Cora, she wouldn't thank you for it. Would you rather have no granddaughter at all.

Cora Oh for pity's sake stop being so dramatic Maeve. She'd get over it. All this waiting to be caught, it's as if we'd committed some sort of crime. I'd rather just give myself up.

Maeve I believe they call it coming out these days.

Cora I don't care what they call it. I just want to have it out in the open.

Maeve And lose your family? Families are too important to lose Cora. Look at me and my family separated by the water. There's enough to separate us without this. Anyway this is ours Cora. Just ours. Something nobody knows but us. I like sitting at work looking at you, knowing that later I can wrap my arms around you. I like that soft secret place we find ourselves in. Nobody's discovered it but us. It makes it all the more special.

Cora Are you saying it wouldn't be special anymore if anybody knew?

Maeve Of course not. I don't mean that. You know what I mean Cora.

Cora I think we should be able to do what we want if it's our business.

Maeve Well darling we do, don't we?

Cora Oh, I'm not saying we don't. But let's not make it into a dirty secret.

Maeve Listen to you Cora. You should be ashamed of yourself. Do you think I could love you so much if I thought it was that? Why do you have to hurt me by saying those things?

Cora Because I'm fed up with it. I don't think . . .

Maeve Why do you need the whole world to know, tell me that! Isn't it enough for you that we love each other as much as we do?

Cora No, it's not. Oh, what's the use in arguing like this? I'm going out for a walk.

Tash Are you sure you're OK Maeve? Maybe we should go. It didn't quite work out how we thought.

Evaki I won't tell nobody if that's what you want Maeve. It's just that I was thinking about what my Nan wanted and I reckoned she'd want Mum to know. But Mum can't know about Nan without knowing about you, so if that's what you want . . .

Maeve (*cries the first real cry since Cora's death*) I don't know what I want! I want Cora that's what I want! I want Cora to be here with me, alive again. Talking to me, holding my hand.

Evaki I thought you might like to have these Maeve. (**Evaki** *gives* **Maeve** *the diaries.*) I know they don't bring her back. But there's lots in them I'm sure she wanted you to read. I got to know her much better from reading them. Anyways, we'll leave you now. Sorry I upset you. When you feel a bit better, come round and see us. I won't tell mum nothing until you say it's all right.

Maeve I know Cora would have wanted her to know. I know that. To hell with it. Go ahead and tell her. If she can't take it we'll have to cross that bridge when we come to it.

Cora Maeve! Maeve! I love you more

and more each day. If only you could feel it.

Maeve My goodness. I've surprised myself. I feel a whole lot better already.

Cora *returns to the coffin. Everyone else gathers around it for her funeral.*

Cora This is what it should have been like.

Maeve *takes centre stage. Everyone pays their respects and sympathies to her.*

Jean I'm awful sorry Maeve. It's hard on you.

Maeve *holds her head high.* **Sharon, Tash, Evaki** *and* **Jean** *exit.* **Maeve** *pays her last respects to* **Cora**, *then exits. Lights down.*

Chronology

This chronology gives details of all Gay Sweatshop productions, the people involved, the dates of opening nights and major tours. Owing to lack of space it has not been possible to list the hundreds of touring venues at which the company has played.

1974
Mar Letter appears in *Gay News* from Inter-Action. Planning meetings held over the following months leading up to lunchtime season of plays at the Almost Free Theatre, Rupert St, W1

1975
17 Feb Homosexual Acts lunchtime season opens produced by Inter-Action with Gay Sweatshop at the Almost Free Theatre.
Limitations by John Roman Baker. Dir. Roy Patrick. Cast: Maggie Ford, William Hoyland, Jeremy Arnold. Des. Norman Coates.
10 Mar Thinking Straight by Laurence Collinson. Dir. Drew Griffiths. Cast: Anthony Sher, Peter Small, Linda Beckett. Des. Norman Coates.
31 Mar Ships by Alan Wakeman. Dir. Gerald Chapman. Cast: Andrew Tourell, Anthony Smee, Elaine Ives-Cameron, Jim Duggan, Iain Armstrong, Timothy Welsh, Barry Parman. Des. Norman Coates.
21 Apr Ships run at the Almost Free extended until 10 May.
Thinking Straight opens at the Act Inn.
12 May One Person by Robert Patrick at the Almost Free. Dir. Stewart Trotter. Cast: Michael Deacon.
Fred and Harold by Robert Patrick at the Almost Free. Dir. Stewart Trotter. Cast: Barry McCarthy, Peter Whitman.
Thinking Straight opens at Mickery Theatre, Amsterdam.
19 May Haunted Host by Robert Patrick (evening performances at the Almost Free) Dir. John Chapman. Cast: Joseph Pichette, Ned Van Zandt. Des. Norman Coates.
Ships opens at Mickery Theatre, Amsterdam.
11 June Passing By by Martin Sherman at the Almost Free. Dir. Drew Griffiths. Cast: Simon Callow, Michael Dickinson.
Summer Campaign for Homosexual Equality asks Gay Sweatshop to take a play to the CHE conference in Sheffield.
23 Aug Mister X by Roger Baker and Drew Griffiths opens at the Sheffield CHE conference. Cast: Philip Howells, Drew Griffiths, Alan Pope, Gordon MacDonald.
Oct 17–Dec 19 Mister X on tour.
Nov During a Women's Season at the Leicester Haymarket there is a one-off performance of *Any Woman Can* by Jill Posener. It is directed by Kate Crutchley and Miriam Margolyes plays the main role.

1976
Jan/Feb Jill Posener, Kate Crutchley, designer Mary Moore are the first women to join Gay Sweatshop.
24 Feb Lunchtime season of plays at the ICA opens. The season is extended and eventually continues until July 17th.
Mister X – the first play in the season – at one performance, plays to 184 people which is a record for a lunchtime play.
16 Mar Any Woman Can by Jill Posener at the ICA. Dir Kate Crutchley. Des. Mary Moore. The play was performed with a cast of four or five and the following is a list of the actresses who performed the play at various points in its Gay Sweatshop production: Brenda Addie, Helen Barnaby, Donna Champion, Kate Crutchley, Nancy Diuguid, Patricia Donovan, Vanessa Forsyth, Sandra Freeman, Patricia Garwood, Sara

Hardy, Elizabeth Lindsay, Penlope Nice and Julie Parker.
6 Apr *The Fork* by Ian Brown at the ICA. Dir. Gerald Chapman. Cast: Linda Beckett, Jeffrey Chiswick, Jim Hooper, Anthony Sher. Des. Mary Moore.
27 Apr *Mister X* returns to the ICA.
The Fork opens at the Traverse, Edinburgh.
10 May *Mister X* and *Any Woman Can* at the Oval House.
18 May *Randy Robinson's Unsuitable Relationship* by Andrew Davies at the ICA. Dir. Kate Crutchley. Cast: James Marcus, Sandra Freeman, Martin Friend, Andrew Branch, Georgina Melville. Des. Mary Moore.
28 May *Any Woman Can* at the CHE conference Southampton.
Indiscreet by Roger Baker and Drew Griffiths opens at the CHE conference Southampton. Dir. Drew Griffiths. Cast: Alan Pope, Philip Howells, Gordon Macdonald, Drew Griffiths.
8 June *Stone* by Edward Bond at the ICA. Dir. Gerald Chapman. Cast: Kevin Elyot, Tony Douse, Anthony Sher, Anna Nygh. Musicians: Robert Campbell, Tom Robinson. Des. Mary Moore.
17 June *Mister X* at Theatre in the Mill, Bradford.
22 June *Mister X* at Birmingham Arts Lab.
29 June *Indiscreet* at the ICA.
12 July *Any Woman Can* at the King's Head.
10 Aug *Mister X* at Oxford Theatre Festival.
30 Aug *Mister X* opens at the Edinburgh Festival on the Fringe (Hill Place Theatre)
6 Sept *Any Woman Can* opens at Edinburgh.
Autumn Tours of *Mister X* and *Any Woman Can* with the companies meeting up to do double-bills at selected venues. The touring company of *Any Woman Can* was: Helen Barnaby, Nancy Diuguid, Sara Hardy, Julie Parker and Jill Posener. This company was joined by Faith Gillespie to perform a *Women's Poetry Show* which opened at the Orange Tree in Richmond and was also performed on the tour.
29 Sept *Indiscreet* at the Oval House.
12 Oct-6 Nov *Mister X* at the Mickery Theatre, Amsterdam and on tour in Holland.
15 Nov-27 Nov *Mister X* and *Any Woman Can* play Project Arts Centre Dublin.
Oct-Dec *Any Woman Can* on tour.
7 Dec *Jingleball 1* at the ICA (lunchtimes)
21-24 Dec *Jingleball* at the ICA. Dir. Michael Richmond. Cast: Bob Stratton, Julie Parker, Nancy Diuguid, Kate Crutchley, Gordon MacDonald, Drew Griffiths, Helen Barnaby, Sara Hardy. Music: Alex Harding and Tom Robinson.
28 Dec-2 Jan *Jingleball* at the Roundhouse downstairs.

1977
30 Jan *Any Woman Can* and *Mister X* return to Dublin to give councillors the opportunity to see the plays before voting on the Project Arts Centre's grant.
7 Feb *Age of Consent* at the Royal Court Theatre as part of a season of plays for schools entitled *Everyone Different*. Devised by the company and Drew Griffiths. Dir. Kate Crutchley. Cast: Bob Stratton, Sara Hardy, Tony Brooks, Helen Barnaby, Keiran Montague, Ian Godfrey, Gordon MacDonald. Des. Mary Moore. Vocals: Tom Robinson. This production toured until 4 April.
13 May *Care and Control* researched and devised by the company, scripted by Michelene Wandor at the Oval House. Dir. Kate Crutchley. Cast: Kate Phelps, Michael Kellan, Natasha Fairbanks, Helen Barnaby, Kate Crutchley, Nancy Diuguid. Des. Mary Moore. Music by Terri Quaye. On tour until 17 July.
26 Aug *As Time Goes By* by Noël Greig and Drew Griffiths at the CHE conference, Nottingham. Dir Noël Greig. Cast: Bruce Bayley, Drew Griffiths, Gordon MacDonald, Alan Pope, Philip Osment, Philip Timmins. Music: Alex Harding. Des. Paul Dart.
30 Aug *As Time Goes By* on the Edinburgh Festival Fringe at the Heriot Watt Theatre.
5 Sept *Care and Control* second tour. Cast: Libby Mason, Martin Panter, Sara Hardy, Marilyn Milgrom, Jill Posener, Patricia Donovan.
26 Sept *As Time Goes By* at the ICA.
Oct-Dec *As Time Goes By* on tour.
Dec *As Time Goes By* tour of Germany – Berlin, Munich, Frankfurt and Hamburg.

1978
15 Jan-5 Feb Gay Times Festival at Action Space Drill Hall organised by Gay Sweatshop men. Performances of *As Time Goes By* plus cabarets: *Urania*, A Thirties cabaret, *Manmad*.
The Sixties by Paul Dart.
The Life, Works and Loves of Lytton Strachey by David Thompson.
Also workshops, discussions, performances by guest companies and screenings.
Feb-Apr *As Time Goes By* on tour in the UK and Ireland including performances as guests of Project Arts Centre at Trinity College, Dublin. Cast: Bruce Bayley's parts played by Martin Panter.
20 Apr-14 May *As Time Goes By* at the Mickery Theatre, Amsterdam and on tour in Holland. Cast: Drew Griffiths' parts played by Martin Panter.
3 May *What The Hell Is She Doing Here?* devised and written by the company at the Oval House and on tour until July. Dir. Angela Langfield. Cast: Ella Wilder, Sara Hardy, Francia White, Eileen Dixon, Kate Jason-Smith.
Aug *Jingleball* at the Oval House. Cast: Jill Posener, Kate Crutchley, Bob Stratton, Drew Griffiths, Gordon Macdonald, Elizabeth Lindsay, Sandra Lester, Stephanie Pugsley. Musicians: Alex Harding (piano), Angela Stewart-Park (drums)
20 Aug *Jingleball* on Edinburgh Festival Fringe at the Heriot-Watt.
27 Sept *Iceberg* devised by the company at the Oval House. Cast: Noël Greig, Sandra Lester, Stephanie Pugsley, Angela Stewart-Park, Philip Timmins.
27 Sept *Warm* a thirties cabaret devised by the company at the Oval House. Cast: Bruce Bayley, Noël Greig, Drew Griffiths, Gordon MacDonald, Philip Osment, Philip Timmins.
Oct-Dec *Iceberg* on tour.
9 Nov *Iceberg* at Belfast Fringe Festival at Queens University.
Dec *Iceberg* on tour in Germany. Cast: Noël Greig's part played by Philip Osment.

1979
8 Mar *The Dear Love of Comrades* a play with songs by Noël Greig at the Oval House. Music by Alex Harding. Dir. Nancy Diuguid. Cast: Ray Batchelor, Peter Glancy, Noël Greig, Stephen Hatton, Philip Timmins. Accompanist: Alex Harding. Des. Paul Dart.
Mar-July *The Dear Love of Comrades* on tour.
29 May *The Dear Love of Comrades* at Munich Theatre Festival.
Aug *I Like Me Like This* by Sharon Nassauer and Angela Stewart-Park at the Edinburgh Festival. Dir. Helen Barnaby. Cast: Dee Welding, Trudy Howson, Anne Wilkins, Ros Davis, Vicky Ryder. Piano: Sharon Nassauer. Drums: Angela Stewart-Park. Musical Dir. Sharon Nassauer. Des. Kate Owen.
Autumn *I Like Me Like This* on tour.
12 Nov *Who Knows?* By Bruce Bayley, Sara Hardy and Philip Timmins at Royal Court Theatre. Dir. Philip Timmins. Cast: Kenny Irvine, Michelle Golaz, Peter Hall, Gary James, Chris Lada, Kate Oliver, Christine Richmond, Jayne Roberts, Lizzie Windsor. Des. Paul Dart.

Gay Sweatshop

1980
Jan *Who Knows?* on tour.
11 Sept *Blood Green* by Noël Greig and Angela Stewart-Park at the Albany Empire. Dir Noël Greig. Cast: Elaine Loudon, Gordon MacDonald, Caroline Needs, Stephanie Pugsley, Philip Timmins. Des. Kate Owen.
Sept-Nov *Blood Green* on tour including performances in Dublin, Cork, Belfast and Coleraine.

1981
31 Mar Gay Sweatshop stops operating.

1983
18 Apr Reading of *Poppies* by Noël Greig at Gay CND weekend conference.
27 Oct *Poppies* opens at Oval House. Dir. Noël Greig. Des. Kate Owen. Cast: Robin Samson, Philip Osment, Philip Timmins, Ralph Smith, Simon Deacon, Robert Hale, Dave Tomalin.
Nov-Dec *Poppies* on tour.

1984
10/11 Feb *Poppies* at Albany Empire (benefit for Greenham)
13-18 Feb *Poppies* at Tricycle Theatre.
New Management Committee formed which is made up of Noël Greig, Philip Timmins, Martin Humphries, Kate Owen and Philip Osment. Planning starts for 10th anniversary festival to take place in 1985.

1985
5 Feb 2nd production of *Poppies* opens at Drill Hall Arts Centre. Dir. Philip Osment. Des. Kate Owen. Cast: David Newlyn, Gordon MacDonald, Peter Shorey, Stephen Ley, David Benedict, John Wilson, Richard Sandells.
4 Mar-11 May *Poppies* on tour.
16 Apr *Telling Tales* by Philip Osment (originally performed June '82) is produced by Gay Sweatshop as the inaugural production in the theatre at the London Lesbian and Gay Centre. Cast: Philip Osment. Des. Rick Fisher.
11 Oct *Raising the Wreck* by Sue Frumin at Pegasus Theatre, Oxford. Dir. Paddi Taylor. Des. Kate Owen. Cast: Bernardine Evaristo, Hazel Maycock, Sara Ridd, Denise Thompson, Marjolein de Vries.
15 Oct-2 Nov Gay Sweatshop Times Ten Festival at Drill Hall Arts Centre. Festival committee: Gay Sweatshop Management Committee plus Diane Biondo, Bernardine Evaristo with help and advice from the GLC disabilities unit and added assistance from Oscar Lumley-Watson, David Benedict and Paul Pettigrew.
Plays given staged readings:
Skin Deep by Nigel Pugh directed by Nigel Townsend.
Chiaroscuro by Jackie Kay directed by Joan Ann Maynard.
England Arise by Carl Miller directed by David Benedict.
Ties by Tasha Fairbanks directed by Philip Osment.
Compromised Immunity by Andy Kirby directed by Robert Hale
Boy by Greyum Pyper.
Julie by Catherine Kilcoyne directed by Maggie Ford.
Meet My Mother by Michelene Wandor with guest appearance by Miriam Margolyes.
Lifelines by Nicolle Freni directed by Libby Mason.
Aliens and Alienists by Rho Pegg directed by Cordelia Ditton.
Dreams Recaptured by Martin Humphries directed by Noël Greig.
Hitting Home by Diane Biondo directed by Paddi Taylor.
Pinball by Alison Lyssa directed by Nona Shepherd.
Angle of Vision by Deborah Rogin directed by Philip Osment.
A Quiet End by Robin Swados directed by Noël Greig.
More by Maro Green and Caroline Griffin directed by Kate Owen.
Education: Part One by Ibo directed by Paulette Randall.
Also poetry readings, performances of *Raising the Wreck*, workshops and performances by guest companies and cabaret.
Nov-Dec *Raising the Wreck* on tour.
11 Dec-15 Gay Sweatshop Times Ten Productions at Oval House:
Skin Deep by Nigel Pugh. Dir. Nigel Townsend. Cast James George, Peter Seton.
Julie by Catherine Kilcoyne. Dir. Maggie Ford. Cast: Karen Parker.
Boy by Greyum Pyper. Cast: Greyum Pyper, Maggie Nicholls.

1986
Jan *Raising the Wreck* on tour.
Jan-Feb Performances of *Julie* and *Skin Deep* at various London venues.
26 Mar *More* begins London tour at Wesley House (GLC Women's Centre). Dir. Kate Owen. Cast: Cordelia Ditton, Maro Green. Des. Caroline Burgess.
24 Apr-10 May *More* at Drill Hall Arts Centre.
3 Jul *Compromised Immunity* by Andy Kirby at the Albany Empire. Dir. Philip Osment. Des. Tony Reeves. Cast: Richard Sandells, Madeline Blakeney, Pip Stephenson, Peter Shorey, David Benedict, Alan Hooker, Duncan Alexander. Lighting Des. Matt Shadder. Cos. Des. Caroline Burgess.
7 Oct *Compromised Immunity* at the Drill Hall.

1987
11-22 Mar Gay Sweatshop Times Twelve Festival at the Oval House
Plays given staged rehearsed readings:
The Gleaners by Maria Aristarco directed by Maggie Ford
Where to Now? by Martin Patrick directed by Cordelia Ditton.
This Island's Mine by Philip Osment directed by Philip Osment.
Seven Seas by Adele Saleem directed by Adele Saleem.
The Legend of Bim and Bam directed by Kate Owen and Richard Sandells.
A Crossed Line by Christopher Eymard directed by David Benedict.
Twice Over by Jackie Kay directed by Sally Aprahamian.
Canada Flash by Paul Doust directed by Philip Osment.
Also *Raw Hide* a performance piece created by Emlyn Claid. Plus poetry readings, guest performers and cabaret.
22 Mar Launch of POSH, Gay Sweatshop's fundraising scheme set up by Ags Irwin.
28 Apr Touring production of *Compromised Immunity* opens at Leicester Haymarket Studio Theatre. Dir. and Des. as above. Cast: Richard Sandells, Sarah McNair, Pip Stephenson, Peter Shorey, David Benedict, Duncan Alexander. Tour continues until 27 June.

1988
24 Feb *This Island's Mine* by Philip Osment with music and lyrics by Sharon Nassauer at the Drill Hall Arts Centre. Dir. Philip Osment. Des. Kate Owen. Mus. Dir. Sharon Nassauer. Lighting Des. Matt Shadder. Cast: William Elliott, Trevor Ferguson, Diane Hall, Suzy King, Margaret Robertson, Richard Sandells, Dougray Scott.
15 Mar-24 Apr *This Island's Mine* on tour.
14 June *This Island's Mine* Scottish tour. Diane Hall's roles played by Irma Inniss.
21 June *This Island's Mine* at the Drill Hall.
27 Sept *Twice Over* by Jackie Kay at Drill Hall Arts Centre. Dir. Nona Shepphard. Des. Kate Owen. Cast: Adjoa Andoh, Pamela Lane, Thelma Lawson, Amanda Martin, Mary Ellen Ray, Cleo Sylvestre.
18 Oct-5 Nov *Twice Over* on tour.